ISBN 978-1-330-08391-8
PIBN 10021666

English
Français
Deutsche
Italiano
Español
Português

www.forgottenbooks.com

Mythology Photography **Fiction**
Fishing Christianity **Art** Cooking
Essays Buddhism Freemasonry
Medicine **Biology** Music **Ancient**
Egypt Evolution Carpentry Physics
Dance Geology **Mathematics** Fitness
Shakespeare **Folklore** Yoga Marketing
Confidence Immortality Biographies
Poetry **Psychology** Witchcraft
Electronics Chemistry History **Law**
Accounting **Philosophy** Anthropology
Alchemy Drama Quantum Mechanics
Atheism Sexual Health **Ancient History**
Entrepreneurship Languages Sport
Paleontology Needlework Islam
Metaphysics Investment Archaeology
Parenting Statistics Criminology
Motivational

THE
COUNTRY BANKER

HIS CLIENTS, CARES, AND WORK

FROM

AN EXPERIENCE OF FORTY YEARS

BY

GEORGE RAE

AUTHOR OF BULLION'S LETTERS TO A BANK MANAGER

No man is so foolish, but may give another good counsel sometimes; and no man is so wise, but may easily err, if he will take no other counsel but his own.—*Ben Jonson*

WITH AN AMERICAN PREFACE

BY

BRAYTON IVES

NEW YORK
CHARLES SCRIBNER'S SONS
1886

GRANT & FAIRES
PHILADELPHIA

PREFACE TO THE AMERICAN EDITION.

An extensive and flourishing system of banking is an indisputable proof of the existence of great and general wealth and material prosperity. There may be individual instances of success among those who act as bankers in communities where the masses are poor, but in such cases it will be found usually that their occupation partakes largely of the nature of money-changing, which is the first step beyond barter, or the beginning of all mercantile transactions. While it will be remembered generally that the first mention of money-changers occurs in the Bible, it may not be known to so many that, in Greece, the temples were the first banks. Delphi and Olympia offered superior advantages, in the way of security, as places of deposit for gold and silver, and, at the same time, as the gathering places of pilgrims and devotees, they gave both useful and profitable occupation to the money-changers. Joint-stock banks are said to have been suggested originally by Xenophon, who proposed to stimulate, through them, commercial adventure.

Commerce cannot exist on a great scale without banks, and as Italy and Holland acquired eminence in manufactures and trade, Venice, Genoa and Amsterdam became prominent centres of banking business. And then, as England gradually wrested the commercial supremacy from the continental nations she gained undisputed con-

trol of the financial world. Next to royalty, the most
famous and influential institution of the British Empire is
the Bank of England, or, in vulgar phrase, "The Old
Lady of Threadneedle Street." Connected with, and
both supporting and dependent upon it, are those great
joint-stock banks, which, with their numerous branches,
control the financial enterprises of England and her col-
onies. Their transactions are enormous in magnitude,
and their influence on the prosperity of the communities
in which they are situated is beyond computation.

But while no one is indifferent to the attractions of a
plethoric bank account, or the indulgence of a liberal
banker, few have an accurate knowledge of the practical
working of the business, or care to read about it. To
the average reader, "discount," "balance sheet," "trade
bills," and "overdrawn accounts," suggest only dry and
uninteresting details, unless, indeed, he happens to have
a personal interest in the latter item. And it must be
admitted that the average writer on such subjects lacks
the ability to overcome their inherent difficulties and
treat them in an attractive manner. To this rule, however, it seems to me that "The Country Banker" is a
notable exception. Without being pedantic, or too tech-
nical, the author has given an accurate and minute
account of the methods by which the branches of the
London banks are managed, and, at the same time, he
has written a book which is so admirable in style that it
presents strong claims to public attention, viewed solely
from a literary standpoint. If there were no other merit in
the book, the excellent quotations from Seneca, Quarles,
Fuller, and others, would make it well worth reading.
The author's experience of thirty-five years in a bank did
not convert him into a machine, nor make him unmind-

ful of everything except money-getting. Out of banking hours he must have read many good books, and thought carefully over their contents. We find everywhere signs of his keen knowledge of human nature. He recognises and demonstrates the fact that successful bankers must have some, at least, of the cardinal virtues; that they must be courteous, honourable, prudent and industrious. When the public become convinced that they possess these, it accords them that mysterious confidence called credit, the acquisition of which is absolutely essential to the transaction of their business. It is mysterious because it seems to follow no rule. Some men can never gain it, and yet no one can point to an overt act on their part which is dishonourable. Others, again, win it easily, and seem to trifle with it, but it clings to them with tenacity. In most cases, when once given it is not withdrawn, and the reason is that it is usually deserved. With comparatively few exceptions the history of banking is a record of honourable dealing.

The business of banking in this country may be said to be still in its infancy. It is only within the past twenty-five years that it has had anything like a system. While there were many rich and solvent banks previous to 1861, the majority were far from strong and succumbed easily to commercial disturbances. To-day, however, they work harmoniously, and with steadily increasing influence. In connection with them and the trust companies, private bankers bring to public notice, and foster all the great enterprises of the country. Every year the relations of these organizations to the public become more intimate, and it is of the highest importance that they should be managed not only with honesty but with intelligence. The investigations which followed the failure of the Marine Bank in May, 1884, drove many weak banks and banking houses into liquidation, and left the others in better condition than before.   While the recollection of the acts of those who, either through weakness or vice, wrecked the institutions under their control, is still fresh in men's minds, the reading of wise, practical suggestions, such as are contained in " The Country Banker " must exert a beneficial influence, both on the public and on those to whom the public intrust their money. And it is a subject of congratulation that these words of wisdom are written so skillfully that readers may gain much useful knowledge, and, at the same time, enjoy a literary treat.

BRAYTON IVES.

PREFACE.

My purpose in writing this book is not to formulate afresh the fundamental principles of banking, but rather to show these principles in operation;—to exhibit, so to speak, the machinery of banking in motion.

In pursuance of this endeavour, I have availed myself of illustrative matter, gleaned from the incidents of an experience, now stretching over forty years, of the life and work of Country Banking, in its relations with customers and shareholders, the officials in its employment, and the general public.

My desire is less to advance special views of my own, than to exemplify, from fresh points of observation, the accustomed lines and recognised limits of prudent banking; a rational observance of which would have rendered the bank failures of our time fewer in number, less scandalous in their revelations, and less calamitous in their results.

A small portion of the present work was published anonymously thirty-five years ago. It was comprised in a little book with a large title,* which has for many years been out of print; but such portions of the text as were found available, after the lapse of a period exceptionally fruitful of banking change and vicissitude, have for the

---

* "The Internal Management of a Country Bank, in a Series of Letters on the Functions and Duties of a Branch Manager." By Thomas Bullion. (1850.)

ix

most part been rewritten and abridged, and used as material in the present publication; the completion of which, the occupations of a busy life have prevented until now.

I use the epistolary form in the work because it gives scope to a more familiar treatment of what most people regard—mistakenly, I think—as a subject devoid of human interest.

I desire to add that where I seek to elucidate precept by example, which is the leading purpose of the book, I do not draw upon imagination for my materials. With slight modifications, in point of time, place, and circumstance, the transactions quoted have had their equivalents in fact; whilst my human exemplars, if they have less claim to authentic history, are not wholly indebted to these pages for their existence.

G. R.

REDCOURT, BIRKENHEAD.
April, 1885.

*** THE call for a Second Edition within a few weeks of the date of publication of the first, has come upon the Author so unexpectedly, that he has to crave the indulgence of the reader if the present reprint be less weeded of defects and otherwise amended, than it might have been, had more time been available.

June, 1885.

CONTENTS.

COUNTRY BANKER.

LETTER I.

THE FUNCTION OF MANAGER.

Let a man be sure to drive his business rather than let it drive him. When a man is but once brought to be driven, he becomes a vassal to his affairs: they master him, which should by him be commanded. OWEN FELTHAM.

THE management of the Branch in Oxborough of the District Union Bank is an important position to have reached before you have well left behind you the days of your youth. Your advancement is hailed by your friends with pardonable enthusiasm, and is naturally a subject of honest pride and gratification to yourself. But increased rank and additional pay in the service of banking have their drawbacks. You will find that they bring with them a serious heritage of unaccustomed duties and anxieties; and it is certain that the success of your management will largely depend upon your early recognition of the fact, that the interests concerned in your appointment far exceed your own in range and importance.

To the good people of Oxborough you will stand in the delicate relation of arbiter of credit. Thousands of pounds will every week be paid across your counter in discounts and advances to a variety of persons, and you will have to satisfy your mind in every case, before parting with the Bank's money, that it is required for legitimate business use, and not for rash and foolish speculation.

It is hardly necessary to suggest that in your dealings with the public there must be a total absence of bias—religious, political or social. When a man brings you his banking account, you do not require to know whether he goes to church or chapel, nor how he voted at last election, nor who his grandfather was. The hundred pounds at the credit of honest Grimes the farrier, who signs himself 'William Grimes ✕ his mark,' are of the same use in banking as if the money stood at the credit of a peer of the realm. There is no respect of persons in banking. Your doors are open to all sorts and conditions of men, except that you draw the line at dishonesty. You will have no dealings with a rogue, if you know it. You will not open even a deposit account with a stranger unless he be satisfactorily introduced, lest you find that you have been entertaining a rascal unawares, who is making use of the cheque-book which you have supplied him with, to victimize half a score of innocent people.

You do not abate your rate of discount on Brown's paper the fraction of a farthing because he is your friend; neither would you add a fraction to it if he were your enemy.

In banking the scope for the feelings is limited. You discount a bill, or you lend a man money, or you refuse to do either, as the case may be, not as a matter of sentiment or affection, but purely as a matter of pounds shillings and pence.

To your Directors you will stand in the fiduciary relation of manager of the funds which they may authorize you to employ in discounts and advances at Oxborough Branch.

As these ripen day by day and return in money to your till, you replace them with fresh discounts and advances, and these again with others, and so on in endless succession. In this way you turn your resources over several times a year, and thereby incur a fresh series of banking risks at every turn. Opportunities for making bad debts will thus come to you in abundance and variety. It is not too much to say that they will offer themselves to you daily throughout the year. It will be the daily study of your business life, therefore, to learn to distinguish at a glance those transactions in banking which are safe and legitimate, from those which are unsafe and pernicious.

To acquire this knowledge and apply it with unfailing success, and thus avoid the worst pitfalls which lie in your business path, your perceptive faculties must be acutely awake and your wits in faultless working order all the year round. The slightest tendency to a mental folding of the hands to sleep during banking hours must be wrestled with at once and overcome.

The Manager who is not at all times vigilant to note every change in the circumstances of his customers, the aspect of their accounts, the quality of their bills and the value of their securities; but gives way to mental indolence, and lends a loose ear to applicants of easy conscience for plausible advances, cannot fail in time to bring loss to his Branch and trouble upon himself The needy drawer, the sanguine acceptor, and the ardent indorser soon find him out, and he becomes their prey.

There is, no doubt, as you suggest, a possibility of being over-cautious; but in banking that is one of the cardinal virtues, compared with the opposite evil and mischief of being over-credulous.

On every occasion, when you have the shadow of a fear as to the safety of any given transaction, there is only one rule and it is without exception—you must give the Bank the benefit of the doubt. When the reasons for and against a proposed transaction are so evenly poised in the scales of your judgment that the balance hesitates to incline either way, a solution of the difficulty will sometimes be found by making the enquiry within—Would you make the advance if the money were your own ?

In the course of your management you will not always

be the medium of pleasing intelligence from your Directors to your clients. You have to intimate to Mr. Bareacres, perhaps, that the loan of a few thousand pounds for a year or two at three per cent. without security, for which that gentleman has applied to the Directors, cannot be granted. The fact probably is that, apart from other fatal objections to the transaction, Mr. Bareacres is not safe for anything like the amount. But you are not obliged to tell him so. Without impugning his credit to his teeth, the refusal of the loan, even if conveyed to him in the mildest language, will be disappointment enough to a man of sanguine disposition; which I take to be the normal temperament of that variety of borrower, who makes periodical applications to bankers for ridiculous advances on impossible terms.

Mr. Bareacres will either accept the decision of your Board with a good grace, or he may resort to irritating comment, in which case it will be well to put a guard upon your temper. Amongst other remarks he may suggest perhaps that your Bank hasn't the money to spare? Nevertheless it would be a mistake to fly into a passion or bandy words with him. Rather accept the sneer as a drollery on his part, and offer to lend him twice the money on approved security and rational terms. He will thus be discomfited on ground of his own choosing, and leave you master of the situation.

In a certain great English town many years ago, there flourished two managers of banks, so widely opposed in temperament and manner, that it was a common saying in business circles that it was pleasanter to have a transaction declined by the one than to have your wish granted by the other. The one, people said, was a courtier, the other a bear. It might be as well perhaps if you took a note of this; because even 'manners and deportment' would seem to count for something in the final rounding off and finish of the complete Bank Manager.

And whilst you are careful to curb your own temper under any strain to which it may be exposed in the course of your business, you will require from your subordinates at the Bank the exercise of a similar restraint; because no amount of affability on your part will reconcile a client to its absence on theirs. Let it be understood at once and with emphasis, that the 'insolence of office' shall have neither place nor tolerance at Oxborough Branch. You have a right to expect from your staff that courteous civility in their intercourse with the customers of the Bank which, it is to be presumed, they exercise in their intercourse with each other.

It would not be seemly, for example, that half a dozen people should be kept waiting at your counter whilst your cashier, Mr. Coigne, is absorbed in the morning paper, or in a surreptitious volume from Mudie's, or in correcting the proof of his forthcoming article on the currency for the Oxborough Gazette. Neither ought he to look calmly on, whilst a client from the country is working himself into much heat and perplexity, in a futile attempt to fill up one of your blank forms, which, although in themselves of undeniable use, are not models of clearness to the agricultural mind. Instead of holding himself coldly aloof, Mr. Coigne would exercise a truer dignity were he to accord a word or two of advice, or even a helping hand, to a customer thus bewildered. It would be little for Mr. Coigne to give, but much for a nervous client to receive; for, even amongst educated people, some are to be found, to whom the simplest processes of banking are still subjects of secret wonder and curious misconception.

LETTER II.

PERSONAL CREDIT.

My meaning in saying he is a good man, is to have you understand that he is sufficient: yet his means are in supposition.
MERCHANT OF VENICE.

THE leading subject of your daily education as a banker will be to learn whom to trust.

Given a certain individual as principal or surety in a proposed transaction, the question which you have to solve is—how many hundreds, or how many thousands, as the case may be, will he be 'good for' to the Bank ; at what figure can you safely put his individual responsibility ?

To insure a reliable solution, you have first to ascertain what the man is 'worth'—that is to say, what he would have remaining for himself, in money or money's worth, after clearing off the whole of his debts and other liabilities.

For the most part you will have to rely for this knowledge on hearsay and the opinion of others. You will consequently have to sift the information which you may gather as to the position of individuals, with the utmost care, because on no other subject of daily gossip is there a greater tendency to exaggeration or mischievous credulity.

You will have early occasion to observe, amongst other things, that the opinions afloat as to the means and position of people are mostly of stereotyped character. The origin of these opinions is always more or less obscure : but when it once comes to be said—it does not seem to matter when nor by whom—that So-and-so is good for so much, his worth will pass current for that amount for

6

years without challenge ; until some day he collapses, to
the ruin of some, the injury of many, and the wonder-
ment of all.

When therefore you are confidently assured, by some
one who professes to know, that Mr. Bounderby, for
example, is worth twenty thousand pounds, put your
informant to the question.   Let him tell you in what
form Mr. Bounderby's worth exists—whether in land, or
houses, or business capital, or shares, or money lent, or
otherwise, and whether his property, real or personal, is
free of charge or incumbrance.   The probability is that
your informant can give you no such information ; and
that in that respect he is the mere echo of antecedent
echoes.   His opinion will be found in most cases to
rest on that most unreliable of authorities—everybody.
Everybody says so : therefore it must be true.

If he seeks to cover a retreat from his first position by
a flank movement in the direction, let us say, of Mr.
Bounderby's expectations, and assure you that he will
have a large amount at his father's death, your informant
must still be put to particulars ; because this reversion
may not be absolute : it may be tied tightly up on
Bounderby himself for life and go to his wife and
children afterwards.

'Let the greatest part of the news thou hearest,' says
Quarles, 'be the least part of what thou believest : lest
the greater part of what thou believest be the least part
of what is true.'

Ask the first farmer you meet next market day what
he considers Squire W— to be worth, and he will quote
you a figure, in all likelihood, absurdly wide of the mark.
You yourself know the Squire's rental to a pound,
because he banks with you.   You also know that the
estate is strictly entailed and that his income dies with
him, and therefore that the worthy Squire's reputed
wealth is a popular delusion.

Ask your leading tradesman what he considers the
means of his customer Colonel H— may be, and he will
tell you that the Colonel must be rich, because he lives

like a gentleman, and never owes his tradesmen a shilling. Nevertheless, when the good Colonel dies, would it surprise you to learn that he has lived up to his income all his life and left nothing ?

When you are assured that Maltby has made ten thousand pounds in hops, do not believe it. Divide by ten, and in nine cases out of ten you will be nearer the mark. But register the fact in your memory, because if Maltby has made money this time, he has an equal chance of losing it next.

Be equally sceptical when you are assured that Bouncer has lost a 'pot of money' in something else, until you have had the rumour verified; because a gain or loss in business, in these days, becomes magnified in passing from mouth to mouth to ridiculous excess, and is hardly surpassed in quickness of growth by Falstaff's men in buckram.

When any rumour reaches you, therefore, either to the credit or discredit of a man, have a care, before acting upon it, to sift it to the bottom: carefully weighing the probabilities for and against, and the evidence on which they rest, as if you were hearing a cause in a court of law. Business calumnies especially are of extraordinary vitality. You shall expose and stamp one out as you imagine, and in a few months it will come back to you again from some distant quarter as fresh and brazen as if you had never crushed it under an angry heel. Whilst you have conceived it dead and buried, it has been merely absent on a tour of the district.

But in many instances the only information which you will obtain will be of a nature which you cannot put to the proof. It will be of the vaguest kind and often contradictory. One informant will appraise a man as good for so much : another will value him at half the money. Either may be right—you cannot tell : or both may be wrong, and the truth lie midway between them : but it will be mere conjecture either way.

In such cases a prudential rule to find the measure of

a man's safety, from a banker's point of view, would be to follow the method suggested in Maltby's case : given the popular estimate of a man's worth, divide by ten, and the quotient will be the result required.

You smile at this novel adaptation of the rule of division : but give the figures a personal application, and they will not perhaps look so entertaining. Given a man reputed to be worth £5000, but of which you have no actual proof, would you feel justified in lending him more than £500 without security out of your own pocket?

Never trust to a man's means or safety as seen through the telescope of rumour ; you will find his truer diameter, as a rule, by reversing the glass.

As regards annuitants of all kinds, clergymen, naval or military officers, professional men and salaried officials of every degree, it has to be borne steadfastly in mind that their incomes die with them. If, therefore, they have laid nothing aside, and have no property beyond their life incomes to fall back upon, they are manifestly ineligible to a bank, either as borrowers on their own behalf, or as sureties for other people.

If they are living within their revenues, the balances of their accounts with you will always be in their favour : but if their accounts once get on the debtor side of your books, the means of repayment must be regarded as obscure, and the date of redemption as indefinite.

Take O—, for example, a most respectable man, but without property or means beyond his professional income which he spends in full : out of what conceivable fund is he to repay the several hundred pounds for which he has been allowed to creep into your debt without security? It cannot be the proper business of a bank to enable any man who is wholly dependent upon an income which terminates with his life, to anticipate and spend that income, or any portion of it, in advance, and thus assist the borrower in placing a burden upon his back—a veritable Old Man of the Sea—which he can never shake off.

In seeking to know whom to trust on the strength of hearsay, it has to be confessed that we have not found this source of knowledge to be altogether satisfactory or conclusive. But in the case of people who bank with you, you have in your ledgers a record which will enable you, in many cases, to check and rectify the estimate of their means and position which is current out of doors. A man's bank account will not necessarily disclose what he is worth: but its entries, debtor and creditor, will serve as tracks to indicate with some degree of clearness the line of progress along which he is moving towards either failure or success. Your customers are unconscious diarists of a portion of their lives. Every account in your books is a record, more or less graphic, of the financial history and progress of the customer, contributed by himself

In evidence of the teaching which your ledgers thus afford, let us take the account of your client, Mr. Giles Borax. He has recently retired from a lucrative business, and his wealth is popularly rated at any amount from a hundred and fifty to five hundred thousand pounds, according to the more or less fervid imagination of your informant. But the items on the credit side of his account will be a safer guide to the fact, than the most confident assertions of rumour. These items mainly consist of dividends on money in the Funds, or invested in leading railway and other shares or debentures. It will be an easy task to calculate from these the approximate value of Mr. Borax's property. If his revenue from all sources be £10,000 a year, you will not be far from the mark if you take it all round at twenty-five years' purchase, which would put his worth at a quarter of a million—less mortgages or other charges, if any, upon his property. Semi-annual debits, identical in amount, to the same payees, will sufficiently indicate the existence of incumbrances if there are any such.

If you are curious to know whether his net income exceeds or falls short of his expenditure, you have

merely to compare the balance with which he com-
mences the year with that with which he ends it : first
excluding any transactions on capital account from
your figures. He may have been laying money out on
loan or investments, for example ; or calling money in :
in either case, these items will be excluded from your
calculation.

It is, no doubt, possible, as you suggest, that Mr.
Borax may not pass all his rents and revenues through
his account, and that any estimate in that event, based
upon its figures, would be defective. So much the worse
for Mr. Borax ; but the defect will be on the side of
safety, so far as you are concerned. It will make
him appear to be, by so much, less opulent than he
really is.

You find serious difficulty, you say, in these occasional readings of accounts ; because some of your
customers draw their cheques in blank—that is, in
favour of a number, or the initials of the payee, instead
of his name. It does not follow, however, that cheques
are thus drawn with intention to deceive. The parties
may desire to keep their money transactions to themselves ; and, if they are never in your debt in any form,
they have a plain right to do so. But if they are debtors
to the Bank, and especially if their indebtedness be uncovered by security, their right to work their accounts in
the dark ceases, and the habit should be given up. If
you trust them with your money, you have a right to at
least a general notion of what they are doing with it. It
is true that, even when an account is worked on the
anonymous principle, it is easy to gather from the indorsements and other inscriptions on the cheques themselves, much of what you desire to know : but that is no
reason why the man who borrows the Bank's money
should be allowed to work his account in cipher, and
put you to the trouble of finding the cipher out. His
cheques ought to reveal their object by proper mention
of names or purposes, and not in the darkened speech
of numerals.

In your reading of any account you have carefully to guard against a mere off-hand and superficial glance at the figures. As a case in point, let us take the account of Stokes & Co., by whom your Bank made a bad debt in the time of your predecessor, Mr. Littleworth. What misled Mr. Littleworth was the fact that the firm had always a substantial balance at their credit. He inferred from this that they had capital in their business even to overflowing, and his astonishment was great when they stopped payment one day with some hundreds still at the credit of their cash account. Nevertheless it was so. Stokes & Co. were dealers in timber, bought it on six months' credit, and got immediate possession of the article. This they proceeded to dispose of to their customers, and drew upon them against sales, and the proceeds of the bills thus drawn they placed straightway to the credit of their bank account. They succeeded in this way with the greatest ease in keeping a good balance at their credit, seeing that they had always the produce of their sales in hand, long before they had to pay for the timber themselves. By reference to the account, Mr. Littleworth might have noticed that the acceptances passed through it during the twelve months preceding their failure reached £20,000; and the acceptances, having each six months to run, it followed that Stokes & Co. were constantly in debt some £10,000 for timber supplied, the bulk of which they had sold to weak joiners and impecunious builders. When half a score of these came to grief, by reason of a collapse in building enterprise, the modest capital of Stokes & Co. vanished, and gave place to a balance deficient of many times the amount; whilst the £500 at their credit on your books still left the Bank to prove for an unpleasant amount on a batch of worthless bills.

You have to beware, therefore, of placing too much reliance on the balance usually at a man's credit as a test of his means, until you have first seen how the balance is created. If you find that he pays mostly by acceptance, and rarely in cash, you will conclude that his balance in your hands is merely fugitive, and virtually in pawn to other people. It is money placed with you in advance to meet coming liabilities. His trading position, in other respects, may be perfectly sound and solid: but the balance at his credit is not of itself conclusive evidence of the fact. It is, indeed, practicable for a clever rogue so to manage affairs as to be insolvent for years, yet all the while maintain a respectable balance in his bankers' hands.

LETTER III.

THE TESTIMONY OF A BALANCE-SHEET.

He that can tell his money hath arithmetic enough : he is a true geometrician can measure out a good fortune to himself : a perfect astrologer, that can cast the rise and fall of others, and mark their errant notions to his own use.

ANATOMY OF MELANCHOLY.

WE have thus far taken count of the means which are afforded us by hearsay of knowing whom to trust. We have found in a man's bank account a useful corrective of information concerning him from without. In cases of men retired from business, we have even found it an authentic witness of the means of which they stand possessed.

But in the case of a man in business, or trade, although his bank account will go far to show what he is doing, it will not show what he is worth. Given his exact position at a certain date, his account will indicate, with some degree of accuracy, whether from that date onwards, he is improving his position, or receding from it; but we have yet to learn, in actual figures, and on authentic evidence, what that position is.

Even where an informant, in whose integrity you have implicit reliance, assures you that he knows So-and-so to be worth £10,000, because he has seen his balance-sheet, the information still comes to you at second hand, and, as we shall see presently, may without iuten-tion be seriously misleading. It is not enough to be thus assured, however truthfully, that a man has so much capital in his business. To take the true measure of his position, you must know, in addition, the total amount of his liabilities, and especially the nature of his assets : because the liabilities may be dangerously in

14

excess of his capital on the one hand, whilst the assets may not be in a sufficiently available form on the other.

A man's duly certified balance-sheet is the one reliable voucher of his actual position : all other information that we can gain respecting him, must be more or less at second hand and imperfect, and it may be delusive. But there is no mistaking the figures of an honest balance-sheet. Only, as a banker, you must see and weigh them for yourself, and not through the eyes and understanding of somebody else.

When a man comes to open an account at your Bank, with the declared purpose of borrowing your money in one form or another ; a reasonable opening, it appears to me, presents itself for the suggestion, that an exact knowledge of his position would greatly conduce to your mutual comfort in the years to come. The business connection thus commencing may be of lifelong continuance : the greater need, therefore, that there should be entire confidence between you. You are prepared to accept the figures of his balance-sheet as the basis of that confidence, and if he is wise he will not reject your condition. I say, if he is wise, because, for one thing, it is certain that when you become his bankers, you will be applied to from time to time for information as to his means and standing. If you know what these are, from actual figures, you can reply to such enquiries with a confidence which would be wanting, had you to rest your opinion upon mere hearsay or conjecture. Instead of a balance-sheet, the intending customer may offer to furnish you with referees ; and these gentlemen may be entirely respectable and assure you of their unqualified belief in his respectability, sufficiency of capital, and so forth ; but all this will come to you second-hand, and from parties who themselves have it only on report. They may be in a position even to specify the sum of his capital to a pound ; but, as we shall see, this is of itself no certain guide to his actual circumstances, without a knowledge of the surrounding figures.

The solid man of business, who, from pride or pre-

judice, hesitates to disclose the position of his business
affairs to the confidential ears of his bankers, damnifies
himself in two ways: on the one hand, he lessens the
full measure of credit which he might obtain from them
should he ever desire to borrow: on the other, he fails
to furnish them with data whereon to speak of his
position, with knowledge and decision, in reply to
enquiries from without. A man lays bare the secrets of
his constitution with candour to his physician, lest, in
the absence of an exact knowledge of the case, inapt
remedies might be applied. For a like reason, a man
should be equally frank with his banker; otherwise, in
the absence of a complete knowledge of his position,
you may ply him with stimulants, when purging would
be better; or bleed him to commercial death, when a
timely stimulant might save his existence.

There are those, no doubt, who have cogent reasons
for keeping the condition of their affairs a sealed book
from their bankers ; but it would be unsafe nevertheless
to assume, in every case, that because a man refuses to
show you his balance-sheet, he is therefore in a bad way.
There are people of secretive habit, who would regard
with dread the possibility of even their bankers getting
to know, not how poor, but how rich they are. But the
persons who take this peculiar view of things are few in
number. Men in large and active business, and requiring at times large banking facilities, see the wisdom of
laying of their own accord their actual position before
their bankers, and having a friendly talk over the
figures. Every man should know that by this course he
secures to himself in times of pressure and panic a
larger measure of help, should he require it, than if his
capital, however ample it might be, were still an unknown
quantity to his bankers.

If it is asked on what ground we claim for banks this
intimate and exceptional knowledge of other people's
affairs, it might be sufficient to reply that we make no
exclusive claim to the information. We seek it for ourselves, it is true, but we have no desire that it should be

withheld from everybody else, nor from a single person who has a right to know it. The information thus acquired you have constantly to impart in confidence to other banks, for the guidance of their customers and themselves. A Banker's Opinion of people, in business or out of it, is in daily and universal request throughout the land; and as the reliance placed upon that opinion is well-nigh absolute, it had needs be sound. It is always as sound as the banker can make it, but not always as reliable as he could wish it to be.

The materials on which he has to form a judgment may, as we have seen, be imperfect. His customers may be shy of giving him assurance of their actual position in the only authentic way, that is, by the witness of their balance-sheets.

He is thus left to frame his opinion, partly on hearsay, partly on the testimony of his own ledgers, and partly on his own observation. But in the absence of a genuine balance-sheet, an opinion thus constructed must, as a rule, be more or less conjectural.

We can understand the smaller class of country trader having a coyness about showing his balance-sheet to his bankers, because he may never have made one, or been instructed how to draw one up, and, therefore, has no balance-sheet to show. But in the case of men in larger ways of business, who have to give much trust themselves, it is difficult to imagine a less judicious form of reticence. It ought to be obvious to them that if every bank knew the exact position of every customer, on the evidence of actual figures, it would be known everywhere with certainty whom to trust and whom to avoid: and thus our annual tale of bad debts in trade, now mounting up to millions, would, beyond question, be largely diminished. It would not exempt us from loss consequent on unforeseen vicissitudes in trade or commerce: but it would give a check to that system of blind credit, which leads us all round into a class of bad debts, the more irritating because they could to a large extent be made avoidable.

The prudent trader will balance his books, if not annually, at least every second or third year, on the same principle that the commander of a ship takes soundings at times, to know whereabouts he is. There ought to be no excuse for the trader who neglects a like precaution. An honest man will desire to shorten sail the moment he finds himself in difficulties. He will thus round the cape of adversity in more hopeful trim than if he drives blindly on to utter wreck, and the just wrath of his creditors. He who will not be ruled by the rudder, says the Cornish proverb, must be ruled by the rock.

A trader's balance-sheet has this supreme recommendation to a banker : it does not rest on hearsay or conjecture. It gives you a man's exact commercial measure in authentic figures. It shews you what liabilities he is under, and the nature, as well as the sum of his assets,— an essential point; because, as we shall see, a man's capital may be set forth—and honestly set forth—in thousands, or tens of thousands, and yet consist of materials without value or avail from a banking point of view.

The printed form of balance-sheet, in use at your Branch for many years past, is short, simple, and comprehensive. It has been the means of saving your Bank from many a bad debt; whilst it has enabled your authorities to judge where to help, as well as to withhold, in trying times; and thus avoid the indiscriminate rigours of panic.

PRIVATE AND CONFIDENTIAL.

Balance sheet of————————————————

————————————————at————————·18————

Assets :—		Liabilities :—	
Book Debts . . . . . £		On Acceptances . . . . £	
Stock in Trade		On Open Account . . .	
Property		Owing to Bank	
		Other Liabilities	
Total . . . £		Total . . . £	
		Surplus or Capital . . . £	

The book debts must exclude all bad and doubtful ones. The stock-in-trade may be taken, according to circumstances, at prime cost or market value. The particulars of the items comprised in the term Property, are to be set forth at length, and at their present values on the back of the document: whether they consist of shares, bonds, or land, or of buildings, machinery, plant, furniture, or fixtures. If any portion of the property is incumbered, the amount and particulars of the incumbrance are to be stated.

The assets insured against fire, and in what offices, are likewise to be given—a point of special importance—because there are many persons, both in trade and out of it, who, rather than pay eighteen-pence a year on every hundred pounds' worth of their property, will run the chance of their goods and chattels vanishing any day or night in flame and smoke—thus taking the hazard of fire at the tremendous odds of 1333 to 1. It is unnecessary to remark that where stock-in-trade, plant and machinery, furniture and pictures, or other aliment of fire constitute the bulk of the assets, a man of good substance might be reduced in a few hours to insolvency ; and an estate worth fifty shillings to-day, be reduced to five shillings in the pound to-morrow.

The Society of Friends have a custom whereby the question is periodically put to each head of a family in their communion—Have you made your will? If the larger community of English creditors, either through their travellers or otherwise, were every now and then to put the question to their debtors—Are you insured against fire? they would be putting a question of equal urgency and moment to their debtors ; whilst the creditor himself might thus avoid having to look for his debt some day amongst blackened walls and smouldering heaps of calcined rubbish.

A man may have responsibilities outside his business, which will have no record in his books. · He may be a guarantor for other people's debts, or a friendly indorser of other men's bills ; and as he anticipates no trouble in respect of them, they will probably find no place in his balance-sheet; hence the heading, Other Liabilities, in order that such contingencies may not be left out of sight.

The form of statement under review is sufficient for all purposes: the merest tyro in book-keeping could fill it up: and he who runs might read it.

When you are assured, therefore, by customers whose balances are uniformly on the wrong side of your ledger, that they cannot fill the form up, not knowing how; you will be apt to suspect that their book-keeping is not what it ought to be, or that they have good reasons for withholding from you an exact knowledge of their affairs.

Let us now see what the three balance-sheets selected for analysis reveal to us. They each show the same amount of capital, and the same indebtedness to the Bank without security: but in other respects they differ from each other more or less widely.

The first statement of the three, that of Mr. Daniel Hyde, tanner, gives us the following figures, as the summary of his position :—

Assets :—		*Liabilities :—*	
Book Debts	£6,000	On Acceptances	£2,500
Stock in Trade	6,000	On Open Account . . .	1,500
Property (Free)	3,000	Owing to the Bank . . .	1,000
		Other Liabilities	nil.
	£15,000		
			£5,000
		Surplus or Capital . . .	£10,000

Mr. Hyde, then, is 'worth' £10,000. He could pay every debt he owes, and still have that amount left of his own. But that is not all: he could discharge his debts at any moment with the greatest ease, because four-fifths of his assets are in readily convertible form.

To put it differently, Mr. Hyde's means exceed his liabilities in the proportion of three to one. He could pay his creditors sixty shillings in the pound. Mr. Hyde is of the stuff that safe bank customers are made of. He is not only a substantial man, but his substantiality is as available as it is ample. It is not such advances as the overdraft on Mr. Hyde's account which disturb a Manager's rest in the night watches.

We come next to the balance-sheet of Messrs. Railton & Co., iron merchants :—

Book Debts	. . . . . . £3,000	Acceptances	£16,000
Stock in Trade	 24,000	Due on Open Account .	3,000
Warehouse and Fixtures		" to Bankers	1,000
(Free)	3,000		£20,000
	£30,000	Surplus or Capital . . .	£10,000

Liability on Bills discounted, £15,000.

In amount of capital and debt to the Bank, this balance-sheet is identical with the preceding one, and the assets are as readily convertible into money. But beyond these points all resemblance ceases. Messrs. Railton & Co. are in a more extended position than Mr. Hyde. Their stock in hand is four times as great as his. A depreciation of 10 per cent. in its value would cause them a loss of £2400, or one-fourth of their capital; whereas the same contingency would cause Mr. Hyde a loss of only a seventeenth part of his.

Again, Mr. Hyde has no bills running. He never draws a bill. He is therefore under no liability to you on that score. But Messrs. Railton are responsible to you on their indorsements to the extent of £15,000. What amount of risk these may involve will depend upon the quality of the bills, and the ability of the acceptors to meet them: but if we put it roughly at £1000, for the sake of argument, that must be regarded as so much latent overdraft. Messrs. Railton therefore will virtually be liable to you for £2000 in all; nevertheless, other things being equal, they would still have resources sufficient to pay their debt to you four times over.

But other things might not be equal. A not unexampled fall in the price of iron might, as we have seen, sweep away a fourth of Messrs. Railton's capital;

whereas an equal fall in the price of leather would hardly make an impression on Mr. Hyde's. It has to be observed, moreover, that whilst his capital is twice the amount of his indebtedness, their indebtedness is twice the amount of their capital. Not that their position, as it now stands, involves risk to you or to anyone : but it is less solid, less invulnerable than Mr. Hyde's, and more subject to vital change in stormy times.

We now come to the balance-sheet of Mr. Abel Trowell, builder :—

Book Debts	£3,000	Acceptances		£5,000
Stock, Buildings in progress, &c.	5,000	Due on Open Account .		2,000
		” to Bank		1,000
Property . . £30,000				———
Less Mortgages . 20,000				£8,000
———				
10,000		Surplus or Capital . . .	£10,000	
———				
£18,000				

Equally with the two preceding statements, Mr. Trowell's shews a capital of £10,000. His statement has likewise another coincidence—he is owing you £1000 without security. But when you look at the nature of the assets out of which your advance is to be repaid, you may well have intermittent qualms as to the safety of the account.

Mr. Trowell, you report, is nearly completing a block of houses on his own account, and, when finished, he is to raise a sum on mortgage of the property, which will enable him to pay you off, and place a good balance to his credit over and above. When this happy change takes place in the aspect of Mr. Trowell's account, you will no doubt think twice before you allow the balance to go to the debit side again without security. His property is already mortgaged to the hilt—that is to say, he has raised all he can upon it. As far, therefore, as his financial requirements are concerned, his property is entirely unavailable. Whether there be any value in the equity, will only be known when the property comes to be realized; but, in the meantime, the £10,000 set forth by Trowell as the value of this asset will be of as little use as an equal number of brickbats in payment of his acceptances, or his men's wages, or his debt to you, or to other people. This item must, therefore, be struck out of his available assets. There will remain £3000 in book debts, and a dubious asset of £5000, consisting of materials and buildings in progress: making together £8000 to meet active liabilities of the same amount. It is, therefore, manifest that if Mr. Trowell should fail to receive any expected instalment under his building contracts, or any sum promised on mortgage, he may find himself in difficulties any day, even as to the payment of his men's wages, to say nothing of the £1000 he is in debt to you or the £7000 he is in debt to other people. It would be difficult to imagine a more noteworthy example of a man nominally worth £10,000, but financially insolvent, from a banker's point of view.

In your private valuation of every trader's assets, as set forth in his balance-sheet, you must take into account the possibility of his failure, and the effect of that misfortune upon their value.

The stock and book debts of Messrs. Railton & Co., for example, would suffer little or no depreciation on being realised; but the realisation of the stock and book debts of a country draper would have a widely different result. The stock may be honestly set forth in the balance-sheet at cost price, but much of it may have gone out of fashion, and become unsaleable, except at a ruinous discount; so that, between the nominal value of a draper's stock in trade and what it will fetch at auction, you must provide for a very wide discrepancy. You will likewise have to make a large abatement from the sum of his book debts. His principal debtors will consist of traders smaller than himself, the majority of whom will break when he breaks; and as regards the residue of his debts, consisting of small sums owing here and there over a wide district, the bulk of them will be absorbed in the cost of collection. It has also to be considered, that a trader is not so rigorous in choosing whom he will trust, as you are bound to be, and that he will regard as good many a debt which you would look upon as more than doubtful. It is to be feared, therefore, that, as a rule, he fails to purge his balance-sheet sufficiently of these; so that on the whole the realisation of a draper's book debts is a disappointing and disastrous process.

The assets of an agriculturist have likewise to be taken with a considerable margin for contingencies, because his growing crops may be blighted by unfavourable weather, or a murrain may make havoc in his sheepfolds, or the foot and mouth disease decimate his cattle.

Again, when shares constitute a portion of the assets, you have to take note of their quality, and their liability to change in value. A customer whose holding of shares consists of first-class English railway stocks, evidently holds a security more solid in value, and stable in price, than if his shares were in ships at sea, or at works, or mines, or in the uncovenanted scrip which is trafficked in beyond the pale of Capel Court. It is of consequence, moreover, to note whether the shares involve a liability to further calls, and, if so, whether the liability is of definite amount. If unlimited, it will matter less what the nature of his other assets may be, because this form of liability may some day sweep them bodily away.

There are likewise assets of a perishable nature, and there are those which a caprice in taste may render well-nigh valueless: and it is certain that there are more descriptions of property liable to waste and depreciation, than to improvement in condition or enhancement in price.

It comes in brief to this—that your estimate of a man's position must rest not merely on the present, but on the prospective value of his assets and property; so far as that value may be affected by the special causes of change to which each form of asset may be liable.

You raise the point—whether a bank known to place reliance on the balance-sheets of traders, as a basis for advances, without security, would not expose itself to the arts of any schemer who chose to victimize it, by a deliberate falsification of his position? No doubt any one who has the courage to play the rogue, may construct a balance-sheet which shall induce you to treat him as a man of substance, when in fact he is a man of straw, and no better than a sharper. But as he might equally persuade you of this by word of mouth, his doing so by means of a balance-sheet will not at all events place you in a worse position; but it will place him at a perceptible disadvantage. He will have put his name to a statement on the shewing of which you have lent him money. He has put his liabilities down at perhaps half their actual amount, and his assets at twice their actual value. The statement is, therefore, false and fraudulent. Your cunning knave has been too clever by half He has been obtaining money under false pretences, and is liable to the consequences of that offence, certified as it happens to be under his own hand. From mere verbal lying and misrepresentation he might wriggle out: but not from a balance-sheet proved to be false, bearing his own signature, and used for a fraudulent purpose. So far therefore from the unprincipled amongst the trading community seeking to hocus you in this way, they are more likely to shun a bank which exposed them to this dangerous formality. The commercial bird of prey will not scruple to attack you whenever you give him the chance; but not in this way. He will avoid what he will designate the 'balance-sheet dodge,' as the experienced rat will avoid an obvious trap.

The probability of your being decoyed into loss by the lure of a spurious balance-sheet is so remote as to be scarce worthy of serious thought. But even, if out of every hundred of these statements one should prove false—that would not amount to a reason for refusing all belief in the other ninety-nine, and therefore dispensing with their use.

LETTER IV.

THE CREDIT OF LIMITED COMPANIES.

JARVIS. *He says he has been at a great deal of trouble to get back the money you borrowed.*

HONEYWOOD. *That I don't know : but I'm sure we were at a great deal of trouble in getting him to lend it.*
THE GOOD-NATURED MAN.

A LIMITED company, the capital of which is wholly paid up, is virtually in the position of an individual who has put his all into his business. You cannot get anything more out of him, nor out of the company, under any form or force of pressure.

Let the three balance-sheets which we have just discussed be those of three limited companies, with their capitals paid up in full: and the same rules of analysis will apply. What is true of the balance-sheet of Daniel Hyde would be equally true if it were that of Daniel Hyde & Co., Limited; and so likewise of the other two. The fact that in one case the capital has been paid up by a number of people, and in the other by a single person, does not of itself in any way affect the position of things. Daniel Hyde & Co., Limited, so long as the balance-sheet shall continue item for item what it is, would be entitled to the same amount of credit as Daniel Hyde himself .

The majority of limited companies, however, leave a portion of their capital uncalled. Your clients, the Imperial Slab Co., do so, and their last balance-sheet gives us the figures following :—

Assets :—		Liabilities :—		
Cost of quarry	£10,000	Due for Purchase		
Goodwill	5,000	Money . .	£9,000	
Book Debts	3,000	" on Mortgage		
Stock	2,000	Debenture .	5,000	
	£20,000	" to Bank . .	1,000	
				15,000
		Surplus, or Paid-up Capital		5,000
		Capital still to call		5,000
				£10,000

The gross assets are £20,000 : but to find the amount of these which are available to pay the debts of the company, you must strike off first the £5000 for goodwill : a nebulous form of asset which may be worth nothing. At the best, it is merely an asset in supposition—a charge upon the future profits of the company, if any. There is no other fund out of which it can be recouped to the shareholders.

From the gross assets, thus reduced to £15,000, you have next to strike off the cost of the property : because you cannot pay the purchase-money, or the debentures, or the Bank balance, with the lease and plant of a quarry, however valuable they may be. They will first have to be turned into money, and that may not be the work of a day nor of many days. The available trading assets of the company are thus reduced to £5000, to meet liabilities more or less deferred, but which have to be met some time, amounting to three times that sum. The liabilities, in fact, exceed the immediately available assets by £10,000.

To provide for this deficiency, the company, as a first step, will have to call up the remaining £5000 of its subscribed capital, because it has already exhausted its legal power of borrowing on debenture. Whereupon the point which first presents itself for inquiry is this: Are the shareholders good for the money? To solve the question, with even a distant approach to accuracy, you will have to procure a list of their names and places of abode, together with the number of shares held by each. You will then have to enter into correspondence with banks in all parts of the country, to ascertain the ability of each shareholder to pay his quota of the call ; a process not always rewarded with conclusive information, but undeniably troublesome. Moreover, there may be able, but unwilling contributories, who, rather than pay up, may force the concern into liquidation : in which event, the exact date for the repayment of your advance will become, to say the least, obscure.

And there is a worse danger than this possible. The whole of the £5000 may be already under notice of call, and mortgaged to some other bank or finance company, without your knowledge : and such a mortgage, as the law now stands, would hold good as against you and all other outside creditors.

But let us assume that the uncalled capital is not mortgaged in the case of the Imperial Slab Company : and that the liquidation is a friendly and inexpensive one. Let us further assume that the call and the trading assets, amounting together to £10,000, on being realized, shall yield within ten per cent. of their nominal amount ; although the likelihood of such a result makes a severe demand on one's doctrine of probabilities. There is, therefore, £9000 in Court to deal with.

But the whole of this will be required to pay the balance of the purchase-money, for which the vendor has no doubt a first lien. It is not likely he would have parted with the property on any other condition. There is still, it is true, the property itself to fall back upon ; but when you come to realize a quarry, or any other description of property, which can only be worked at a loss, the price originally paid for it ceases to be a factor in any reliable estimate of its worth. Moreover, whatever may be the result of a sale, the debenture holders have a prior claim to yours on the proceeds. It is conceivable that these may be sufficient to satisfy their claims, but the probabilities with one accord point all the other way. In any event, they have no interest in the property fetching a single farthing beyond what will suffice to pay themselves, and will only be too thankful, when the biddings reach that point, to see the hammer fall without more ado. In any probable event, therefore, you will be left out in the cold, without a penny piece towards your debt, or any one to proceed against for a farthing of it.

In thus dealing with this balance-sheet of a limited company, we have taken everything at the worst that could happen to its shareholders or the Bank; unless indeed, the Bank were to buy the quarry in, and take to working it on its own account. The future of its advance from that moment would pass beyond the reach of human estimate.

It is only fair to admit that the Imperial Slab Co. is one of an exceptional class. In ratio of number, there are probably as many sound limited trading companies as there are sound private firms, or individual traders. Nevertheless, the difficulties, complications, and risks, which we have been reviewing, should be present to your mind, whenever you seek to measure the trustworthiness of any limited company by the shewing of its balance-sheet.

There is yet another risk which you have to consider when you make advances to a limited company, which is this:—Its articles of association may not give it the power to borrow from a bank; but even if they do, the exercise of the power may be hedged round with difficult forms of legal observance, of the due performance of which you can never be perfectly assured. Even with the exercise of the greatest caution, you may find some day that you have made an advance to a limited concern, for which neither the company itself, nor its Manager, nor any one else, is legally responsible. Except, therefore, where the undertaking is one of acknowledged success, with ample capital and immediately available trade assets, sufficient at all times to discharge its trade liabilities, you require the personal guarantee of its Directors, when you make advances to a limited company.

These gentlemen will know whether such advances are within the scope and limit of their borrowing powers, and what resources will be at hand to meet the advances when due. They will always be on the right side of the hedge, because they can protect themselves ; but, without their guarantee, you may some day find yourself on the wrong side of it, with ño debtor in tangible form betwixt you and the horizon. In all other cases, there is usually something to go upon, or somebody to go against, and a residuum and dividend of some sort. But in the case of a concern like the Imperial Slab Co., you find yourself in the condition of an exhausted receiver, with the vacuum for your debt.

LETTER V.

COVER FOR DEBT.

Nor do we let fall our pen upon discouragement of contradiction, unbelief, and difficulty of dissuasion from radicated beliefs and points of high prescription : although we are very sensible how hardly teaching years do learn, what roots old age contracteth into errors, and such as are but acorns in our younger brows, grow oaks in our elder heads and become inflexible unto the powerfullest arm of reason. SIR THOMAS BROWNE.

WE have now explored the various paths of inquiry which are open to a banker when he seeks to ascertain what a man is worth and what this worth consists of. You have to rely for this knowledge on hearsay, or on the shewing of a man's bank account, or on the witness of his balance-sheet. On one or other of these sources of information you have to place your reliance, when you seek to measure the responsibility of any individual, as a borrower on his own account, or as a surety for others.

But although the information thus obtainable, as to the sum and substance of a man's worth, may be exact and true at the time, it may not continue to be true. An advance may be safe at the time it is made, but the circumstances of the borrower may readily change for the worse without your knowledge. It is true, that in the great majority of cases, you will have the means of detecting this change, without further guidance than the shewing of a man's bank account : but there remains this difficulty—the knowledge may come too late. You may come to the conclusion that a man's affairs are going the wrong way, and call his account up : but his affairs may by that time have drifted so far into insolvency that your call cannot be responded to. The knowledge that a man's circumstances are becoming involved will doubtless have this value—it will put a

31

stop to any increase in your advance to him: and in many cases the knowledge will come to you in time to enable you with due diligence to recall and to recover your existing advance: but, as I have just said, the knowledge will not be available in every case: it will not always come in time.

A man may commence business with ample capital, conduct his bank account with the strictest regularity, never exceed by a pound the limit of overdraft allowed him without security, and yet, after a few years, shall make a bad failure, to the dismay of his bankers, and the surprise of all. He has been speculating secretly in shares, or produce, or something else, and has managed to keep all trace of such transactions out of his bank account, and therefore from the knowledge of his bankers. Whilst they are serenely reliant on the splendid figures of his latest balance-sheet, one asset after another has furtively melted away and disappeared in the unknown depths of his 'differences.'

The case is fortunately exceptional. For one man who suddenly abandons a sound and legitimate business and a respectable position in life, to cast his all into the vortex of speculation, there are tens of thousands who are never afflicted with this form of insanity: but although such cases are abnormal, they cannot be left out of count, if you are to reckon with and guard yourself against every contingency.

Our banking losses are always exceptional. We never make an advance which we expect will become a loss. It is always, therefore, the unexpected which happens, when a bank makes a bad debt, and it arises invariably at some point which has been left exposed,— on some account which has been left unguarded by security. And the only way effectually to safeguard this, the weakest point of country banking, is never to make an advance to any one, except on security of approved quality and adequate value.

You act upon this principle when you employ the Bank's money in the discount of bills. You do not part

with it on the individual security of the last indorser.
He virtually provides you with bail, in the persons of
the acceptor and other obligants on the bill.

This being so, when you employ your money in discounts, it does not appear on what ground you should
ever lend it on overdrawn account without any security
at all.   On the contrary, the need for cover is greater :
because in the case of a bill there is actual value behind
it, in addition to the personal security of the obligants :
whereas an overdraft need not necessarily rest on any
value at all beyond the responsibility of the borrower
himself   Moreover, the bill has a brief and definite term
to run.   The circumstances of the parties to it will only
have some three months in which to change for the worse,
before it comes to maturity.   But money advanced on
overdrawn account without security to an agreed-on
limit, is not usually subject to such prompt repayment.
The debtor on this form of advance has therefore a
longer time for getting into trouble, if his affairs should
tend in that direction.

It may be unpleasant to have to refuse an advance to
a gentleman of good family but restricted means, with
whom you are on terms of friendly intercourse.   But in
banking, as we had occasion to remark at the outset, the
scope for sentiment is limited.   The feelings need no
more be touched by refusing to lend a gentleman money
without security, than by refusing to make a bet, or to go
a cruise, or make a tour with him, or anything else that
is simply inconvenient.   It may be an amiable weakness to think otherwise ; but if a bad debt is to be
the fruit of this amiability, the sooner your disposition is
soured the better.

You admit the principle of requiring cover to be
sound, but you hold that it would be unwise to enforce
it in every instance, unless you are prepared to see some
of your most valued accounts going over to your neighbours, The Old Bank, Messrs. Yewtrey & Co.

You are assured that they seldom act upon the rule,
and act upon it in a liberal spirit when they act at all.

But if this assurance has come to you through customers of your own, to whom a similar laxity on your part would be an obvious convenience, you will no doubt entertain it with a proper infusion of distrust. In the ordinary course of your business, you must be prepared frequently to hear, from one quarter or another, that your terms are less liberal, and your conditions more stringent than those of other banks. In almost every instance the reproach, when inquired into, will prove to be groundless. In some cases it will have arisen from misapprehension: in others from idle talk: and in some few from deliberate mis-statement. Nevertheless, a rigid adherence to the rule in every case, would, no doubt, result in a certain loss of business, which no bank is willing to face, even although the loss should consist exclusively of a batch of overdrawn accounts uncovered by security.

As banking usage in the provinces prevails at present, therefore, you feel obliged continually to depart from the only rule which would render your advances safe under all circumstances. You feel constrained, because other banks do so, to depart from a principle which would make each of your overdrafts secure, whatever reverse of fortune should overwhelm the debtor himself.

You quote in reply the dictum of an old writer: ' He ought to be well mounted who is for leaping the hedges of custom.' That is true; but the fact that you are constantly forced by custom out of the safe lines of banking, affords no reason why we should not discuss the usage on its merits. It may be that its unsoundness and danger, if made manifest to all, might lead to its gradual limitation, and in time to its final abandonment.

Let it be admitted then, as it may be, without controversy, that there are people in Oxborough who would be safe beyond all doubt for advances without security: nevertheless, it is equally beyond cavil that no one is as safe without security as with it. If every advance on your books were covered by adequate security, it is clear that in respect of such advances you would stand abso-

lutely exempt from the risk of loss : but the moment
you begin to make exceptions to the rule, by granting
advances to this client or to that, without security, you
leave the solid ground of safety for the treacherous
swamps of banking risk.

Bear in mind that every advance which you make
without security, will rest for its safety on the unerring
accuracy of your own judgment as to the means and
character of the borrower. But in such cases is your
judgment—is any man's—infallible? Is it equal in any
case to good collateral security?

In making your selection and choice of the trust-
worthy amongst your customers—in separating the
sheep from the goats—your experience will be more
than human, if you do not take to your bosom a black
sheep now and then. And the irony of the thing will
lie in this—your losses, when they do happen, will come
to you from your chosen ones—from those in whom you
have placed your business faith, and to whom unhappily you have lent the Bank's money without security.

Let us suppose that you have advanced £1000 for
three months without security to a client believed at the
time by everybody, yourself included, to be a man of
substance, and undoubted for the amount. Let us
further suppose that this estimate of his means turns out
to have been a delusion, and that the man fails, and is
made bankrupt and pays five shillings in the pound.
Now your clear profit on the transaction, taking all things
into account, will not have much exceeded a £5 note.
To secure this modest recompense of reward, you have
risked £1000 and actually lost £750. You will have
to make 150 fresh advances of a thousand pounds each
—that is to say, you will have to incur fresh uncovered
risks to the amount of £150,000 to redeem your loss.

Now, are the chances 150 to 1 in favour of almost any
man, that he will repay an advance when due? Or to
put it differently : out of any 150 unsecured advances, is
it a moral certainty that all will be repaid? You may
be correct in 149 cases : but if you are wrong in one, the

loss on that one will swallow up the profits on all the rest and strip you of even the semblance of reward for all your risk, work, and anxiety.

The only rule, therefore, which insures safety in ,every case, is never to make any advance without security. It is not enough that you may do so in hundreds of cases with impunity, because, as we have just seen, the fruits of your success may be swept away at any time by one reverse.

And the proper time to stipulate for security, it has to be observed, should be before the opening of an account —not afterwards. To allow an overdraft to remain unsecured for a time, and then require it to be covered, will incense a client with the belief that you have heard of something to his disadvantage : and it will be difficult to persuade him to the contrary. You trusted me before, he may fairly protest,—why distrust me now? And thus a requirement, which, if stipulated for at first, would have been without offence, may become a grievance and affront.

When a man of property borrows money from a private person, the usual basis and condition of the loan is a mortgage on the property of the borrower ; not as a favour, but as a matter of course and ordinary business custom. This being so, it is difficult to see on what ground a banker is expected to lend his money to any-one without a similar formality.

It may be argued that there is a material difference betwixt a temporary advance, such as is generally obtained from a banker, and the permanent loan which is usually obtained on mortgage. There is this difference certainly,—there is less chance of anyone wasting his substance in three months than in three years. Nevertheless, the private lender can part with his money with greater safety for years than you can for months, because under all circumstances he has his mortgage to fall back upon : whereas you have nothing. He has protected his advance with sufficient cover against all weathers ; whilst yours stands naked and exposed to every wind of adversity.

It will **not** be wise, therefore, to lay much weight on
the temporary nature of your uncovered advances, as an
element of safety.   Some of the heaviest bad debts
known to English banking had their inception as
temporary advances.

It is a point worthy of consideration, also, that if you
excuse certain of your customers from giving security
whilst you exact it from others, you can hardly fail now
and then to be guilty of injustice.   You cannot in every
instance hope to draw with perfect exactness the line
which divides those who are safe, and those who are unsafe, without security.   You require security from Mr.
Smallfield because you suspect him to be poor ; but you
let Mr. Manifold have what he wants without security,
because you account him to be rich.   You are justified
in this as custom rules at present : but would it not be
a less invidious course to require security from both
alike ?   Mr. Smallfield must know that you do make
advances to other people without security, and he will
deem it a hardship that an old client, like himself, should
be denied a like indulgence.

Moreover, you will find that men of substance are less
opposed to giving security than men of limited means
are.   The chief objectors indeed to giving security for
advances are those who have none to give.   They will
tell you with calm effrontery that men of their standing
object to the thing on principle, and that to demand
security from men of refined commercial instincts is to
expose their feelings to moral outrage.   You will know
how to deal with these susceptibilities when occasion
offers, and how to put them to a just appraisement.

If it were represented to Mr. Manifold that the giving
of security in his case would be purely a matter of form,
but that it would strengthen your hands in demanding
it in cases where security would be indispensable ; he
would at least appreciate your difficulty, and would in
all likelihood comply with your request.   And what Mr.
Manifold would do, others would be equally ready to do,
if the reason of the thing were plainly and frankly put

before them.   When it came to be understood by traders
and others of visible means, that by giving security for
advances, they placed you in a position to enforce the
same condition on traders and others of invisible means;
it is reasonable to conclude that-they would comply with
your rule in their own interests.

The unsecured advances of English banking, from the
outset, were doubtless made with an assured faith in
every case that the borrowers were individuals, or firms,
of acknowledged means and unimpeachable credit.   It
is not to be imagined that any Manager or Board
of Directors, ever made an advance in the deliberate
expectation and belief of its becoming a bad debt.
Unfortunately, however, as we have seen, it is always in
the matter of advances made without security, that the
unexpected happens.

That would be a remarkable return, if it were to be
procured, which should shew the net result to English
banking of uncovered advances.   Place in one scale the
aggregate of profit, and in the other the aggregate of
loss upon such accounts, and who can doubt for a moment
which scale shall instantly and with a vengeance kick
the beam ?   The losses upon uncovered advances, within
recent memory, have been of a magnitude sufficient, one
might suppose, to impress upon the minds of bankers,
with an emphasis that should be lasting, the danger of
such advances ; and the expediency of rendering security
henceforward an indispensable condition for money lent
or advanced.

To give general effect to the principle would, no doubt,
require a greater degree of concert and a livelier sense of
a common danger, on the part of English banks, than
exist at present; because no bank can act upon the
principle rigidly, whilst its competitors play fast and
loose with it, without a certain loss of business.   Those
persons who have come to regard an uncovered overdraft,
less in the light of a favour than as a matter of custom and
right, would no doubt exclaim against the adoption of
a system that would restrict them to a narrower range

of operations : and they would without scruple take their custom elsewhere, provided they found banks prepared to take them at their own valuation, and adopt their accounts on their own terms.

But against the loss of income thus occasioned place the loss that might arise some day on one or other of these uncovered accounts : and it is at least a possibility that your present loss might prove an eventual gain. Better lose the profit on a naked overdraft now, than its principal amount hereafter.

It is at least a reasonable contention that a bank which had the courage, in this matter, to take custom by the beard, and resolutely decline, after a certain date, to make any advance without security, would not be a loser in the long run. It would necessarily do less business for a time, but the profits made on its reduced business would at least be beyond attack : so that its shareholders would probably receive the same dividends as heretofore, and with greater certitude of continuance, because there would be no desolating inroad of bad debts every now and then, to swallow profits up.

Would it be an impossible thing for the Banks in any given town to come to an understanding that after a certain date they would make no advances upon fresh accounts without security? Such a course would leave the existing business of the Banks intact, to work itself out on existing conditions ; but it would lay a basis for the business of the future, which would give it a degree of safety and solidity in this particular direction which the present system lacks.

The necessity, moreover, that all advances by banks should be covered by security is increasing with the increase of competition in banking. The continued attenuation in the rates of banking profit in certain directions, which is the outcome of this competition, is gradually narrowing the margin for bad debts. As your profits diminish, so must your risks, and notably that class of them which consists of advances without security.

You ask whether character is not in itself a security : whether there are not persons, even of limited means, to whom it would be safe for a bank to lend money without security—persons who would shrink with honest repulsion from undertaking any liability which they did not see their way rigorously to fulfil.

No doubt there is security, of a kind, in honest intention : but honesty itself may be overthrown by unforeseen disaster. A man may borrow money from you and resolve with all his · might to pay it back again. He sees his way, he believes, with perfect clearness, at the time, to do so. But no amount of honesty will endow a man with second sight ; it will not enable him to see further than his neighbours through a stone wall ; neither will it shield him from business misfortune.

To make advances on the strength of character, moreover, requires the banker who ventures upon this line of business to be a reader of men : but this is a faculty with which bankers are not supremely gifted. On the contrary, my experience is that bankers have the full average capacity of being taken in, when they go beyond the safe line of advances on security, and venture upon the quicksands of personal credit.

If a customer, even of slender means, applies to you for a temporary advance without security, and can satisfy you that his difficulty is accidental, and that the means to recoup your advance will reach his hands immediately, and you have dealt with him a sufficient number of years to be assured of his integrity and righteous dealing, you might be justified in making an exception in his case. You are merely making an advance against money virtually in sight and which will be in your hands in a few days ; unless indeed he turn rogue at the last moment, and cancel at a stroke the honest repute of a lifetime. But such· exceptional and temporary help is a widely different transaction from lending such a man money without security, to trade with and put into his business, practically for good.

You ask whether the profit on an account ought not,

in some measure, to regulate the amount of risk taken
upon it: that ·is to say—whether you would not be
justified in making a larger advance, other things being
equal, upon an account that brought you in £50 a-year,
than upon one which brought you an annual profit of
only £10.

The advance upon any given account must be regulated absolutely by its safety, and not by the return of
profit which the account may yield. When you find
yourself troubled with the fear of losing a good account,
unless you agree to continue, or enlarge the advance
upon it without security : the question will narrow itself
to this,—will you rather risk the principal of the debt
than lose the profit upon it? Will you let the fear of
losing even the most profitable account ·on your books
induce you to continue or enlarge a risk upon it which
you would not otherwise take? There can be only one
answer to the question, and the answer must be—No.
But the temptation is great, and therefore has to be
jealously watched and steadfastly resisted. It is one
of the most insidious allurements against which you will
have to set your face in the conduct of your business.
The profits on such accounts are pleasing to the eye :
but too frequently they prove bitter to the taste, and
become the Dead Sea fruit of banking.

But although you cannot allow the profit on the most
valuable account to obscure for a moment the cardinal
question of its safety, there is one important concession
which you make in the working of such accounts,—you
treat them as sacred from touch, even in the exigencies
of panic, so long as the circumstances of the holders or
their securities suffer no change for the worse. The
holders, thus exempted from the fear of having their
overdrafts called up, can make consecutive and more
lucrative use of them. In consideration of the larger
profit which you derive from such accounts, you enable
the operators upon them to reap a corresponding
advantage.

LETTER VI.

OVERDRAWN ACCOUNTS.

As it shall not be lawful for each man to be a usurer who will, so shall it not be lawful for all to take money at use—not to prodigals and spendthrifts, but to merchants, young tradesmen, and such as stand in need, or know honestly how to employ it.
ANATOMY OF MELANCHOLY.

GIVEN, you say, a responsible tradesman applying for leave to overdraw his account to a certain limit, the annual operations on the account chargeable with the usual commission being ten times the amount of advance, and the advance itself being secured by the guarantee of persons safe for the amount;—given these conditions, you desire to know why you may not accept such an account as soon as offered, instead of having to refer it in the first instance to your Head Office for approval.

It may at once be conceded that you do not stand alone in your manifest leaning towards this class of account. It contributes largely to the revenue of a Branch: it has therefore a special attraction for officers of spirit, who are still in the fervour of their managerial youth. The larger the number of overdrawn accounts —thus runs the argument—the larger the profits: and the larger the profits of a Branch, the higher the Manager will stand in the estimation of the Board: therefore—the nearer he will stand to the next rise in his salary.

The pleasing fallacies which this formula involves will come up for hearing and judgment in due course. Meanwhile, let us deal with the overdrawn account on its own merits.

And first as regards the plea of safety. No doubt the

42

paramount consideration with a banker when he makes
an advance is the certainty of its repayment. It may be
taken for granted that no one in the possession of his
ordinary senses would lend his money without this
certainty—without a conviction that he would be repaid
his loan with interest to the uttermost farthing.   But
with a banker, there are considerations beyond these.
The safety of any particular account or series of accounts
is one thing : the financial safety of his bank is another.
It involves no paradox to affirm that a bank may not
have a single unsafe account in its ledgers, and yet be in
an unsound position itself   A bank, to be in a perfectly
sound financial position, should be able at all times to
meet, with ease and amplitude, the demands which may
be made upon it at any time by its depositors.   If
therefore it has to look to ledgers-full of overdrawn
accounts—no matter how safe they may be—as its
principal means to meet a rush, or even a heavy drain
upon its deposits ; its position might conceivably be one
of actual peril.   A drain upon the resources of a bank,
whose business was chiefly confined to the discount of
negociable bills, could be met by simply contracting the
volume of its discounts ; but you do not necessarily
diminish your existing overdrafts a single pound by
refusing to grant fresh ones.

No doubt the overdrafts, as a rule, have been granted
on the understanding that they might be called up at
any time.   But to call up an overdrawn account, and to
obtain payment of it, are distinct and not identical
operations.   Between the date of recall and the receipt
of the money, there will lie an uncertain interval,
extending over weeks or months, or even years, as the
case may be.

If the borrower has accustomed himself to make use
of the overdraft only now and then, to meet a casual
excess of engagements over his means in hand to meet
them, repayment will be prompt.   If he has used the
overdraft as a permanent addition to his floating capital,
repayment will be a slower, but still a measurable

process in respect of time. But if he has fixed it in his trade—in buildings or machinery, in plant, fixtures, or book debts, the time of repayment will be altogether uncertain ; and even highly lucrative overdrafts of this description, you will confess, would be but a poor resource from which to meet an active drain upon your deposits.

You remind me that there are the sureties to fall back upon. I will go further, and admit that they may eventually be good for the obligation ; but this in no wise proves their ability to redeem the guarantee when required. I apprehend that no sane person puts his name down as surety for a thousand pounds, or any other amount, in the expectation that he will ever have to pay the money. The consequence is, that a surety as little thinks of providing for such a contingency, as he does for paying off the National Debt. As a rule, therefore, it is the nature of sureties to be unprepared to meet such engagements.

Overdrafts, then, and especially those of a permanent character, are deficient in that first requisite of a banker's assets ; namely—ready convertibility into money in case of need.

It is a further objection to permanently overdrawn accounts, that they limit the extent of assistance which you might otherwise afford to the monetary wants of your district.

Let us take the case of your customer A. B. by way of illustration. He is allowed an overdraft of £1000, of which he steadily avails himself to the full. Your advance in his case is practically a dead loan. As long as he retains the money, it is certain that you cannot lend it to anyone else. But if you had conditioned with him that his account was to be overdrawn only now and then to the stipulated limit, the money would have been at your disposal during each interval to lend to other people.

Let us take the average duration of permanent overdrafts at the moderate period of three years ; and contrast a thousand pounds thus advanced to an individual, with a like amount advanced every three months to a succession of individuals. By the one process, it is obvious that you assist one man only, to the extent of a thousand pounds within the period; whereas by the other you assist a dozen men to the extent of a thousand pounds each.

Not that there must therefore be no more overdrawn accounts—no more banking cakes and ale. Within certain limits, which we shall have to discuss by and by, they are an allowable and necessary feature of English country banking. We are here taking account merely of their financial incidence as banking assets.

And is the privilege of overdrawing one's bank account uniformly of advantage to the person thus favoured? The privilege wisely used is no doubt a valuable one: but it is often misused, to the ruin of the borrower himself, and the injury of other people.

Let us take from your ledgers a case in point. Samuel Titson, draper, Oxborough, has been allowed an overdraft on his account for so many years, without question, that he has, practically, ceased to regard it as a liability. The amount has consequently become as 'fixed' in his trade as the £500 with which he boldly started in business ten years ago. A fatal ambition to out-draper all Oxborough has brought him a prodigious business, but it has raised his liabilities to corresponding figures: so that when it dawns at last upon your predecessor Mr. Littleworth, that the overdraft has become excessive and ought to be reduced, and he applies for its reduction accordingly, the astonished Titson is on the eve of applying for its further enlargement.

Now if Titson were wise, he would cease forthwith to pile up stock and book debts on borrowed money. He would reverse the process, and bring his liabilities within safer compass. But he only cares to think how best to meet this unexpected and upsetting demand of the Bank. He therefore arranges with the travellers for the wholesale houses with whom he deals, for the renewal of his acceptances to them due next 'fourth,' and thus gains sufficient command of his daily receipts to effect the required reduction in his overdraft. The Bank is appeased for the time, and Mr. Titson thus completes his first stage on the road to the Gazette.

He cannot have proceeded far, before he discovers that the reduction of his overdraft has not diminished his liabilities as a whole by a single pound. It has simply varied their distribution. He has reduced his debt to the Bank by going further into debt to other people. His friends, the travellers, begin to come their rounds again with remorseless punctuality, and if his difficulty was great in fencing them off, the previous journey, it is fourfold greater now : because whilst their demands have doubled in amount, his excuses for delay have lost half their force. He cannot now rely upon receiving much from his book debts before the turn of the year ; but he can draw upon his debtors for what they owe him, and upon the more affable of them, no doubt, for a good deal more. With these bills and a sprinkling of cash, backed by promises of enlarged orders and payments in full next time, Titson wheedles his travellers into unwilling contentment, and thus finds his way to the end of the second stage.

Early in the third, the Bank is again at his doors for a further reduction ; and the first batch of his renewed acceptances are rapidly becoming due and must be met in cash, come what may. Dealing as usual with his difficulties as they arise, and taking no thought for the morrow, Titson now decides upon a vigorous move : he resolves to have a clearance sale. The lovers of bargains at 50 per cent. below prime cost flock to the shop, and enough is realized to meet all pressing claims. Mr. Titson thus tides on ; but only towards increasing difficulties and final collapse.

A distant creditor, exasperated at last by repeated promises which are never kept, now issues a writ, and even the stout heart of Titson sinks within him. A traveller he could cajole, the Bank he might put off, an acceptance he might renew ; but a writ, he knows, means for him money down, debt and costs on the nail, or ruin swift and irretrievable.   Thus driven to the wall, money-less and desperate, and giving ear to evil counsel, he finds refuge in a cognovit, which pacifies the obnoxious creditor for a time ; and thus Mr. Titson accomplishes the fourth stage of his career.

The writ has barely been satisfied, when the bills drawn by Titson upon his customers begin to return to the holders with a persistent uniformity of dishonour—the reason being, that they had for the most part been accepted on the understanding that Titson was to meet them when due—the acceptors, meanwhile, sending him their 'takings' as they came in, without reference to the bills at all.   His own acceptances, further renewals being denied him, now begin to be dishonoured.   The Bank, thoroughly alarmed, becomes increasingly urgent; whilst creditors at a distance, finding that Mr. Titson's signature to a cheque is no longer regarded even on a second or third presentment, become uneasy and resent-ful.   Thus beset on all sides, and driven to the wall, an assignment for the general behoof is wrung from him at last.   Several large creditors, however, finding that others have been paid in full, whilst they have been left in the lurch, decline to come in, and so the affair terminates in bankruptcy and sixpence in the pound.

LETTER VII.

INSOLVENT TRADING.

Debt! Why, that's more for your credit, sir; it is an excellent policy to owe much in these days, if you will note it.
EVERY MAN OUT OF HIS HUMOUR.

THE unprofessional reader of this correspondence, if there be any such person, may regard this story of a draper as a mere flight of the imagination; but no English country banker will have much difficulty in recognizing in Samuel Titson a familiar acquaintance.

It has to be admitted that the blame of his career did not rest altogether with Titson himself. In respect of the money lent him by the Bank, for instance, he merely made the same improvident use of it which most persons in his position and with his lights would have done. That is to say, he put it into his trade as so much capital. He never reckoned upon the Bank calling it up, and made no provision for such a contingency. Had your predecessor kept Titson's overdraft strictly to its original and proper limit, he at least would have saved the Bank from abetting Titson in his mania for extension. As it was, Mr. Littleworth, good easy man, had unbounded faith in Titson's energy and business habits. His periodical report on the account might have been stereotyped, for it invariably ran thus:—'Perfectly safe, business increasing, making money fast.' As a matter of fact, the author of this report was Titson himself, who gave it to Mr. Littleworth, who repeated it to the Directors as his own; which in one sense it was, because there is no doubt that he honestly believed it to be true. In this belief he allowed the overdraft to increase, not in

48

"Perhaps no man in the country is better qualified than Mr. Knox to perform a work of this kind, and surely, within the limits proposed for himself, it would have been difficult for anyone to perform it more satisfactorily. The Volume is a careful and thorough review of all legislation and of judicial decisions and public discussions relative to the questions of currency since the organization of the Government."—NEW YORK TRIBUNE.

"Probably no man in the country is better qualified than John Jay Knox to write a history of the various issues of paper money which have been authorized by the United States government."—NEW YORK JOURNAL OF COMMERCE.

"The book is indispensable for reference in all discussions of the currency question."—HARTFORD COURANT.

"We should be puzzled indeed to refer elsewhere for the information that it collects in most available shape, and we trust that its modest title will deter nobody from the perusal of a work of great historical value."—ST. PAUL PIONEER-PRESS.

"This is a welcome addition to the meagre literature pertaining to the history of national finance. In a Volume not greatly exceeding 200 pages, the author has given a Very interesting and accurate account of the Various issues of paper money by the national government. The work is strictly a history and not a record of the author's theories or opinions. The subject is Very important, and, since the Supreme Court has finally settled the constitutionality of the legal tender legislation, we are likely to hear much in the near future concerning the issue of government notes."—NEW YORK BANKERS' MAGAZINE.

"* * * This bare outline of the subjects treated in Mr. Knox's able and useful Volume affords but a slight idea of the wealth of historical facts, dates, and information, and of the sound financial doctrines that is embodied in the luminous essays that forms its brief and comprehensive chapters."—HARPER'S MONTHLY.

"The recently published book of Mr. Knox, entitled 'United States Notes,' is an admirably clear and dispassionate collection of historical facts bearing upon the subject. We have to thank the author, although a little outside the main purpose of the work, for the fullest and best account of the distribution of the surplus in 1837 that has ever been written."—FINANCIAL CHRONICLE, NEW YORK.

"The subject is treated historically, and the book will not only prove invaluable to students of finance, but is worth a place on the shelves of every banking-house and public library."—TORONTO WEEK.

"A second and revised edition of the Valuable work on 'United States Notes,' by ex-Comptroller Knox, with the figures brought down to 1885, has just been published by Charles Scribner's Sons. An edition has also been brought out in London."—THE NATION.

"Mr. John Jay Knox's book on 'United States Notes' has had a rapid sale, and a second edition of it is now in course of issue. The work is of great practical value to the banker, the merchant, and the economist."—NEW YORK DAILY COMMERCIAL BULLETIN.

⁎ *For sale by all booksellers, or sent by mail, post-paid, on receipt of the price, by*

CHARLES SCRIBNER'S SONS, PUBLISHERS,

743 AND 745 BROADWAY, NEW YORK.

proportion to a corresponding increase in Titson's capital, duly ascertained, but in proportion to the operations on the account.　He appears to have divided these by ten, to find the amount which the bank might safely advance to Titson without security and without enquiry.　When the operations were £5000, the limit of safety would be reached at £500.　When they rose to £10,000, the limit would be reached at £1000, and so forth.　He computed Titson's success by the volume of his business, and determined his stability by the rule of three.

It does not appear to have struck him that Titson's principle of trade was the 'nimble penny,' and that his only chance against the old-established drapers of the town was to go in for small profits and quick returns.　Titson held that twenty transactions, on which the profit was a shilling each, were equal to a single transaction on which the profit was a pound.　Working on this maxim, the operations on his bank account necessarily increased, hand over hand.　But their rapid increase held no warning for Mr. Littleworth.　He **was** content to measure Titson's stability by his spread **of** canvas, rather than by his weight of ballast.

When the matter came to be looked into, it was seen that the Bank had virtually been in partnership with Titson for years, and doing an active business in the drapery line without knowing it.　But the co-partnership had this curious disadvantage :—the profits, if any, would go to Mr. Titson : whereas the losses would fall upon the Bank.

Now there are mercers on your books, who work their business on capitals of their own, and seldom trouble you for advances : was it fair to them to enable a man of straw, by means of excessive banking facilities, to half ruin their business for a series of years ?

You suggest, in reply, that the man who has to pay for the use of capital, cannot well undersell the man who is working with his own.　But Titson did, and thousands do.　Moreover, Titson did not pay for the capital lent him by the Bank.　He paid you neither principal nor

interest.   He fought his competitors in trade with what
was found money to him, although it was lost money
to you.

The man who is regardless how many shillings in the
pound he may some day pay his creditors, has a palpable
advantage over those who are scrupulous to pay their
debts to the last shilling.   He has the difference—the
sum of his delinquency—to play with.   If he is owing
£20,000 when he calls his creditors together, and his
assets have shrunk to £5000, he has manifestly had
£15,000 to do with as he thought fit.   He may have
added a ward to a hospital out of it, or a spire to the
church, or enlarged the parish schoolhouse, or done any
other act of munificence with other people's money.
To steal a sheep and give the trotters away for God's
sake, is an old Spanish saw.   In the case of- our
insolvent it has become a modern instance.   He could
afford to be generous.   Out of every sovereign owing to
his creditors, he has appropriated fifteen shillings to himself and left five shillings for them.   But he may not
have devoted any portion of his deficiency even to acts
of spurious beneficence.   He may have preferred to use
his creditors' money to speculate or gamble with, or to
settle upon his wife, or spend in riotous living, or to hide
away until the thing should blow over,—that is to say,
until the denuded creditors should have had their dividend, and he his discharge.

But Titson, it has to be admitted, did none of these
things.   He devoted the difference betwixt his debts and
his dividend—say nineteen and sixpence out of every
pound—to the single purpose of driving competition
out of Oxborough, by selling for years together below
cost price.   No wonder his competitors in business
were indignant with your Bank, when the extent of its
advances to their aggressive rival became known.

You submit that the case of Titson is exceptional;
because a man who uses borrowed money, not knowing
when he may have to pay it back, will, as a rule, be more
careful how he lays it out than if it were his own.   It

may be so with borrowers of tender conscience ; but that is not an universal quality, nor is it one on which it would be prudent for a banker to lean exclusively for the repayment of an advance.

Moreover, there are persons with a certain obliquity of business vision, who profess to regard a loan from a bank and a loan from a private person, as things morally distinct. To an individual, they will tell you, the loss of the money might be ruin : but to a great joint stock bank it would be only so much to each proprietor, a mere bagatelle, which he would never feel. 'In the name of Mercury, the great god of thieves,' exclaims Sydney Smith, 'did any man ever hear of debtors alleging the wealth of the lender as a reason for eluding the payment of the loan?' Advances, without the most ample security, to persons holding these views, will no doubt be marked in your private register as doubly hazardous, and shunned accordingly with steadfast resolution.

We were once told by a man with whom we had made a bad debt,—a man of fair intelligence and average honesty,—that we need not be so angry with him, because, if we would cast up the interest and commission he had paid on his account during the last five and twenty years, we should find that we had lost little or nothing by him !

LETTER VIII.

OCCASIONAL OVERDRAFTS.

What surprised me most was, that, though he was a money borrower, he defended his opinion with as much obstinacy as if he had been my patron. VICAR OF WAKEFIELD.

IT is not to be assumed that every one makes the like improvident use of an overdraft that Samuel Titson did. As a rule, experience points the other way. The customers of a country bank are not all Titsons. His congeners in trade, no doubt, are to be found here and there amongst the constituents of every provincial bank; but the majority of people in business have a wholesome dread of getting beyond their depth. They, therefore, avail themselves with thrift and only upon occasion, of the facilities offered by the overdrawn account.

The non-arrival of a ship when due, for example, the detention of a mail, the non-receipt of a promised payment, and other such incidents in the daily course of business life, are proper occasions for a timely advance from one's banker. So, likewise, when rent day has come round before the farmer has sold his wheat or his fat stock; or when the mercer, the woolstapler, the tanner, or any other trader, is replenishing his stock of raw material or manufactured goods; in these and in like cases, the banker may reasonably be expected to assist with an advance, in proportion to the means of the borrower, his habits of business, and the circumstances of the case. If these are perfectly known to you, you will rarely make an unwise advance.

52

You tell me that there are persons of undoubted means and position, who would not submit to be cate-chised as to the object of an advance ; and that sometimes the first notice you have of an overdraft being required, is the presentment of the cheque which creates it. But in nine cases out of ten you will know, without asking, whether the proposed advance will be in the strict course of a man's business : and in the remaining case, if the borrower be of undoubted means and position, there will be no need to catechise him. He has probably overdrawn his account by inadvertence.

Your active accounts are chiefly those of men engaged in business or trade, and no man will lightly risk his commercial credit by issuing a cheque that may come back to him through several banks, with the damaging inscription—' Refer to the drawer,' on the face of it.

No doubt there are persons of another stamp, whose accounts have a constant tendency to get on the wrong side of your ledger ; and who will trade upon your indul-gence, not to the extent of their means, which would be easy of estimate, but to the extent of their audacity, which is incalculable. The short and easy method with such is to dishonour, without scruple, the first cheque which exceeds, by however little, the balance at their credit. No doubt they will hector and bully. Mr. Horace Larkyns, whose cheque you have dishonoured for a ' dirty hundred,' will menace you with the direst penalties of the law for this outrage to his feelings, and stain upon his honour. But you have the sub-stantial fact to set against this windy bluster, that the hundred pounds are in your till, and not in the outraged Mr. Larkyns' pocket. You can there-fore regard the indignant closure of his account with outward serenity, and the loss of it with inward satisfaction.

And you will do wisely to make it a rule absolute, whenever you are invited to lend the Bank's money, in any shape or for any purpose, to satisfy your mind that

the means will exist, in available form, to repay the
money when due.   In most cases you will know this
without inquiry.   You will know that the money you are
parting with, will go to purchase an equal value of produce, commodities or property, or to pay for purchases
of such already made.   The means to meet the advance
when due, therefore, will be in the possession or control
of the party to whom you lend the money.   In cases
where this is not apparent, it will be your business to
inquire.   You are not obliged to lend money in the
dark.   When a man comes to you for the loan of a few
hundreds, or a few thousands, as the case may be, unless
the transaction is clearly in the direct line of his business, you have a right to know for what purpose the
advance is wanted.   Without this knowledge, what
assurance have you that the money may not be spent in
furnishing a house, or dowering a child, or opening a
quarry, or sinking a mine, or in some other way which
shall be equally successful in locking your money up
beyond human reach?

You cannot in every case, it is true, move in a right line
towards a given principle in banking.   Circumstances,
like a contrary wind, may cause you at times to deviate
a point or two from your direct course; but you can
always keep heading towards it.

When Squire Oakfield, for instance, sends his cheque
in without notice, and overdraws his account a thousand
or two, although he has thus violated one of the cardinal
principles of your Rules and Regulations, it would not
be wise, however regular it might be, to dishonour the
cheque; because the Squire is at once a wealthy and a
choleric gentleman, and probably believed that by overdrawing his account he was bestowing a favour rather
than receiving one.   You cannot afford to quarrel with
the Squire.   You will prefer to follow a famous example
for the moment, and turn your blind eye upon the strict
letter of your instructions; because, in addition to himself, his agents and tenants, and many of his nearest

relatives bank with you.   There is a time for gathering stones, and a time for throwing them away; but this would not be a prudent occasion for the scattering process.   Once cast away the Squire's goodwill, and drive him to the other bank; and without any hostile action on his part, he will soon have a perceptible following.

Again : a certain account may of itself be less operative than your rules stipulate for; and yet it may not be politic to call the balance up.   Like the Squire's, certain accounts have roots.   Your unprofitable client may have friends and relatives amongst your customers, and in pulling his account up, you may root others up along with it.   In this, as in the previous case, you will guide your course, not by the value of the one account, if it be absolutely safe, but rather by the value of the group.

The overdrawn account exists, as we have said, and will continue to exist as a prominent feature in English country banking.   And to this there is no objection, within certain limits.   We have thus far been analysing this form of advance, not with a view to its extinction, but to its limitation.   The objections to it rest on financial grounds, and amount to this—that overdrafts, as a rule, are the least convertible form of a bank's assets, and therefore should never exceed a certain percentage of its resources.   What that percentage ought to be, we shall have occasion to discuss when we come to the management of a head office.   Meanwhile the fact that there is such a percentage and limit furnishes an answer to your opening question, Why every proposal for an overdrawn account must be referred in the first instance to your Head Office for consideration : because it is manifest that if all your Branches had the power of granting overdrafts at will, the limits assigned by your Head Office to the total overdrafts of the Bank, might at any time be seriously overstepped.

The first question which a Branch manager puts to himself in respect of a proposed transaction is, Will it be safe?   And the second is, Will it pay?   But at head-

quarters a third question lies beyond, and takes
precedence of these, and is this—Will it suit? The limit
assigned by your authorities for any particular class
of transaction, may have been already reached, and
the door closed against further increase for the time
being.

LETTER IX.

RECALL OF ADVANCES.

While the money is hoped for, and for a short time after it has been received, he who lends it is a friend and benefactor : by the time the money is spent, and the evil hour of reckoning is come, the benefactor is found to have changed his nature and to have put on the tyrant and the oppressor. It is an oppression for a man to reclaim his own money : it is none to keep it from him.

DEFENCE OF USURY.

THE Portuguese have a saying, If you would make an enemy, lend a man money, and ask it of him again : and there is no country bank in England which has not had occasion at times to digest the truth and pungency of the adage.

When the building committee of a church, or chapel, or school, come to you for an advance to complete the structure, in anticipation of promised subscriptions, and offer their joint and several guarantee for the advance; it will be difficult to refuse it, because the committee may include some of your most valued customers, who might resent your refusal as a slight to themselves. They will be slow to comprehend why you should refuse to advance a sum of money for a beneficent object, on the security of gentlemen good for many times the amount. Nevertheless, if the subscriptions do not come in, and you have in the end to come upon the guarantors for payment of the money, you will be fortunate if you do not more or less offend them all. Your application will be a provoking reminder to each, of his over-sanguine trust in promised contributions. Some will offer to pay their quota of the guarantee at once, provided you will

57

free them from further responsibility; but this you cannot do, because the liability is joint as well as several, and no one can be released, without vitiating the security, until the whole is paid.   Others will hold back, from a natural indisposition to pay a debt for which, personally, they have had no consideration, and for which they have an indistinct notion, perhaps, that they are not morally responsible.

Advances, therefore, for whatever object, on the security of a number of obligants, although they may be abundantly safe, are not always expedient.   They are almost certain in the long run to bring you into unpleasant relations with some of the parties, and more particularly with those who refuse to understand why a large bankcannot permit a loan to outstand for any length of time, so long as it is safe.   They refuse to see that the Bank is doing them a service in pressing for early payment.   It does not occur to them that their co-obligants are mortal, and that every obligant who dies practically bequeaths his liability to the survivors.   The signatory who would have the thing outstand for twenty years, if need were, might find himself the sole surviving debtor in the end ; and would then seethe thing, no doubt, in a proper light, when it was too late.

You ask what is to be done in such cases?   You cannot, you state, refuse such advances, and you cannot recall them without giving offence.   It only remains for you to point out, at the time, the unpleasant possibilities which such advances involve, and to dissuade committees from borrowing at all, if you can.   If they disregard your advice, as they probably will in most cases, the consequences will be of their own seeking.   You will thus acquit yourself of having been a silent observer of the transaction, or an accessory to their imprudence.

There are borrowers in plenty who do not trouble themselves to reflect how or when an advance from a bank is to be repaid.

The proper business and use of a bank, in their estimation, is to lend money to any amount, no matter for what length of time, nor for what purpose. They cannot imagine why it should concern a bank how the money is laid out, nor how long it may remain unpaid, so long as the loan yields interest, and is covered by security. You will have to reason such people out of delusions like these. If you fail, you have a conclusive argument always at command—you can refuse to lend the money. You can refuse to countenance transactions which may lead the parties into trouble. You are not obliged to furnish people with weapons to break their own heads with.

When overdrafts are allowed for specific periods, be it for weeks or months, or any other sections of time, you will have to see that such advances are repaid when due. If your practice in this respect be lax, the majority of your customers will not be slow to profit by your example. If you are loose and inexact in your requirements, they will not strain after rigid punctuality themselves. They are not likely to assail you with reminders that their debts to you are overdue, and implore you to call them up.

It is no doubt possible, as you suggest, to be over-exacting in this particular ; but that is on the assumption that you act in the matter without discretion. This is not required of you. A certain latitude is allowed to every Manager. You cannot in every case, as we have seen, enforce the strict letter of your instructions without respect of persons, circumstances or results. The law of successful management should not possess the rigidity of cast iron : it should rather have the property of highly tempered steel. It should have a certain degree of flexibility—a certain margin within which to play.

In the application of this particular rule, you will find that there is a time to bind and a time to loose. There are those amongst your customers, and they are the great majority, who must be held strictly to their engagements in respect of time : but there are others, who may safely be left to fulfil such engagements at their own time, even if it should vary a little from yours.

But there are people, who have had the use of the Bank's money, it may be for years, who will resent your calling it up, whenever you do so, as an injury and affront. It matters not that the advance may be long overdue, or that the security has become depreciated, or the transactions on the account insufficient, or that you wish to reduce such advances generally. The borrower will refuse to be conciliated. Is it possible—he will ask you, with unconscious insolence—that a large bank like yours can want the money? If not, why put him to inconvenience, so long as he pays you good interest for it? Have you lost confidence in him? If . not, why disturb an arrangement which has gone on for so long without a word of objection on your part? The man who takes this perverted view of things will be transformed into a life-long enemy, whenever the Bank shall insist upon having its own again, whether his position be sound or the reverse. If sound, he will impute the withdrawal of your advance to personal spite. If, on the other hand, he has to go into the Gazette, he will revile the Bank for having rendered that step necessary. It would not be an unheard-of thing if he went a step further and charged you and your advance with his ruin —a rancorous accusation, when your accuser is about to repay your good nature by a dividend the minuteness of which is a satire on your credulity.

It betrays a curious twist of moral vision, but it is not the less a fact, that when one of your customers fails, and compounds with his creditors, certain of your other clients have a feeling that they, too, are entitled in some vague way to consideration. They would try a little failure of their own, perhaps, but unfortunately they are perfectly solvent, and known to be so. This is certain: that if you let Sharples off with half his debt to the Bank—that is the way they will put it—they will have an indistinct notion that they ought not to be overlooked altogether, and will persuade themselves that the obligation to pay twenty shillings in the pound is, in their case, inequitable, and of the nature of a hardship.

Persons subject to this infirmity of commercial vision, would look upon the plunder of a bank by a fraudulent neighbour as scarcely amounting to an impropriety.

You tell me, indeed, that joy is openly expressed in certain quarters in Oxborough over every bad debt you make, and that popular sympathy is always with the debtor. You think it hard that the evil which your predecessor did should live after him, and be visited upon you.

The business conscience of Oxborough is evidently deficient in tone, and needs a corrective ; and this you can administer best, by the simple process of making no more bad debts. Instead óf furnishing your detractors with periodical occasion for rejoicing, you will thus put their malice to diet on emptiness, and achieve a lawful revenge. Happy are they, says Benedick, that can hear their detractions, and put them to mending.

LETTER X.

BANKRUPTCY.

If, like an ill venture, it come unluckily home, I break; and you, my gentle creditors, lose. . . . Bate me some, and I will pay you some, and, as most debtors do, promise you infinitely.
EPILOGUE TO HENRY IV. PART 2.

IT is right on principle that a man should reduce his account on the very day he promised to do so; but it is not incumbent on you to serve him with a notice in bankruptcy on the very morrow of his default. He may have failed to keep his promise through the default of others. You will at least give him a hearing before you hand him over to the rigours of the law. If Black has died penniless, with a balance against him on your books of some £20, and his principal assets consist of the beds his widow and children lie upon, I conclude that you will rather write the debt off as bad, than sell the forlorn creatures up—on principle.

You remind me that I have urged that the scope for the feelings in banking is limited. That is true. I held and still hold that you do not lend money, neither do you recall it, in obedience to the emotions. If men are entitled to credit, you give it to them; if they are not, you refuse it. If they are able to pay you back and will not do so, then put the law upon them without scruple and without remorse. I was not referring to the slippery customer who has sufficient means to pay his debts, but a persistent repugnance to doing so. There need be no parleying with defaulters of this type; the shortest rope of procedure will be long enough for them. My remark had reference solely to the involuntary and helpless debtor—to cases where the quality of mercy would yield a preferable result to the pound of flesh.

It is, no doubt, possible to be over abrupt in calling up an advance. If it has existed for years, and the borrower has had no reminder that it might be called up at any time, he has just ground for complaint, if, without reasonable notice, you peremptorily demand repayment of the money. If by this course you drive him to extremity, and compel him to file his petition, and it turns out that he was in a position to pay everybody twenty shillings in the pound, but for your insistance, you will have aroused the enmity, not only of the debtor himself, but of all his friends, and the business of the Bank might thereby suffer detriment. A bank that should acquire the reputation of forcing solvent people into the Gazette, would certainly lessen the number of its better class of applicants for advances.

Nothing more retards the progress of a bank than unpopularity; nothing, on the other hand, brings it a steady accession of business with more certainty than its standing well with the community. The bank which has the good will and the good word of every one is sure to make progress. But to insure this kind of popularity, it must be incapable of harsh dealing. It must not be over-grasping or too insistent in every case upon its exact legal right—the strict letter of its bond. In banking, as in other things, there is a law within the law : and that bank will do best for itself and its shareholders which can at times be generous as well as just.

Where an advance therefore has existed for years, it will be politic, as well as just, to give reasonable time for its repayment, provided the advance be fully covered by security. Even in cases where no security is held, it may be expedient to exercise forbearance, when the customer can satisfy you beyond a doubt, that his estate would yield a substantial surplus, even under a forced realisation. But when he cannot assure you of this, and is obviously in difficulties, or drifting towards them, the sooner his affairs are taken in hand by his creditors, the better for himself and them. Beware of nursing the account of a needy customer, whose solvency you have the slightest reason to doubt, however confidently he may affirm, or seek to prove, that a little more help will see him through.

It is in the nature of a man in difficulties to take a sanguine view of his position. Do not let him persuade you to look at matters through his spectacles. Use your own eyes. By using his, you may be induced to place yourself in his position, adopt his liabilities, and be morally fathered with his delinquencies. Neither be persuaded into paying other creditors off who are pressing him, from a fear that their persistence may embarrass him and imperil your own debt. You will not improve your position by letting them out and yourselves further in. When a man's affairs get into confusion, it is not the business of a bank to provide him with the wherewithal to pay the urgent in full, and leave the less urgent to take what they can get. If your debt has become doubtful, do not add to its amount, even on good security, unless it be rendered clear to you beyond all question, that by help of a further advance, every one, yourselves included, will receive twenty shillings in the pound.

When the balance of an account or bill stands overdue, and the debtor has taken no notice of your demand for payment, more than once repeated, your steps for recovery must be prompt; otherwise a more energetic creditor may step in before you, or the defaulter himself may abuse your indulgence, by secretly making away with what means he has. Unhappily there would be nothing strange in this: but even where parties are incapable of this form of dishonesty, if their affairs are in a bad way, the sooner they are wound up the better for all concerned, the parties themselves included. If traders and others were brought to book at the first symptom of insolvency, they would be deprived of the power of dissipating their assets in satisfying the claims of peremptory creditors, or giving fraudulent preferences to friends or relatives, or making secret hoards against

the rainy day to come. Their assets, if put under arrest
in time, and placed beyond the reach of wasteful sacrifice and unlawful distribution, would enable the parties
to offer a reasonable composition to their creditors, and
start afresh, with the help of some, and the good wishes
of all.

And better, surely, a composition in almost any case
in these days, than see a small estate thrown into bankruptcy, there to undergo the process of liquidation by
that unrivalled absorbent, and see it come forth again,
after many years, the mere skeleton and shadow of its
former self.

For the helpless English creditor, the choice would
seem to lie betwixt legal absorption on the one hand,
and illegal plunder on the other. The dishonest knave
who offers you half your debt in payment of the whole,
and who, you have reason to suspect, has most of the
other half hidden away, richly deserves the knout; but
there are difficulties. Before you can punish, you must
establish your suspicion, which may possibly be incapable
of legal proof. You may thus waste the substance of the
estate and not even scotch your snake. To punish a
fraudulent debtor nowadays involves the process of
splitting one's nose to spite one's face. To put a small
estate into the Court of Bankruptcy, is to imperil all
chance of a reasonable dividend; so that the much
enduring creditor is almost tempted to exclaim,—
Better ten shillings in the pound with robbery, than
bankruptcy with nothing.   .

The Comptroller in Bankruptcy, in his report for
1881, gives the total of bankruptcies for that year as
9727. Of these 15 per cent. paid dividends of two and
sixpence each and upwards: 24 per cent. paid dividends
ranging from two and sixpence each downwards to two-
pence halfpenny: whilst 61 per cent. of the whole—sixty-
one estates out of every hundred—paid nothing at all,
but vanished bodily and for ever from the sight of men.
To the eyes of English creditors wistfully expectant of
dividends, the portals of our Court of Bankruptcy might

aptly bear the inscription on that other place of shadows
—Abandon hope all ye who enter here.

Such being our experience of bankruptcy, as a machine
for the realization and distribution of insolvent estates,
it has occurred to many that the less we have to do with
it the better. Some would even go the length of
abolishing it altogether and making a fresh start. But
this is not the view of others, who have given much
thought to the subject, and whose capacity of judgment
is unimpeachable. They believe that the working of the
institution can be improved. Its present machinery is a
labyrinth of complication, a cover for fraud, a very sink
for costs, and a contrivance for procrastination and delay
only rivalled by the Court of Chancery itself

It is the intention of the new Act, and the hope of its
promoters, to change all this. Nevertheless, even under
it, every estate of the value of £300 and upwards, may,
by possibility, at one stage or another, engage the attention of the Chief Judge, or the services of the Official
Receiver, the creditors' trustee, the committee of inspection, and the auditors of the Board of Trade.

It will appear to some that to subject the liquidation
of a small estate, even to the action of this modified
apparatus, is suggestive of breaking a fly upon the
wheel.

The new Act, if successful, will largely increase the
transactions of the Court, and the moneys of bankrupt
estates in its hands. The balances of provincial insol-
vencies have heretofore been kept with the local banks:
but these institutions will no longer have the exclusive
use of these moneys, to lighten the inconvenience and
pressure which arise from local failures. Under the new
Act, they will have a formidable competitor in the
Government itself, for the holding of these funds in
future. It is in fact virtually provided that the funds
shall in every case go to the Bank of England, unless
the creditors shew cause to the contrary. How often
they will take the steps required to shew cause, and how

often they will prevail upon the Board of Trade, to allow the funds of an insolvent estate to be banked on the spot, has yet to be seen.

It is too late to raise the question whether a simpler method of dealing with insolvency might not have been devised.   The evils of the old system were manifold and flagitious.   Let us hope that, in our haste to rid ourselves of these, we have not created others instead ; and that in avoiding Scylla we have not chanced upon Charybdis.   One thing is certain, whatever the end may be : in casting off the unspeakable Trustee, we have put ourselves under the heel of the Board of Trade.

LETTER XI.

TRADE BILLS.

Mistrust no man without cause, neither be thou credulous without proofe; be not lyght to follow every man's opinion, nor obstinate to stande in thine owne conceipt. EUPHUES.

WHEN your client, Mr. Vincent Cartridge, the paper manufacturer, offers you for discount his bill for £256 13s. 4d. at three months' date, on Messrs. Booker & Co., of Birmingham, wholesale stationers; he proposes a transaction which you could dispose of at a glance, if it were the only bill betwixt the parties which you would hold, and the only responsibilty which either of them would be under to the Bank. In that case, you would merely have to satisfy yourself as to the responsibility of drawer and acceptor. If that were unquestionable, you would discount the bill: if it were not, you would decline the transaction.

But this is not the only bill, by a good many thousand pounds, which you would hold from Mr. Cartridge: neither will the present be his first and only draft on Booker & Co.: there are already several of them in your hands. You cannot deal with the bill now offered, therefore, as an isolated transaction, but as forming a portion of a larger liability.

And in taking the measure of this liability, it is not enough to look at its mere total, or to be satisfied with the individual safety of the various obligants on the bills. There may be other features in a man's account and bills, in which you may detect matter for question, and in respect of which you may require enlightenment.

In evidence of this, let us take the account of a former

client of your Branch, Mr. Philip Bargood. The history of his trading is written in your books with much clearness and force to those who care to read it. The leading facts, indeed, may be said to be set forth in capitals.

Mr. Bargood commenced business in 18— with a capital of £5000. For the first two years, he carried on a moderate trade, and bought nothing on credit. But in the third year he began to extend ; he became still more extended in the fourth, and in the fifth year reached a degree of inflation which rendered eventual explosion inevitable.

The considerable balance which stood at his credit with you for a good portion of the first two years, becomes rapidly diminished in the third, disappears altogether in the fourth, and in the fifth year is replaced by a balance against him. His acceptances, meanwhile, exhibit a corresponding swiftness of growth in number and amount. He no longer buys for cash. He buys on credit, and accepts for everything. His discount account shares in the general tendency of his affairs to expansion, and shews a large and rapid increase. Mr. Bargood, whilst availing himself to the full of his own credit, is giving credit far and wide to other people.

But apart from these leading features of the account, there are minor incidents to be noted, the significance of which alone, might have opened Mr. Littleworth's eyes to the headlong course along which Bargood was hurrying. To those who have the capacity and the will to look, there are 'eye-openers' to be met with, even in a bank ledger, although not of a mirthful cast. They incite the observer rather to wide-eyed and angry astonishment.

The amount of bills drawn by Bargood on Laxey & Co., for example, ought to have challenged attention. Instead of being drawn to the extent of a few hundreds in all, which was their original and sufficient limit, they came in the end to be drawn for as many thousands.

But if the increase in the total of these bills held no warning in it for your predecessor, the regularity with which each was discounted, a few days before another of similar amount became due, ought to have awakened him to the fact, that the paper on Laxey & Co. was being kept afloat by a series of renewals.

Nor is this all.   There appears amongst Bargood's acceptances, an occasional one to Laxey & Co., thus indicating the existence of cross-paper between the parties.   Whilst Bargood at Oxborough was raising money, by drawing fictitious bills on Laxey & Co.—bills for 'value received' in nothing—they, on their part, were hocussing their bankers with bills drawn by them on Mr. Philip Bargood for a like consideration.   It never occurred to Mr. Littleworth that these bills were being manufactured, simply to raise the wind; still less, that they would be represented by that element alone, when the wrecks of the two estates came to be marshalled for final distribution.

On 5th January, 18—, to refer once again to the account, you will find a debit of unusual amount—To A. B., £1500.   A few months later on, this mysterious payee figures for another £1500; and once again a cheque in his favour for a similar sum is debited.   Now the other cheques drawn upon the account, from first to last, are of moderate amount; in no instance exceeding a few hundred pounds.   These abnormal debits, therefore, would have justified the inference, that they represented transactions lying outside the regular course of Bargood's business.   And why drawn in blank?   His other cheques are openly drawn in favour of somebody, or in payment of something; but who was A. B., and why his initials only, and not his name?

The dark horse—the A. B. of the cheques—was, of course, Mr. Bargood himself.

The money went into a mine, which he and his co-adventurers ardently believed would prove a second Golconda, and make village Rothschilds of them all; whereas, the mine proved to be only rich in water.   It yielded that in fathomless quantity; the pumps were worked night and day for years, and the shareholders were pumped out, but the water never.

When Bargood came to a stoppage and final break-down, and the facts which we have glanced at became known to the Directors, Mr. Littleworth was allowed to resign the position which you now occupy.

The moral to be drawn from his experience is this—that the manager of a Branch, to be fit for his position, must look deeper into a customer's account, from time to time, than merely at the balance at its debit, or the sum of its activity. He must read between the lines, now and then. The man's balance may be in order, and his bills within their authorized total ; but the Manager is not therefore to shut his eyes to every other feature of the account, until certain of its aspects become so ominous, that they are challenged from head-quarters. The Manager has the supreme advantage of being on the spot. Every transaction on every account, is open to his inspection from day to day. He has opportunities, therefore, which your chief Manager and Directors have not, of detecting those irregularities which indicate the departure of a man from the straight line of his busi-ness, and are often the incipient symptoms of in-solvency.

Had Mr. Littleworth thus supervised the account and bills of Philip Bargood, and drawn the attention of the directors to each irregular or disquieting transaction as it arose, the curb would have been applied in time, and Bargood saved from ruining himself and a score or two of other people, besides landing the Bank in a serious bad debt.

You suggest that Mr. Bargood, instead of retiring his acceptances to Laxey & Co. through his account at Oxborough, might have done so through some other bank, and have thus effectually concealed from Mr. Littleworth and everybody else the fact of their being renewals. That is true : but the difficulty would have been to find a bank in all England that would transact this more than questionable description of business.

You are distinctly required, by your code of instruc-tions, to refuse to advise or take up the drafts or accep-

tances of any but your own customers.   This is only in
pursuance of an old principle of English country banking, that a man should only have one banker.

Many years ago, it is true, a bank took up for some
years running, for a man who did not bank with it, his
drafts upon a distant acceptor.   When it transpired, at
last, that the bills thus provided for as they fell due,
were a series of forgeries, which the drawer had discounted with his own bankers, and which the other
bank had thus enabled him to keep afloat; it became
apparent, that a departure from sound banking usage
had betrayed one bank into rendering possible a felony,
which resulted in the plundering of another bank of
many thousand pounds.

In applying the various tests which are suggested by
the instructive account of Mr. Bargood, to the draft of
Cartridge on Booker & Co., the fate of which is still in
abeyance, you may find that the paper under discount to
Cartridge is already at the highest point sanctioned by the
Directors.   Or it may be, that the bills of the acceptors,
already in your hands, have reached an amount beyond
which you are unwilling to go.   Or, again, it may happen
that a bill for the same amount, between the same
parties, is about due ; which might imply, although not
necessarily, that the bill now offered is a renewal.   It
may be drawn against an entirely fresh transaction, to
which it has merely a chance nearest in amount.   The
drafts of Bargood on Laxey & Co. were not open to this
construction.   They were so uniformly alike, in point of
date and amount, for several years running, as to pre-
clude the idea of accidental likeness or fortuitous
identity.   Or, finally, you may have remarked amongst
the bills retired by Cartridge a stray acceptance of his
to Booker & Co.—a circumstance which could not be
accidental, and would have to be challenged forthwith.

It may be, that the Bookers make it part of their
business, to purchase rags for Cartridge and to draw
upon him for the cost.   To this there would be no objec-

tion, so long as the bills were drawn against actual transactions : but this system of reciprocal drawing is open to
flagrant abuse, as we shall have occasion to see by-and-by.

But let us now assume that the draft of Cartridge on
Booker & Co. has been subjected to the tests which we
have indicated, and that it has successfully run the
gauntlet of objection. You can now address yourself
to the fundamental question of safety, with a mind at
rest on all side issues and outlying points of doubt.

And first, as regards the acceptors. You find a
satisfactory account of them in the confidential character-
book of the Branch ; but it is open to the objection that
the record is now some years old.

Without disparagement to Messrs. Booker & Co., it is
allowable to conceive that a firm, which was safe and
sound a few years ago, may not be in the same position
now. Every kind of business is subject to occasional
loss, and as a rule the loss is borne in secret. No one is
in haste to proclaim his trading mishaps from the house-
top. They may be known or suspected on the spot, but
the knowledge will not necessarily travel far beyond it.
You know, because you have the means of knowing
in several ways, how people thrive in business in
Oxborough ; but you cannot exercise this supervision,
in the case of persons who are following their avocations
in distant towns and far-away cities.

If Hobson of Oxborough has made a mess of it in
something, you are more than likely to hear of it,
although he may not speak of it himself, nor put it
in the newspapers : but if Trevethick of Penzance, or
Macpherson of Cromarty, has been quietly going to
the bad in business, the fact will not necessarily reach
Oxborough at all.

It follows, that the opinions which you have received
as to the position of acceptors or others out of
Oxborough, will require frequent revision. You are not
to await the on-coming of a general crash, before you
commence the revisal of your register ; otherwise you

may find a score or two of its reputations in the Gazette, before you have run your pen through records concerning them of fabulous misconception.

And now, as regards the safety of the parties for whom you discount bills. The drawer and indorser of a trade bill is ordinarily the same individual, as in the present case. Mr. Cartridge draws on Booker & Co., and indorses the bill to you, and you consider him good for ten times the amount of the bill. This would be conclusive of the whole matter, if the bill now offered were the only bill you would hold of his : but you already hold Cartridge's drafts upon a variety of people, to the considerable total of £10,000.

You report the whole of his bills as good on their merits : that is to say, as being drawn upon acceptors believed to be able, in every case, to meet the bills as they mature. But acceptors do fail at times, although their selection has been the subject of diligent inquiry and the utmost circumspection beforehand.

It is difficult to estimate the exact amount of risk which thus attaches itself to Cartridge's indorsements ; but the risk is not the less real, because it is not presentable in exact figures.

The question remains—will the £2500, which you consider him good for, provide a sufficient margin for this contingent risk? A rough method of answer will be found, in a synopsis of his bills current. Place those which are beyond all doubt in one column, those which are considered safe in a second, and the weaker bills in a third; and let us assume that we have the following figures as a result :

First Class	£5,000
Second ”	4,000
Third ”	1,000
	£10,000

Take the first class at twenty shillings, the second at
17*s.* 6*d.*, and the last at 10*s.* in the pound; and Cartridge
would stand to suffer a conjectural loss of £1000 on the
whole. That would be the measure of your floating risk
on his bill account.

The factors here used are purely arbitrary; they may
be put higher or lower, as circumstances may direct: but
the method of the computation, although it will not
furnish you with figures of precision, will at least enable
you to form a rough estimate of the risk you are running
with any given discount account.

And the amount of this risk, by whatsoever process it
is arrived at, has to be looked upon as forming a mental
addition to the overdraft of the customer, or a deduction
from the balance at his credit, as the case may be.

But in addition to bills drawn by Cartridge on other
people, you hold £1000 in bills drawn by other people
upon him.

Now a banker, as a rule, would rather not keep both
sides of a man's account. If he discounts a customer's
bills to an agreed-on total, he would rather not be
weighted with his acceptances as well: because, for one
reason, the safety of the drawers of these bills may not
in all cases be without question. The people, for
instance, who draw upon Mr. Cartridge for rags collected
and delivered, are for the most part of small means, and
could not take up his acceptances which you have
discounted for them, should he himself fail to do so. In
estimating your position with him as a whole, therefore,
you have to look upon such weak bills as being little
better than so much overdraft without security.

It is true that you may thus find yourself in a difficulty. If you allow his margin for discounts to be par-
tially absorbed, by transactions of which he is ignorant,
he will have just cause for complaint; on the other hand,
if you refuse to discount his acceptances, by whomsoever
drawn or presented, you may seriously damage his
credit.

The only means of escape from the horns of this dilemma would seem to be—never to get between them. Let there be a distinct understanding with every customer, from the outset, that you must treat such of his acceptances as are brought to you for discount, as an addition to his liabilities on bills, where the drawers are good; and as so much overdraft, where they are weak. If this be clearly understood, your customers will see the unwisdom to which some persons are addicted, of sending their acceptances to their own bankers to be discounted: especially if the drawers are weak.

If you have any difficulty with my paper at your Bank, says Bounderby, try mine: I flatter myself you will find it all right there. Although Mr. Bounderby, by this advice, may seek to magnify his own credit in the eyes of drawers, his intention towards the Bank is entirely friendly. He believes he is doing you a good turn, and is without a suspicion that he is thereby running up a secret score in your bill ledger against himself.

We have now gone the round of inquiry, to which the bill of Cartridge on Booker & Co. has given occasion, and you are in a position to regard the transaction in all its bearings, and to deal with the bill accordingly.

You have a feeling, you remark, that your customers would hardly await your reading up of the general subject after the laborious fashion herein proposed, before giving them your decision. Probably not. They will expect, and are entitled to an immediate answer, yes or no. You will therefore have to do the reading up beforehand. You will have to keep your memory freshly posted up, from day to day, on all the points which we have had under review, so that you may have always at your fingers' ends, the data whereon to rest the fate of almost any bill at a glance. The faculty of distinguishing a bill which is eligible and to be desired, from one which is to be avoided and cast out, becomes developed by cultivation, to a degree bordering on instinct.

LETTER XII.

LOAN BILLS AND NOTES.

And pray, sir, said my friend, do you want all this money ?
Indeed, I never wanted it more, returned I. I am sorry for that,
cries the scrivener, with all my heart : for they who want money
when they come to borrow, will always want money when they
should come to pay.   CITIZEN OF THE WORLD.

THE bill of Cartridge on Booker & Co. being now disposed of, and added to the contents of your bill case,
your attention may next be invited to a discount operation of quite another stamp, but of some prevalence in
the agricultural districts.

Mr. John Bowdler, then, has looked in to borrow a
couple of hundred pounds, for a few months—he is not
particular to a month : and he proposes to draw for
the amount on his friend and neighbour, Mr. David
Starkey, who accompanies him.   Not that Starkey owes
the money ; that is not pretended : but he has agreed to
go bail for the amount without consideration, except that
of good fellowship.   You know Bowdler to be a substantial man.   He has sums out at interest, he has a low-
rented farm, a valuable stock, his manner of living is
frugal, and his expenses are moderate.   Starkey also is
a man of considerable means and one infirmity—an
easy-going readiness to lend his name to oblige a neighbour.   In short the two men are safe for many times the
amount of the proposed bill.

But bill it is not, in the strict sense of the term.   A
genuine bill of exchange represents value given by the
drawer and received by the acceptor : but Mr. Bowdler
draws simply on Mr. Starkey's good nature for the

amount, and means in due time to pay the bill himself.
The document, it is true, has the semblance of a bill.
It is dated at Oxborough, and drawn in regular form for
value received. It is accepted by Mr. Starkey, and
domiciled at your bankers in London, although it has to
be confessed that he knows as little about —— & Co. as
they do about him.

But this counterfeit presentment of a bill of exchange
would never pass muster in Lombard Street. However
cunningly got up, it would still be Bowdler on Starkey
—pig upon bacon—to the comprehension of the
meanest capacity in the bill market.

Not that such bills are never re-discounted. In easy
times, when money is a drug, they may find discounters
at a price. But such paper will become as foolishness
in the eyes of brokers, and as chaff before the wind,
in the winnowing of the first monetary squall.

A further objection to the class of bills now under
review, is the irregularity with which they are met when
due. Now the property which, next to safety itself, raises
the bill of exchange to the foremost rank amongst banking securities, is the certainty of its being paid in money
the day it matures. But on this point it has to be
admitted that Mr. Bowdler is unreliable.

When he puts his name to a bill, he determines its
currency by what he calls a rough guess. If you cannot
let him have the money for six months, he thinks he can
manage it in three—a month or two either way being of
no account from his point of view. His engagement to
meet the bill when it falls due, imposes no greater tie
upon his conscience than a promise to visit a friend in
the course of the summer.

A merchant is acutely sensible that he must meet his
acceptances to the day, or hopelessly blast his credit ; but
this is an unknown sensation to Mr. Bowdler. The processes of presentment, dishonour, and noting for non-pay-
ment, are as inscrutable to him as the order of procedure
in Chancery. He cannot think why there should be so
much ado about nothing, and will ask you almost with

heat, if you fancied him likely to make a purposed journey to pay the bill on a particular day, when he was coming to Oxborough Fair the Friday week following, whether or not.

Not that it will be always so with Mr. Bowdler. It is almost an even chance that he meets the bill a week or two before it is due, as that he takes it up a fortnight afterwards, and meanwhile lights his pipe with your notice of dishonour.

It is another feature of this class of bill, frequently to require renewal. The chief obligant and actual debtor on the bill finds, or pretends to find, when it reaches maturity, that he has miscalculated or been disappointed, or had some unlooked for demand to meet, or has not effected sales, or something else. If you are satisfied with the excuse, you will renew the bill; provided always that no change for the worse has arisen during its currency in the affairs of the man himself, or the other parties to the bill. But in all cases the first renewal, as a rule, should also be the last. The circumstances must be exceptional which would justify your taking a third or fourth renewal of the same bill. Miscalculation, disappointment, and so forth, may be accepted as excuses once, but they pall on repetition. A man may, by inadvertence, book his acceptance as due in May instead of April; but that he should repeat the inadvertence several times running, is beyond rational belief

It is usual to designate paper of the description we are now discussing, as accommodation bills, or kites; but if the epithet is just, it must be admitted that there are diversities of kites. The draft of Mr. Bowdler on his friend Mr. Starkey, for example, is not to be placed on an equality of demerit with the bills of Bargood on Laxey & Co. In Mr. Bowdler's case you knew the transaction intimately; there was no attempt at conceal-ment: but in Bargood's case there was not only conceal-ment, but something that would be deemed fraud, under any less mild dispensation than the bankruptcy laws of England. A less obnoxious term, such as Loan Bills, would better express the quality of Mr. Bowdler's paper and its equivalents.

But you may be offered bills from time to time, the origin of which may not be so apparent—bills which you cannot 'read.' When you are offered a bill, let us say for £95 10s. 3d. drawn by Mr. Skinner, the currier, on Mr. Scales, the grocer, the question will at once suggest itself: What description of value can have passed between the parties? Mr. Scales does not deal in shoe leather, and his personal consumption of that article, even on the extreme assumption of his being his own bootmaker, can never have involved such a figure as is expressed in the bill. The presumption is, that no value has passed in the transaction, and that the value received is purely a figure of speech. The drawer and acceptor, no doubt, intend to divide the proceeds amicably, share and share alike, and to find the money, when due, on the same principle of friendly regard and mutual equality.

Again,—when a customer whose proper business, for example, is that of a corn merchant, offers you his draft on acceptors, whose business is entirely out of the path of his own, the same question will arise—Why is the bill drawn, and against what? Be the acceptor concerned with coal, or copper, or timber, or lead, the drawer can have no legitimate dealings in such merchandise. He is either having a speculation in it on his own behalf, or in conjunction with the acceptor.

You will know without difficulty how to deal with bills of this class; whilst the fact of their existence will heighten the regard which you will thenceforth give to the accounts of their drawers, particularly if their balances happen to be on the wrong side of your ledgers.

And whilst you are careful to note on whom your customers in business draw, you will be none the less careful to observe to whom they accept. You will have no difficulty in judging whether a man is accepting against transactions which are beyond the limits of his proper business. You may thus detect irregularities at their inception, and occasionally protect a customer against himself. He will not care to be thus protected perhaps : on the contrary, if he is a self-willed, sanguine man, he will probably resent your interference and close his account in dudgeon : nevertheless, it would not be without precedent, if he lived to thank you in the end, and humbly make offer of his custom back again. Repentant clients have had to thank their banker before now, for the refusal of facilities which, if granted, would have been their destruction.

Akin in some respects to Loan bills, are the promissory notes of individuals, which are sometimes discounted by country banks against security. Regarded as negociable assets, they are valueless. You could not rediscount them in the most plethoric state of the money market. In any analysis of your financial position, for your private guidance, therefore, you will have to treat them as forming an addition to your overdrawn accounts, rather than to your bills of exchange. Loan bills and notes of hand are virtually overdrafts in disguise.

As a rule, a banker will prefer a short to a long-dated bill. In the first place the risk is less. In the ordinary course of things, more firms will give way in six months than in three. It may be affirmed, without disparagement, that there is always a greater chance of the first house in England standing for three months than for six.

In the second place, the banker, for every one bill at six months', could discount two at three months' date, within the same period, and with the same amount of money; and thus render his resources doubly available to his constituency.

Let us say that the limit for discounts at your Branch is £50,000. If you invested the money in bills with an average currency of three months, your discounts would gross £200,000 in the year; whereas they would only reach half that sum, if the bills had six months to run.

Let us further suppose that, during a monetary pressure, you have to contract your discounts, in order to meet a drain upon your deposits reaching £5000 a month. Now if your bills are all at the longer date, only £8000 of them will reach maturity within the month. To meet the supposed drain, therefore, you will have to contract your ordinary discounts to customers, from £8000 to £3000 a month—an application of your financial brake, sufficient, one would suppose, to spread consternation among half the trading community of Oxborough.

But if your bills were of the shorter currency, then £17,000 of them would ripen monthly : in which event, you could meet the drain of £5000, and still be able to continue your discounts to customers, at the rate of £12,000 a month. There would be pressure even in this case ; but in the other it would be semi-strangulation.

It has also to be considered that, in times of commercial panic and money pressure, even A 1 paper, if it has six months to run, ceases to be negociable in the rediscount market.

As a matter of fact, no banker's bill case is filled exclusively with either short or long-dated bills. The most exclusive bill case must hold some admixture of the latter. No doubt the fewer the better. If the proportions were as 10 per cent. of long, to 90 per cent. of short paper, the banker would be perceptibly nearer the point of financial safety, than if these proportions were reversed.

LETTER XIII.

NEGOCIABILITY OF BILLS.

It is not by augmenting the capital of a country, but by rendering a greater part of that capital more active and productive than would otherwise be so, that the most judicious operations of banking can increase the industry of the country. WEALTH OF NATIONS.

THE transaction out of which the draft of Cartridge on Booker & Co. arose, is one of universal occurrence in the every-day course of business and trade. Cartridge has sold and delivered to Booker & Co. certain goods, against the invoice value of which he has drawn this bill; which is at once an acknowledgment of debt, and an undertaking on the part of the acceptors to pay the debt at the end of three months.

But it suits the arrangements of Mr. Cartridge better to have the use of the money at once. He therefore asks you to give him cash for the bill now—less interest or discount on its amount, for the time you will be out of pocket by the transaction. If you decide to discount the bill, the effect of the operation will be a virtual addition to the working capital of Mr. Cartridge for the time being, equal to the proceeds of the bill.

This fact of itself may hardly seem worthy of note : but when you reflect that every bill thus discounted by a bank becomes an addition, for the time being, to the working capital of the country ; and that the average of bills under discount in England may be safely put at 250 millions of pounds sterling,* the fact broadens into

---

*Mr. Inglis Palgrave, in his Notes on Banking, estimates the average circulation of Inland Bills at 210 millions, and of Foreign Bills at 141 millions for the United Kingdom. It will not therefore be an excessive estimate to put the figures for England alone at 250 millions.

significance. If these facilities were withdrawn, there would be that amount less of business done in the land, in the course of every three months or so. In other words, that portion of the business of the country, which depends exclusively on the discount of bills of exchange, would have to be curtailed, other things being equal, to the extent of some twenty millions a week ; and suffer the enormous shrinkage of a thousand millions a year.

But the money employed by the banks in the annual discount of this prodigious aggregate of bills is not their own. It is held by them from multitudes of depositors, at short notice, and much of it at call, and therefore must be employed in securities of negociable character. The desired class of security is chiefly found in bills of exchange; because they can be negociated and con-verted into money at all times, provided they are accepted payable in London—but not otherwise.

Messrs. Booker & Co. make their acceptances to Mr. Cartridge payable in London, in accordance with English usage ; and the whole of your business clients do the same, with one or two exceptions.

Mr. Howard Bagster is one of these, and is accounted an authority in Oxborough on matters of finance and currency. Mr. Bagster is a provision merchant by trade, and can distinctly trace his last failure to the operation of Peel's Act and the monopoly of the Bank of England. Hence his normal attitude towards banks and bankers, which is inimical. He holds that all traders have a right to make their acceptances payable where they please, and that by making them payable at their own shops, they save a commission on retiring the bills when due : but that, as we know, is a fallacy. When an accept-ance of Mr. Bagster's, for example, nears maturity, it is sent to you for collection, by the bank which discounted it, and you charge your usual commission for paying the proceeds over in London. By seeking to evade the pay-ment of one commission himself, therefore, Mr. Bagster subjects the drawer of the bill to the payment of two,— one to his own bankers, and one to you. That the drawer will ignore this fact, in adjusting accounts with Mr. Bagster, is not within the lines of business usage, nor the limits of reasonable probability.

But we may let that pass; because, even if drawers were found willing to humour Mr. Bagster in this caprice, at their own expense, their bankers are not likely to countenance a form of eccentricity, which is of no advantage to the acceptor himself, and which, if unchecked, might render them, in time, the holders of an undesirable percentage of unmarketable paper.

There is no law to prevent the acceptors of bills making them payable at their own shops, or on their own doorsteps, or, for that matter, at the parish pump, if they are so minded. It is not a question of law, or legal right, but of expediency. The custom which in England requires bills of exchange to be made payable in London, is a necessity of its banking system. The Banks could in no other way continue the daily use of £250,000,000 of their deposits to the public, in the form of discounts, unless they chose to disregard and imperil their own stability.

The vital requisite of the securities in which the Banks invest this portion of their deposit money, is negociability,—the securities must be readily convertible into money, in case of need; and to render bills of exchange thus convertible, they must be payable in London, the discount centre of England.

Bills not payable in London are simply unmarketable. You could not rediscount them at the Bank of England, nor in all Lombard Street, in the easiest of times. They are only a shade more eligible, as banking assets, than equal amounts in overdrafts would be.

If every acceptor were to humour his fancy in the 'location' of his bills; not only every city, town, and village, but every office, shop, and dwelling-house in the three kingdoms might, in turn, become points of redemption for trade paper, and our banking system would be revolutionized.

To meet this new condition of things, a member of

your staff would have to be on the wing, day by day, from street to street, and shop to shop, and from one dwelling-house to another, wherever the bills had to be presented for payment. In this respect, it is true, he would be no worse off than a telegraph boy, or the penny postman: but he would have troubles of his own, which happily for them, they know not of.

If he receives payment of a bill in legal tender, that is to say, in Bank of England notes, or gold of standard weight—well and good: there will be nothing to charge and nothing to discuss. But in nine cases out of ten, he will be tendered in payment, cheques on other Banks, Country notes, Post Office orders, light gold, or loose silver, in varying proportions. If he declines to accept these promiscuous elements of the circulating medium as standard money of the realm, and insists upon making a charge, to cover the expense of their conversion into legal tender, there will be a wrangle in every case. His pocket gold-weigher will be derided, its use contemned, and its accuracy disputed. His refusal of cheques drawn on distant Banks, by persons of whom he knows nothing, will be resented. He will be dared by some, at his peril, to refuse the payment tendered. He will be requested by others to call again later on. He will have to await his turn at every counter, and abide the reception which is usually accorded to the man who calls for an account.

Now by the simple expedient of having all bills made payable in London, the whole of this egregious waste of time, trouble, locomotion, and temper is avoided. You thereby create a common centre of liquidation, towards which the bills from all parts of the kingdom gravitate as they become due, and quietly sink into the great stream of transactions which daily flows through the London Clearing.

You have thus, instead of countless thousands of scattered points, one central and all-sufficient focus of liquidation; and thus, bills in thousands, and representing millions of pounds in the aggregate, are daily met, and their separate amounts distributed amongst

their multitudinous holders, with less friction than
would accompany your ambulatory clerk in his daily
round.

It is not the usage, nor is it the province of a bank, to
wait upon the acceptors of bills, or upon the indebted of
the community in general.   It is the business of the
debtors to bring the money to it.   If a bank had to
wait upon every customer who had an acceptance to
meet, an advance to re-pay, or money to lodge, or a
cheque to cash; there would be a speedy end of banking
altogether.   Its machinery would suffer dead-lock, and
its business come to a stand-still.   A hundred persons, on
the average, transact their business across your counter
at Oxborough every day, with ease and mutual affability:
there is no difficulty, no wrangling, and no friction.   Mr.
Coigne, your cashier, is equal to the work were it twice
as much: but even if he had the shoes of swiftness, it
would be impossible to reverse the operation.   He would
enter upon it at the disadvantageous odds of a hundred
to one.   The customers one by one come to him with
perfect ease; but for him to go to them, individually,
and transact every variety of banking business, at a
hundred different points, in the same day, would be a
performance transcending human ability.

Akin in one respect to bills not payable in London,
are certain instruments known as Cash Orders, drawn
by some of the wholesale dealers in a few of our larger
cities, upon retail customers in the smaller towns, and
sent to local banks for collection.   Like locally accepted
bills, these orders are ostensibly redeemable at the shops
of the parties drawn upon.

But it is not the business of banks to act as house-to-
house collectors of trade debts.   The regular customers
of a bank, to whom it may be supposed to be under
some obligation, do not expect it to wait upon them
when they have a payment to make, a debt to pay, or
an acceptance to meet: they come to the Bank.   It is
hardly reasonable therefore to expect you to wait upon

the parties on whom these orders are drawn, and thus afford facilities to non-customers, which you do not extend even to your regular clients.

Parties thus obligingly waited upon, will be able to dispense with keeping bank accounts altogether. They will make treasuries of their tills and money boxes, and become their own bankers—with what advantage to themselves we shall have to discuss hereafter.

You therefore, on receipt of one of these orders from another bank to collect, send notice to the shopkeeper it is drawn upon, that it lies with you for collection, and will be sent back to the drawer next day, unless taken up in the meantime.

No doubt a lower salaried class of man would suffice as commercial traveller, were country banks to take his duties as collector and cashier off his hands : but whether the saving thus effected by the employer, will be equal to the collateral disadvantages, is at least open to question. All is not gain, it has been said, that is got into the purse.

In numbers of cases, a wholesale house has to depend entirely upon a banker's opinion, as to the trustworthiness of its more distant customers. When the parties keep bank accounts, there is little difficulty in obtaining a reliable opinion : but when they do not, a banker has no greater means of knowledge than any other member of the community. The creditor, therefore, who assists a debtor in doing without a bank account, is shutting a door against himself: he is depriving himself of a means of information, which might be of substantial service to him at times, and perhaps save him every now and then from a bad debt.

LETTER XIV.

PERSONAL SECURITY.

Be very wary for whom thou becomest security, and for no more than thou art able to discharge, if thou lovest thy liberty. The borrower is a slave to the lender : the security is a slave to both. QUARLES.

IF a Banker has a claim, in common with any other lender of money, to have his loans covered by security; it follows that the security thus taken ought to suffice, under all circumstances, to secure repayment of the advance which it is taken to cover. How far this self-evident proposition was present to the minds of former Managers of Oxborough Branch, on all occasions, will appear more clearly, as we proceed to analyse the batch of securities, ancient and modern, which you have selected for discussion.

You hold the GUARANTEE of Mr. Rolston to secure repayment of advances to W—— S—— to the extent of £1000.

The report on this security is,— ' Rolston is known to be possessed of means to the full amount of the guarantee.' But, if Mr. Rolston is not possessed of means to a much larger amount, the prudence of taking him as surety for such a sum is more than questionable.

A man's 'means,' so far as they are available for the payment of another man's debt, can only consist of the surplus which his assets would yield, after the discharge of his own indebtedness. In Rolston's case, his assets are set down at £6000, and his debts at £4500. He shows a capital or surplus therefore of £1500.

That would be the surplus of his business as a going

concern : but both it and he would cease to go, the moment you came upon him for the payment of £1000, for which he has had no consideration, and has nothing whatever in hand. He must stop payment: in which event his surplus of £1500 will at once disappear and be replaced by a balance against him.

Every man's estate, as we have seen, has two values :— a value to himself, and a value to his creditors : a value before, and a value after bankruptcy. A trader's stock-in-trade and book-debts, his buildings and machinery, his furniture and pictures, are usually set forth at cost-price, in his balance-sheet, and it would take the same money perhaps to replace them. But force him into bankruptcy, and we know the result. His estate and effects, after passing through that famous mill, will re-exhibit themselves in figures which it will be hard to reconcile, and impossible to identify, with those at which they stood in his books before the grinding.

In your estimate of a surety, therefore, the point to be kept in view is,—not what you might be able to squeeze out of him by process of exhaustion ; but what he could at any time pay, over and above his other engagements, without serious inconvenience or detriment to himself That is the true measure of his fitness as a surety ; and if you take him for more than this, you may do him a fatal disservice, and possibly lay the foundation of a bad debt for yourselves. If Rolston's guarantee had been taken for £150, instead of for nearly seven times that amount, it would have been nearer his mark as a guarantor.

Let it be your maxim, therefore, that a man is good security to a bank for a portion only of what he is worth—a portion which will mainly depend upon the showing of his balance-sheet.

You would take the guarantee of Daniel Hyde, for example, for a larger sum than you would that of Railton & Co., whilst you would decline to take Abel Trowell's guarantee for anything at all: although each balance-sheet of the three shows the same amount of capital.

But you will not always have a balance-sheet on which to base your calculation. You will more frequently have to depend on hearsay, and the result of your own observation. In this event, you will do wisely to revert to the rule which we have already indicated, or a modification of it.

Let us say, for the sake of argument, that a man will be an eligible surety to a bank for the tenth part of his reputed means; let a man, supposed to be worth £10,000, be taken as individually safe as surety for £1000. I do not suggest this as an immutable divisor or rule of estimate. It would be excessive in the case of Mr. Hyde; it would be less than sufficient in that of Mr. Trowell. But in the absence of authentic figures, you are bound to protect yourself with an ample margin, by subjecting a man's reputed means to the moderating effect of a liberal divisor.

Even by the suggested rule, a surety would be exposed to the possible loss of a tithe of all he could call his own—surely a sufficient penalty for an indiscreet act of good nature? This at least is clear: that the higher your divisor in applying the rule, the lighter the strain will be on the resources of a guarantor, and the greater the certainty and promptitude with which your claim upon him will be satisfied.

It has also to be borne in mind, that the good nature which prompts a man to become surety for a relative or friend, is guided more by the feelings than the intellect; and it thus happens that the same friendly hand which has signed a guarantee, or indorsed a bill for A. may have done the like for B. and C. or others. You know that Mr. Bowdler's bill is not the only one which bears the indorsement of Mr. Starkey; but there may be others, who are as free as that philanthropist with their signatures, but less furnished with means.

A personal guarantee, however safe the guarantor may be at the time of its date, offers a less stable form of cover to a bank, than the collateral security of shares or other property: because the position of a surety may change for the worse without your knowledge; whereas changes in the value of property take place in the sight of all men, and you may keep yourself advised from day to day of all movements in price. In the one case, the substance of the security is in your own hands: in the other, it remains in the order and disposition of the guarantor, to do what he will with it. He may be a thriving man, and he may continue to thrive; but it is also possible that he may prove unfortunate: in which event you may some day find yourselves the holders of a document, the maker of which has parted with his substance and left you his shadow instead.

You can dispose of a marketable security at any time, and get the money for it: but to turn a surety into cash, is a less certain process, and not always crowned with satisfactory results.

As regards annuitants, professional men, life-renters, and all other persons whose incomes cease with their lives, if we found them ineligible as principals, we must pronounce them equally ineligible as sureties: unless they have inherited, or saved and set aside, during their lives, sufficient securities or property to provide for their posthumous liabilities.

A man who owns a property for life, for example, which brings him in say £1500 a year, and who requires it all for the expenses of his household, and the education of his children—how is he to repay the £1500 advanced on his guarantee, to some good-for-nothing relative, without loading his life interest with such an annual weight of charge, as will bring daily discomfort and social privation to his family and himself?

Still worse: suppose a clergyman to become surety for a few hundred pounds, the amount, it may be, of his whole year's stipend, for some pious and plausible rogue; and that the unhappy vicar has in the end to make good the debt. In such a case, if he has no property to fall back upon, the result must be either immediate ruin, or some arrangement for deferred payment, which will make him a struggling man for life.

Poor F—— with his salary of £250 a year, a wife and half-a-dozen children, how is he to find the £200 for which he became surety for his brother-in-law, in whom he had a boundless faith, and who has just filed his petition and won't pay five shillings in the pound?

If therefore you would have a business conscience void of offence, you will strive to minimise, if you cannot quite avert, such wretched possibilities in the future.

LETTER XV.

COLLATERAL SECURITY.

He that lendeth to all that will borrowe, sheweth great good will, but lyttle witte. Lend not a penny without a pawne, for that will be a good gage to borrowe. EUPHUES.

THE samples of collateral security which you have selected for discussion, do not admit of treatment as a group. They are so various in quality, and fruitful of suggestion, that it will be necessary to deal with each on its merits.

DEPOSIT OF TITLE DEEDS. You hold the title deeds of the farm of Greenfields as cover for an advance of £2000 to the owner, Mr. Miles Thornton. Your predecessor reports on the transaction :—'Mr. Thornton is needy : but the property is amply worth £2500.'

Mr. Littleworth does not explain how he arrived at this valuation. He may possibly have yielded to his easy way of looking at things, so that it would scarcely be a surprise, if the valuer in this case should prove to have been Mr. Thornton himself.

As regards the important question of title, the deeds have not been examined, it appears, by the solicitors of the Bank. Mr. Littleworth was satisfied that the deeds must be in order and the title perfect, because the property had been in the possession of the Thorntons for more than a century.

But this assumption might involve more than one serious fallacy. It is possible, for example, that the property may be subject to settlements and other charges, the instruments creating which need not accompany the title deeds, nor be accompanied by them.

Again : the name of your client has probably run in the family for generations, so that the mere name,—the Miles Thornton of the deeds,—may be that of some paternal ancestor : in which event, for anything that Mr. Littleworth knew to the contrary, Mr. Thornton may prove to be his own grandfather.

Once again :—in the case of so old a title, it is possible that one or other of the deeds may have been mislaid or lost ; a fact of which Mr. Thornton himself may be ignorant. But such a mischance would make a flaw in the title, which might render it impracticable for you to realize the property.

As a further excuse for not having the deeds properly perused by the Bank solicitors, whereby all these untoward possibilities would have been set at rest, Mr. Littleworth had a feeling that Mr. Thornton would not have submitted to the expense. But on this ground, Mr. Thornton might with equal reason have demurred to paying interest on the advance. This gentleman came to borrow £2000 from the Bank on certain conditions ; one of which was, that the advance should be covered by deeds of property of sufficient value. He could not in reason assume, that the Bank would take his deeds 'in the lump,' without even looking at them, as a security of proved value. Would Mr. Thornton have lent money of his own, on the security of a brown paper parcel, purporting to contain deeds of sufficient value to secure repayment of the money lent?

But Mr. Thornton is an honourable man and incapable of stating an untruth ? With all submission that is not the question. There may be a missing link in the title, as we have said, without his knowledge. If instead of deeds, Mr. Thornton had brought money in a bag, and stated that it contained, in all, a couple of thousand pounds, which he desired might be placed to the credit of his account ; would he have felt his honour touched or his veracity impeached, if Mr. Littleworth had proceeded there and then, which without doubt he would have done, to tell over and verify the contents of the bag?

In banking you take nothing for granted, of which the proof is within reach. Whatever may be the point on which you seek assurance, there is no excuse for your resting on assumption, when you can fortify your judgment by the superior logic of facts.

But let us assume that Mr. Thornton has a good title to the property, that it is free from incumbrance, and that you have a good equitable lien upon it. In the event, then, of his inability to repay the advance,—will you be in a position to recoup yourself the £2000, plus interest and charges, with reasonable certainty and despatch?

You have first to obtain power of sale. You have to persuade Mr. Thornton to concur in a sale,—if you can overcome a man's natural repugnance to part with a property which has been in his family for generations. Or you may induce some other creditor to make him bankrupt. Or lastly, you may file a bill against him in Chancery. Such are the courses open to you, when you seek to realize your security—under what the law, with pleasant irony, styles an 'equitable' mortgage.

But the right to sell and convey being obtained, by persuasion, or bankruptcy, or a Chancery suit, you are not to conclude even then, that your path to realization is finally cleared of obstruction. Even on the supposition that the valuation of the property on which you have relied is not excessive—it will be known to all Oxborough that the Bank is the seller. Traditions of fabulous bargains made at sales of property by banks, will demoralize intending buyers; and the highest bid at the sale may not be within speaking distance of your reserve : you will buy in the property in disgust, and become mortgagee in possession, and receiver of the rents,—subject to leave of Chancery.

What the net amount of these will be, after deduc-

tions for repairs, additions, and what not, no man can
tell. But the fact that the tenants have a joint stock
bank for their landlord, will no doubt have a stimulat-
ing effect on their requirements; and the result will
be dispiriting, regarded as a rate of interest on your
debt.

But this will be a point of minor importance. The
leading fact to bear in mind is this—that so long as you
retain possession of the property, the money you have
advanced upon it is as effectually locked up and unavailable for your ordinary business purposes, as if it were at
the bottom of the Pacific. You cannot discount bills, or
make fresh advances, or cash cheques, or pay deposits
with title deeds, however valuable they may be. They
must first be turned into money by public sale or private
treaty. The process may be distasteful and cause the
loss of a portion of your debt: but better have the living
money back again in your coffers, even at a sacrifice,
than tied up beyond the reach of use, and yielding a
return, varying with the seasons and the voracity of
tenants, from three per cent. per annum, to within sight
of nothing.

The laws which regulate the devolution, sale, and
transfer of real property in England, involve processes
so tedious and complicated, and so fertile of cost and
risk, that real estate is rather shunned than sought after
as a cover for debt by many English Banks. For the
bulk of their advances they give the preference to
securities, the transfer of which is easy and inexpensive,
and without complication or risk in title,—securities
which, for the most part, can be turned into money on
any account day throughout the year.

And bankers will continue to give the preference to
such securities until something is done to facilitate
and cheapen the sale and transfer of real property in
England. That lands or houses can be rendered as
easy of transfer as a share in a railway, or a bill of
exchange, or a ten pound note, is not to be supposed;
but that the conveyance, as it too frequently obtains,

could be shorn of its obscure verbiage, ridiculous tauto-
logy, and bewildering length, ordinary people believe to
be within the sphere of rational hope, and not beyond
the limits of human capacity.

Much has been done, no doubt, in this direction of
late years. The form of mortgage, for example, in use
at your Branch, in lieu of the old 'memorandum of
deposit,' is printed on the face of half a sheet of ordinary
letter-paper. It has proved as effectual at law, nevertheless, and in all other respects, as if it covered five
skins of parchment, like the mortgage of forty years
back for £150, and costing £25,*—a monstrosity in
legal form now happily sharing oblivion with the ancient
unity of Doe and Roe, and other eccentricities of our
legal past.

RAILWAY STOCK. We come next upon what may
properly be termed your champion sample of banking
cover—£1000 London and North Western Railway
Stock, present market price £1625, to cover loan of
£1400 for three months to O. D.,—Stock registered in
name of the Bank.

This fulfils every requirement of a first-class banking
security. It affords to a lender, simplicity of title,
cheapness and ease of transfer, readiness of sale,
reasonable steadiness of value, and ample margin for
loss.

In the matter of title, that of railway shares is a
marvel of clearness and brevity. It does not require
weeks or months to deduce and 'settle;' nor several
skins of parchment for its laborious recital, in a language
which is devious and obscure except to the legal mind.
The deed by which railway shares are conveyed from
one man to another, is printed on the face of half a sheet
of paper, and is so simple in construction, that one of
your senior apprentices might fill up and perfect the

* Bullion's Letters, p. 69.

instrument in a few minutes. And the document thus perfected, will suffice to convey and transfer the stock to you, were it hundreds of thousands sterling, as inalienably as if it passed to you under the Great Seal itself

The shares of a leading railway company are also ready of sale. They can be turned into money, any business day throughout the year, on any Stock Exchange in the three kingdoms. They thus possess one of the highest qualities of a banking security— immediate convertibility into money at will.

They have the further quality of steadiness of value. But apart from this, your advances on railway stock, as in the present case, are protected against loss in value, by your margin of 15 per cent., which the borrower is bound by agreement to keep up: and if he fails to do so, you can sell out against him. A loss upon such transactions is therefore impossible, unless we are to imagine a financial convulsion, which shall topple North Westerns down more than £22 10s. per £100 of stock in four-and-twenty hours.

And there is yet another point in favour of this description of security. The shares are paid up in full, and therefore no liability in the shape of calls, or in any other form, can ever attach to them. Were the London and North Western Railway to stop payment to-morrow, the holders of its shares would not be liable for a shilling of its debts.

In brief, the ordinary, or preference, or debenture stock of any leading English railway company, is only second in quality, as a banking security, to Consols or Treasury Bills themselves, in readiness of sale, facility of transfer, steadiness of value, and absence of liability.

SECURITIES TO BEARER. Amongst your securities are certain bonds and debentures payable to bearer. In stability of value, and readiness of sale, they stand high: but they are open to a serious objection: if stolen, they would be as difficult of recovery as so many bank notes. All other forms of security you can register in the name of the Bank, or specially indorse in its favour ; so that, if abstracted, they could not be negociated by the thief, and would therefore be of no use to him.   But there is no way of protecting securities payable to bearer, by registration or indorsement, from negociation.   This being so, it follows that the less you hold of them the better : and if you decide to hold none, it will be better still : at least until some method can be devised, which shall render them unnegociable, equally with other forms of security, in case of misappropriation or theft.

And this leads to the question,—whether a bank, which gives safe custody to this class of security for a customer, is responsible to him, in the event of its being stolen. If so, the simplest way will be to decline the safe custody of such 'perilous stuff' altogether ; or to accept the charge on such terms, as will exempt the Bank from responsibility, whether arising from burglary from without or from fire or malversation from within.

You cheerfully give to all other forms of documentary Securities, belonging to your clients, the same protection which you give to your own, and will continue to do so·: because if stolen they would be incapable of transfer : but if certain of your customers choose to invest in 'bearer' securities, with their unlimited capability of swift and secret transfer, and consequent attractions for the misdemeanant, it is beyond reason to cast upon Bankers the formidable risk which is involved in their safe keeping.

TRANSFERS IN BLANK.   In some instances you are content with a deposit of railway or other shares, bonds or debentures, accompanied by a transfer in blank.   Where you are dealing with parties whom you know to be safe, beyond all question, for the advances, without security, this is an irregularity which may have to be winked at in some cases : but it must be strictly exceptional.

An imperfect security is no security at all while it remains imperfect. It is open to the further objection, that in the manifold transactions which you will have to conduct or supervise, day by day, you may forget, unless you have a memory of superhuman range and tenacity, which of your securities are perfected and which are not. You may thus by inadvertence deal with a customer's account as covered, until you receive a painful refresher to the contrary, some day ; and find yourself compelled to hand your uncompleted security over to his assignee in bankruptcy, to sink into his general estate.

There is this further objection—Companies' stock, accompanied by a transfer in blank, may expose you to as certain loss, if misappropriated or stolen, as an equal value in 'bearer' securities ; because a thief could make immediate use of an instrument so admirably adapted for his purpose, as a stamped transfer in blank, accompanied by the scrip itself. The transfer thus affably left open to be filled up as he shall see fit, amounts almost to an invitation to perfect his felony. It is at least certain that you could not furnish him with a more effectual means to that end.

When there is more than one cash safe at a Branch, the scrip could no doubt be kept in one and the transfers in another, and the bonds and coupons of bearer securities might be kept separate from each other by the same arrangement. This would afford a certain amount of protection against external attack. It would put a burglar to the extra trouble of forcing a couple of safes instead of one ; but if he should ever gain access to either, he will probably have made his arrangements to include both in the night's work.

I assume that when you make advances as against transfers in blank, to suit the humour or the susceptibilities of customers, you do so on the understanding that the security is held by you at their risk in case of fire or theft? You hold the security in its imperfect form to oblige them, and in violation of your general usage: it is only reasonable, therefore, that the risk thereby involved should be theirs, and not yours.

LOCAL SHARES. The next sample of your securities, although of some steadiness in value, is less negociable than railway stock:—Fifty shares in the Oxborough Water Works, to cover account of F. G.

'The shares are fully paid up: transferred into the Bank's name; they pay 4½ per cent., and the last sale was slightly above par.

So far so good. They possess all the qualities of a sound banking security except one: you cannot send them to the nearest Stock Exchange and have them turned into Bank notes next account. You must wait for a local buyer, and this may mean weeks, or even months of waiting. Any attempt to force a sale would probably be futile, and would certainly be detrimental to your security. The more you lower the price, the more the hidden purchaser, if there be one, will hold aloof He will mark your eagerness to sell and prevail against you by a masterly inactivity; unless you change your tactics and play the waiting game yourself If there is no urgency in the case, your retention of the shares will not involve the Bank in any liability. Better, therefore, wait a month or two for a willing buyer, than surrender them at once on usurious terms to some local Shylock.

The objection to your Water Works shares, that is, their unreadiness of sale, applies to the shares or debentures of all merely local Companies, Corporations, or Trusts which are not quoted on the price-list of any Stock Exchange; and the objection extends to securities of every description, which can only be disposed of by private sale, or public auction.

SHIPPING SECURITIES.   Your next example brings us
to the consideration of securities, in our appraisement of
which, it is possible that we may find ourselves at sea in
more senses than one:—'Mortgage on barque *Rapid*,
estimated value £2500, to cover debt of £1700 by L. M.
now insolvent.'

This might be a good security to a shipowner, or
shipbroker, because it is his business to know all about
ships, and to devote his whole time and energy to the
working of them to the best advantage.   But to do so
with success, requires half a lifetime of business training,
and a store of special knowledge, of which, to say you
are well-nigh destitute, would be no reflection on your
general qualifications as the Manager of a country
bank.

The *Rapid*, it appears, is now on a distant voyage,
and is being worked on account of the Bank.   It may
be that the vessel will return after many days, with a
skilful captain, a steady crew, and a splendid freight.
But it is also possible that the reverse of all this may
happen.   A disorderly crew, a ruinous freight, and a fool
for captain, would not be an unknown experience to the
British shipowner.

Amongst other things, you may have to meet claims,
or defend law suits, brought against you by shippers or
consignees, for damage to cargo, occasioned through
the carelessness of captain or crew, or through bad
stowage.

It is also within the range of possibility that the ship
may run aground in a fog, or sustain damage in a gale,
and have to put in for repairs at some foreign port.   She
may thus get 'bottomried' to a formidable amount:
but whatever the amount may be, it will take precedence
of your mortgage: and if the sum bottomried shall
exceed the value of the ship, the Bank will be liable for
the deficiency.   It might thus happen, that the mortgagee in possession of a ship, might lose not only the
amount of his mortgage, but find himself exposed to
further charges.   He may not only have to forfeit the

money he has lent, but find himself amerced for having lent it on a precarious security.

Moreover, the *Rapid* may some day, by evil chance, run into and damage another vessel, or even sink her outright: in which event you will have to reckon with the law for the injury done, and possibly for the loss of human life.

No doubt these and other risks can for the most part be covered by insurance: but is the game worth the candle? Is the periodical disbursing and manning, victualling and insuring, loading or chartering of a ship the proper business of a Bank Manager, or his Board of Directors? Will any rate of banking charge which you can levy on such transactions, amount to a reasonable equivalent for the time wasted or the temper lost over their attendant wrangles, risks, and worries? Better in my judgment sell the *Rapid* on her first arrival in port at almost any price, and thus avoid the pains and penalties which the pursuit of shipowning has ordinarily in store for the uninitiated.

In addition to owning the whole of the *Rapid* you have an interest to the extent of 8-64ths in another vessel at sea. There is one advantage in your holding only a share in a ship: your Board will not be allowed to work her —she will be managed by your co-owners. But there is this disadvantage :—When you own the whole of a ship, as in the case of the *Rapid*, you can sell her at any time, at a price: but you cannot so easily dispose of the fraction of a ship.

If you succeed in selling it at all, it will probably be to one of your co-owners: but it will be at his own time and price, and not at yours. You will then realize the disparity which is sometimes found to exist between value and price: betwixt the value put upon a certain thing by its owner, when he comes to borrow your money, and the price at which you have to part with it, when you want the money back again.

And there is this further disadvantage in owning only

a few shares of a ship: you are entirely in the hands of
your co-owners and liable for any amount of debt in
which they may involve the vessel. On the whole, I
think, as a banker, I would part with these 8-64ths on
attractive terms to the first buyer.

'BILL OF LADING of hides to secure £1450 advanced
to Arthur Pringle.'

You hold the stamped policy of insurance, duly
indorsed : and the present market value of the hides is
£1800. On the presumption that you hold the entire
set of bills of lading, and that there will be no stopper
put on the delivery of the hides on arrival of the ship,
and that they are of a quality to realize the price you
quote—although it is going a long way to assume all
this—you appear to hold sufficient security to cover
your advance.

But it is the business of a broker to make advances on
merchandize at sea, and you will do wisely to leave the
business to those who understand it. The custom of
merchants, or the intricacies of mercantile law, do not
necessarily form branches of a country banker's education. A smattering of such knowledge will come to you
no doubt in time : and will be unobjectionable, so long
as you do not act upon it. If you do, you are more
than likely, to use a popular expression, to put your foot
in it.

In the case in hand, the regular course would have
been for Mr. Pringle to place the bills of lading in the
hands of a broker of repute, and to draw upon him for
the £1450 ; obtaining from the acceptor a letter hypo-
thecating the proceeds to payment of the bill.

But as this course was not followed, it is to be inferred
that Mr. Pringle objected to it. He preferred, no doubt,
to borrow the money through you, at your ordinary rate
of commission, rather than obtain it through a merchant
or broker at more than twice your charge. This was
only natural. Mr. Pringle would have been foolish not

to avail himself of your liberality. But on what ground a Banker should conduct transactions, of which he knows little or nothing, for one-half the commission which would be charged upon them by those who know them perfectly, is not so obvious.

But Mr. Pringle, you explain, is a man of substance, good for many times the worth of the hides, and a valued customer of the Bank in other ways. These considerations, no doubt, change the aspect of the affair, and render a transaction allowable, which would be less defensible on its own merits.

HOUSE PROPERTY. You hold a ' First Mortgage on twenty, cottages in Oxborough, gross annual rental £200, to cover the account of Owen Pegler for £2000.'

It was considered safe, you report, to take the annual rental at ten years' purchase, to find the value of the property. Pegler has failed, and you have been mortgagees in possession for some years. A house-agent collects the rents on account of the Bank, as best he can, but his latest report is discouraging:—one third of the cottages empty : half the tenants more or less in arrear of rent: the interior of most of the houses sadly dilapidated : roofs leaking : plaster falling off the walls : windows broken: doors off their hinges or refusing to shut, and the sanitary arrangements bad and dangerous to health. A whole year's gross rental will not suffice to put things in decent repair.

I would part with this property, if it were mine, at less than ten years' purchase of the nominal rental. Even the net rental, if that were a known quantity, multiplied by ten, would have been an outside value to have put upon it—that is on the supposition that a bank ought ever to be the holder, at any price, of property, the rents of which have to be collected, by so many shillings a week, from poor and struggling tenants, if the rents are to be collected at all.

House or shop property, even of a superior class, is

not a desirable security, on its own merits, for a bank to hold, if it were merely on the ground of its uncertainty of sale. The ordinary purchasers of house or shop property, by which I mean buyers for their own occupation and use, have their fancies, and are limited in number; and failing a purchaser of this class being in the market, when you have an eligible shop, a detached residence, a double villa, or a desirable block to dispose of, you have to resort to the dealer in house property and equities, who will naturally protect himself by a handsome margin, if he buys at all; and the price finally agreed upon will be nearer his ideas of value than yours.

Not that this description of security is uniformly to be rejected. You allow C. B., for instance, to overdraw his account, at any time, up to a certain sum, because his balance-sheet shews him to be safe for more than the amount, and the account is profitable: but as a matter of precaution, you take the title deeds of his house and shop, as a security to fall back upon, in the event of misfortune overtaking him amidst the unforeseen vicissitudes of trade.

LETTER XVI.

SECURITIES WHICH ARE NOT SECURITY.

I trusted so much that I solde the skinne before the beaste was taken, reckoning without mine hoast, and setting that down in my bookes as ready money, which afterwards I found to be a desperate debt.   EUPHUES.

YOUR sample of Securities does not improve in quality as we proceed : on the contrary, the tendency in that respect is downwards.

LIFE POLICIES.   You hold a policy on the life of Noah Hardy for £3000 to secure balance of account.   The present value of this security is some £150, or one third the amount of premiums thus far paid upon it.   Its prospective value depends upon the period of Mr. Hardy's demise.   Should that be the unhappy result of your calling upon him to pay up, the security will be available to its full amount, in a few months afterwards, provided the policy has been assigned to the Bank and notice thereof registered in the books of the Insurance Company.

But the inability to pay a sum owing to a bank has not ordinarily a fatal effect on the life of the debtor. As a matter of fact, the records of your Bank would rather seem to shew that the average rate of mortality is unusually light, amongst parties indebted to the Bank on the strength of Life Policies.   In cases, indeed, where the premiums are paid by the Bank, the debtors frequently reach a patriarchal age.

Whether, as you suggest, the interests which they know to be involved in their speedy departure from this

life, have the effect of rousing an oppugnant and unreasonable spirit on the part of the assured, which gives
a fillip to their constitutions and promotes longevity, is
a speculation which we need not pause to discuss : it is
enough for the purpose in hand, that, in one instance,
you are still paying the annual premium on a policy
which your Bank adopted to cover a bad debt thirty-
eight years ago. If you will put the matter to computation, you will find that so far from saving, you have
thus more than doubled the original amount of this
venerable debt.

The payment of the premiums on Mr. Hardy's policy
as they fall due, being guaranteed by another person, no
doubt improves the value of your security : but the
improvement is only a contingent one. To be effectual,
it requires that the guarantor shall live, and continue
solvent, for five-and-twenty years to come. That is the
official period that persons of Mr. Hardy's present years
and robust constitution are computed to live, and within
which they are officially expected to die : but surely a
prodigious period of time for any banking advance to
run? Three months being the approved average currency of the available resources of a bank, a debt having
five-and-twenty years to run, regarded as a banking
asset, might as well have a currency of centuries or
accomplish the years·of Methuselah.

If Mr. Hardy had offered the Bank for discount his
promissory note at six months after date, even in the
most lax and easy condition of the money market, the
Bank would have taken it with a grudge, if at all, and
as an exceptional transaction : but in making Mr. Hardy
this advance upon his Life Policy, the Bank virtually
discounted for him his promissory note at so many
months after death.

BILLS OF SALE. You hold from Felix Addler as
security for his account, a Bill of sale over his stock in
trade, etc. for £600.

The value of the stock is set down at £1000 : but if another cipher were added to the figures, the security would still be one of the most rickety in law, and the worst in character, which a bank could hold. A security over stock in trade, or furniture, or live stock, or implements of trade, or other articles which are portable, and may be removed, exchanged, or otherwise disposed of to any extent without your knowledge, is practically no security at all. You might as well select a shifting sand, as a foundation to build a house upon ; or have taken a permanent charge upon the coin in Mr. Addler's pocket, for all the certainty you can have that the articles will be forthcoming when required.

SECOND MORTGAGE. Your next specimen is 'Second Mortgage for £1500 on house property in Oxborough: to secure the account of Ephraim Raddle.' The valuation of the property is £5000 and the first mortgage is for £3000. The surplus, or equity, has been mortgaged to your Bank for £1500.

Now the considerations which guide a private lender in such matters, ought to have at least equal weight with a banker. If it would be imprudent in an individual to lend more than a certain sum on a given property, it is difficult to understand how it could be prudent in a bank to do so.

In Mr. Raddle's case, we may take it for granted that he raised all he could on the property, in the first instance. If anyone would have lent him more than £3000 upon it, it is not to be imagined that he would have refused the increase. Apart from the question of expense, he had no doubt experienced how hard a thing it is to find capitalists who will lend money on the second mortgage of anything. We must therefore regard £3000 as the maximum which any prudent lender saw his way to advance upon the property, and this being so, the question arises,—On what ground did the Bank make a further advance upon it of £1500 ? According to the valuation, it is true, there ought to be sufficient value in the property for you both,—enough to pay off the first mortgagee and yourselves afterwards.

But valuation is not synonymous with value. Valuations are commonly arrived at, by multiplying the net rental of a property by so many years' purchase, according to a scale which has no fixed basis, but is purely arbitrary.

Moreover, there are varieties of valuers. Some are more sanguine of view than others. One will put a higher value on a given property than another would. In this particular, each valuator has his own scale and method of appraisement and is a law unto himself. Properties, when brought to the hammer, do sometimes realize the valuation put upon them, but they more frequently yield very much less.

When a man therefore advances money on the mortgage of a property, he usually makes a large mental deduction from the sum of the valuation. The question for him is not its regulation value, but its market price, —the sum it will realize if brought to the hammer.

In the present case the lender mentally deducted £2000 from the valuation, to find the amount it was safe for him to lend. He therefore regarded two-fifths of the valuation as partaking of the quality of moonshine, except as affording him a margin for contingencies. If he was correct in this, you would seem to hold a legal mortgage for £1500 on a value which has its principal basis in the imagination.

It may be that the lender has undervalued the property: but you have to recollect that he has no interest in its selling for more than will recoup his advance, plus interest and costs. He can moreover sell at his own time and at any price, without regard to you or your second mortgage, unless you choose to step in and pay him off. You will thus get the control of the property into your own hands: but you will at the same time add £3000 to the already dubious debt of Ephraim Raddle.

Not that there is never any value in a second mortgage. A second charge for £1500, for example, on Mr.
Starkey's estate, a property worth £20,000, might safely
follow the only previous charge upon it of £5000. But
there is this further risk attendant on second mortgages,
—Mr. Raddle, for example, might execute a third mortgage to somebody else, and this third claimant on the
property might pay the first mortgage off, and tack his
own claim on to it, in advance of yours. He who was
third and last would thus become first and foremost,
whilst you would be practically nowhere.

I am informed and believe that in this I am correctly
stating the law of the matter—with certain qualifications ;
but do not in this, or any other matter, take the law
from me. This is not a legal treatise : I have purposely
abstained, as far as it was possible, from referring to
points of law, because, for one reason, I am not a
lawyer ; and because for another, the perennial manufacture of fresh laws by the legislature is so persistent
and profuse, that even the Judges of the land, it is said,
can hardly keep pace with them.

Not that I would discourage your careful study of the
general principles of the law, as they concern the ordinary transactions of your business, because you will
have occasion for the exercise of such knowledge day
by day. It is not essential to this end, however, that
you should commit to memory the whole of Blackstone's
Commentaries, or even Chitty on Bills of Exchange—a
treatise which covered a thousand pages of stiff reading
even forty years ago. There are handier works than
these now-a-days, the study of which will suffice for all
practical purposes ; but inasmuch as English law, as we
have just said, in its bearings on banking usage and on
banking forms, is subject to frequent change, I would
counsel you to be guided in every case, where there is
any legal doubt or difficulty, by the solicitors for the
Bank. The Bank Manager who shall act exclusively
upon his own reading and interpretation of English law

in these days can hardly fail now and then to have a fool for his client.

Building Land. Following the downward tendency of your selection of securities in point of quality, we come next to—

'Five thousand square yards of building land, with houses thereon, as security for advances to Bricknal & Co., Builders.'

Your history of this account is instructive :—

'At the date of the original advance the land was looked upon as ample security, being admirably situated for residential property of a good class.

'When the Bank applied to the Bricknals for repayment of the original advance of £1000, they stated that if pressed just then they must suspend : whereas if the Bank would enable them to build on the land, by making them further advances, they saw their way to clearing off the old debt and everything else with ease and promptitude. The proposal was entertained, and Excelsior Crescent was commenced. The Bank advanced two-thirds the certified value of work done, and everything went swimmingly. The first block, when completed, was readily mortgaged by the Bricknals for enough to repay the fresh advances made by the Bank, as well as to effect a substantial reduction in the old score. Consequent upon this success, two additional blocks were started without delay : but when these were less than halfway to completion, the Bricknals collapsed, and the Bank was left with two large piles of unfinished property which it had either to complete or abandon. We decided to complete, and the last stage of the Bricknals' account was worse than the first.'

There is nothing surprising in that. When a Board of Directors takes in hand to finish half-built blocks of houses under their own supervision, they have generally, to use a colloquial figure, to pay through the nose. They

8

may flatter themselves with the hope that the property, when finished, will sell for such a sum as will repay their fresh outlay and extinguish the original debt: the more sanguine may even speculate on a handsome surplus, to go to the reserve fund.

It will not be till they have cast the accounts up and realized the total cost of their amateur adventure in house-building, that the truth will reveal itself,—that they had far better have left the half-built structures to go to ruin where they stood, and the original debt to perish with them.

You hold another plot of building land, on which no messuages have been erected as yet, by yourselves or anyone else. At the time the Bank took the land as a security for a certain account, the town, you explain, was rapidly extending in that direction. That is now thirty years ago, and the town, it seems, has stretched entirely the other way ever since.

Your field of two acres, or 9680 square yards, which was looked upon at the time as ridiculously cheap, at half-a-crown a yard, you let for some years as town pasturage, at a few pounds a year rental, whilst waiting for the purchaser who never came; but the fencing so constantly needed renewal, and when renewed was so promptly carried off, to be used as fire-wood by the predatory arabs of the neighbourhood, that you have long since abandoned the attempt to keep it inclosed; and it is now a sort of no-man's land, a play-ground for all the ragged urchins of the place, and the repository for fragmentary pottery, stray brickbats, and general rubbish.

Excepting shares in undertakings which involve liability, it is difficult to imagine a more objectionable security for a banker to hold. You can sell almost anything else, at a price; but unless it is actually wanted by some person at the moment, for his own purposes, you cannot sell building-land, unless you are prepared practically to give it away. You might have sold the land in question, it appears, many years ago, at something less than the half-crown; but to accept the offer, was looked upon at the time by your authorities as throwing the property away, and the opportunity was lost, never to return.

Has it occurred to you that the £1200 locked up in this security, if employed in your proper business, to bring in even 3½ per cent. per annum, would have fructified by this time to £3360; instead of shrinking to a few miserable hundreds?

For a Bank to hold this description of property, for better times and a higher price, is virtually to speculate in it. Its sale is of all things the most uncertain, and the demand for it the most capricious. There is not a town in England where you may not find secluded plots of building-land, which the tide of building has passed by on either side, from no apparent cause, and left in abandoned sterility. As a banker, you are a dealer in money, or in securities readily exchangeable for money, and building-land does not come within this category. It is practically inconvertible into money on rational terms, and ought therefore to have no place amongst a banker's assets.

BUILDINGS AND MACHINERY. You held at one time the deeds of the Atlas Forge to cover advances to G. D. & Co.

'The firm,' you write, 'failed in 18—, and when the Bank came to realize its security, the whole of the machinery, which formed its chief value, was claimed by the other creditors, as belonging to the general estate. The Bank resisted, but to no purpose.

'After a prolonged and costly fight, we were finally left in possession of the walls and roof—'four naked walls that stared upon each other'—and the half-acre of ground they stood upon. We appear to have lost about three-fourths of this debt.'

Smelting works, or factories, or shipbuilding yards, **or**

rolling mills, or blast furnaces; or works of any description, where the chief value consists of machinery, plant, and implements, which cannot legally be mortgaged to a bank, or to anybody else, are securities of a class which all prudent bankers will resolutely shun.

Whatever may have been the original cost of buildings and machinery, or the value of any work as a going concern—so soon as it ceases to be workable at a profit, its value to a lender practically shrinks to that of the land it stands upon, plus walls and roof, and the value in old iron of the fixed machinery.

SECURITIES INVOLVING LIABILITY. You hold, or rather held, only two of these; one of them having happily been numbered long since amongst the things that were.

Your first sample consists of 'Fifty shares of £50 each in the Nonpareil Porcelain Co., Limited, held on account of the debt of Adrian Ware.

'Ware's debt of £500 becoming doubtful in 18—, the Bank took from him such securities as they could get, the above amongst the rest. There was at the time only £5 paid up on the shares, and they stood at £5 premium, and could have been sold at that price: but as the Directors had private information that they would go immensely higher, a sale was deferred.

'We have since paid calls upon them amounting in all to £20 a share : no dividends have been declared for years, and the payment of calls has had no effect on the market price. It has been like the pouring of water into a sieve: in fact there is no market price for them, and we could not even give them away if we would.

'The concern is heavily in debt, and the majority of the shareholders are more or less incapable of paying any more calls : so that there is a possibility of our having to pay the remaining £25 on each share, and thus add another £1250 to our loss by Ware.

'In seeking to save the original debt of £500, we have lost it altogether, and stand to lose £2000 besides.'

There is a quiet force in this narrative which will find its way to the heart of any banker, who has suffered from a like experience; the moral of which would seem to be, that in grasping at a security at the last moment, as drowning men are said to catch at straws, a banker has to beware that he does not clutch a liability instead.

Proceeding still from bad to worse, we finally arrive at 'Lease of the Lower Deep Coal Mine,'—another security, taken for another doubtful debt. 'We worked the mine,' you report, 'on our own account for a good many years, but to no advantage. The quarterly state-ment, it is true, always shewed a substantial profit: but the debt to the Bank was all the while increasing, and increased largely, from the time we took the mine into our own hands.

If an adventure is shewing a steady profit, but is en-larging with equal steadiness its debt to the bank which is carrying it on, the probability is, that outgoings which ought to be charged to revenue, are being charged to capital instead. In this way the working of the most disastrous concern can with ease and success be made to shew a profit. The method is immoral, but it would not be without precedent.

You only sought to work the mine, it seems, until you could find a purchaser for it: but there is one reflection with regard to this description of security, which you will do well to lay to heart, and it is this,—that when a bank takes upon itself the working of a mine, or a forge, or a factory, or any other concern which has ruined the original adventurer, it is a reasonable conclusion that the Bank will not make a fortune by it. If a man can-not succeed in a business, to which he has been trained, and which he thoroughly understands; it is beyond con-ception how another person, or body of persons, who know nothing about it, can hope to do so.

And the money loss which is the almost certain result to a bank, which takes to mining, or any other descrip-tion of business on its own account, is not the only draw-

back. To look after such concerns, diverts a large portion
of the thought and care, which the Directors and Manager
might otherwise apply with advantage to the proper
business of the Bank.

Nor is this all. A bank which elects to mine, or grind,
or smelt, or spin on its own account, converts every one
in the district, who is following any of these lines of
business, into an active and outspoken enemy. Its management is derided, its losses are exaggerated, and its
intrusion on a field of enterprise not its own, is resented
as unfair, and denounced as leading to destruction. And
those who believe all this and publish it abroad, will not
rest content with removing their own accounts from
such a bank. They will use their influence to induce
their friends to do the same. The Bank will thus have
set itself, so to speak, to burn at both ends. At one
end there will be the loss of valuable accounts; at the
other, the absorption of profits in a business alien to its
constitution.

But the worst evil of the thing is this—that once
fairly embarked in a Colliery or any other description
of mining adventure, the necessity for going through
with it gathers force with every fresh thousand sunk:
and a banker's 'alacrity in sinking' under such circumstances has passed into a proverb;—One more shaft, one
short drift, a hundred yards to the main level, and fresh
leather to the pumps, and then—! And then, in ninety-
nine cases out of a hundred, you find yourself precisely
where you were—plus the fresh addition to your debt.

'The fact was,' you further report, 'that if we had
allowed the mine to fill with water and the roofs to fall
in, and the drifts to choke up, the penalties of the lease
were frightful; and as for a purchaser after that, we
should have had to pay a tremendous bonus to anyone
who would take the thing off our hands. In short it was
a case of pump or sink.'

It would be difficult to visit with an excess of repro-
bation, the Board of Directors who should seek to save a
bank from an impending bad debt, by the adoption of

any security which involved a limitless liability. The shares of any unlimited company, of what standing soever, are not banking securities. That is not a security, which may some day become an overwhelming liability.

This must conclude your 'sample.' It embraces specimens of banking security, ranging in quality from the highest to the lowest : from the very best to the very worst. As there can be no higher point reached in the scale of quality than London and North Western Stock, neither in the worst experiences of banking can there be found a worse example than 'Lower Deeps.' There are other securities on your register, which we do not discuss, because they assimilate, more or less, to one or other of the forms which we have dealt with, and are to be gauged by the same rules, when you desire to ascertain their relative eligibility as banking securities.

Glancing backwards over the various forms which we have had under review, they would seem to require at your hands, in dealing with them, a range of ability, an extent of knowledge, and a breadth of judgment, which are given only to men of phenomenal capacity. To begin with,—you are a railway proprietor. That, however, may pass ; it is the only security which will make no serious demand upon your time or attention. But if matters go wrong with Mr. Thornton, you will have to guard against the legal toils which await a mortgagee in possession, or become the actual owner, and possibly the cultivator, of a two hundred acre farm. You are the chief moneyed partner in a porcelain business, with what aptitude for that description of art manufacture does not appear. You are managing owner of the barque *Rapid*, although it is not in evidence what your maritime experience has been, nor whether you could tell the ship's stem from her stern-post. As a general broker, you do a little in hides, and if misfortune should overtake Seth Addler we may have a taste of your quality as carpenter and joiner. Banker, railway proprietor, land-

owner, potter, general broker, ship's husband and joiner
—the admirable Crichton himself would have hesitated
to undertake the management of Oxborough Branch.

It has to be said that the worst of your securities were
taken to cover advances which had already been made,
and had become desperate; but that is no excuse. The
branch manager who shall seek to save the Bank from
loss on any given account, by the adoption of securities
which may become more fatal absorbents of money than
the account itself had been, betrays an ignorance of the
ordinary principles of banking which would be fatal now
a days to his obtaining a diploma for even a senior
clerkship in a bank from the Institute of Bankers,—an
institution, I desire to add in passing, which is designed,
and assuredly destined in my judgment to exercise an important and wholly beneficial influence on the banking of
the future. To our banking youth, especially, membership
in the Institute should be a powerful attraction, because
its diploma will be more and more regarded by Boards
of Bank Directors as an extra feather in the cap of
those seeking advancement.

NOTE.—The reader is not to assume that the securities
criticised in this letter are a fair average sample of their
kind: nor even that, as a whole, they were ever held by
any one bank, or branch of a bank; but that they, or
their equivalents, have figured, at one time or another,
amongst securities held by banks, is not a figment of
the brain, but a fact within the knowledge of the writer.
The worst of them, no doubt, belong to an extinct
Past: but their record may not be without instruction
for us, even in these more enlightened days of banking.

LETTER XVII.

DEPOSITS AND RUNS.

Fancy is the castle commanding the city; and, if once men's heads be possessed with strange imaginations, the whole body will follow and be infinitely transported therewith.　　FULLER.

In common with other banks, you are ready at all times to accept from people the use of money, for which they have no immediate employment themselves; and who believe it will be in safer keeping with you, than in the seclusion of their own pockets. You accept the use of money also from persons in business, although they have almost daily employment for it themselves, but who prefer to place it in the Bank, day by day, rather than trust it to the protection of their own tills or cash boxes overnight.

The people who thus make you the custodian of their floating cash, have a motive for so doing beyond the attraction of receiving interest upon the money. They reflect that, in the event of the bank being burnt down or broken into and plundered, they have still the share-holders to fall back upon to make their money good; whereas, in the event of a personal experience of this nature, they would have nothing to fall back upon but the police.

The trader who retains £50 in his own keeping overnight, rather than pay a trifling commission to his banker for taking charge of the money, and awakes to find his till forced and the money gone, will hardly account the operation a brilliant one, which has saved him fifteen pence at the cost of fifty pounds.

Moneys placed by their owners in a bank, are in the

nature of loans, but not loans in the usual sense of the term.   The ordinary borrower applies to the lender, but in your case, it is the lender who applies to you.   The borrower seeks to borrow, because he is in want of the money; but you are not in want of it, neither do you go about seeking for it.   If it is brought to you, you can no doubt make use of it; if it is not so brought, you can do without it.   There is no favour involved either way.

Moreover, when an ordinary loan is sought for, it is usually for a term of years, and involves a certain degree of permanence; whereas the loans tendered to you are for terms measurable by months, weeks, or days, and sometimes even by hours; and their feature is instability. In brief, moneys placed with a bank are as much deposited for safe custody as lent, and hence for shortness, the term applied to them—Deposits.

You separate your deposits into two classes—into those which you have to repay at any moment on demand, and those which are not repayable without previous notice.   The former you pass to the credit of parties on current account; the latter you place to their credit on deposit receipt.   These receipts are subject to notice of withdrawal, ranging from a few days to a calendar month, according to the usage of different banks and localities.

In consideration of this proviso, you allow a higher rate of interest on the money, than if it were repayable on demand.

The more volatile class of your deposits, namely, the balances of your current accounts, as we have said, are payable on demand; but you have, no doubt, an understanding with your principal clients, that they will not check upon you for large amounts, without previous notice, however brief   No doubt there are those who, either from perversity or want of thought, omit this simple act of courtesy, and will check upon you at times for large sums without a moment's notice.   Accounts of this description will sometimes provoke the query, whether it would not be to your advantage, on the whole, if they were taken elsewhere. It is evident that you can derive but slight advantage from the use of balances so .capricious; inasmuch as they oblige you to keep an abnormal amount of cash lying idle in your coffers, to meet their abrupt and uncertain movements.

The advantage sought by a banker in having the bulk of his deposits subject to previous notice of payment is obvious: it protects him against sudden demands of embarrassing amount, whilst it enables him to employ a larger portion of such funds in discounts and advances.

The only member of the community who may not with impunity request a creditor to call again to-morrow, is the banker—not that he gets payment of the debts owing to him more readily than other people; on the contrary, there would seem to be a pestilent and wide-spread belief, that a banker has untold hoards of money always at command, and can 'wait.' He acts as middle-man, between the lenders and the borrowers of money, and is the general purveyor of cash for the community. But there is this distinction—whereas the banker is bound to refund the money to every depositor the moment it is asked for, the persons to whom he has lent it do not feel themselves under any such peremptory obligation. It is by no means fatal to a trader's credit, to inform his bankers that they must wait; but such an intimation, if made by a banker, would be his commercial death. For him there is no waiting and no mercy—not for an hour. He must pay his debts, the moment they are due and demanded, or close his doors.

There are people without number, who have yet to realize the simple fact that banks, if they are to pay interest at all on moneys deposited with them, must re-lend the greater portion of such moneys at interest to other people.

In spite of School Boards and the march of intellect, there are those who harbour the delusion to this day, that the money which they deposit in a bank—the identical notes and coin—are straightway placed in impregnable vaults, there to remain until the owners want the notes and coin out again; as if money thus disposed of, would fructify of itself and yield perennial fruits of increase.

Mr. Oliver Nayler, the keenest man of business in Oxborough, who has a few thousands at his credit at your Branch, and is amongst the first to join in a run upon you, will admit with effusion that such ideas are absurd, and degrading to the human intellect; but that he requires the money for a particular purpose that day and must have it. It wounds him to the quick to ask for the money without a moment's notice, but he finds there is no reasoning with some people. Moreover, his word is pledged, and he cannot go back from that.

Mr. Nayler is right—there is no reasoning with some people, especially of the Nayler class. You might as well seek to reason with a savage on the war path, as with a depositor ' on the run.' The promptings of avarice and dread so possess him for the moment, that nothing will content him, until he has clutched the actual money, that he may hide it away in the traditional old stocking, or whatever may be the secret place of his hid treasure. How soon the secondary terrors of fancying his house broken into, his throat cut, and the money stolen, will supervene, and outweigh his former fears, will depend on temperament: but these thoughts will come to him before long, in the night watches; and when he comes to re-deposit the money, you will no doubt render its withdrawal subject to the longest term of notice within the range of your instructions.

Your preparedness as a bank, at every hour of every business day, to lend money, or accept the use of it, at interest, to any amount, from tens to tens of thousands—although a service to the community of priceless convenience, is entirely ignored and set aside in the blind selfishness of a run. But whatever sense of heartless requital may be stirred within you by this reflection, you will do wisely to keep it strictly to yourself. Better accept the inevitable with a good grace than with an impotent resentment. Receive your panic-stricken depositors with a smile, however forced, rather than with an angry frown ; because, whether you regard them with one expression or the other, the money they will have there and then, whilst the fit is on them— let whatsoever else happen. ' The robb'd that smiles,' you will recollect; ' steals something from the thief.'

When, after a time, they find that the panic was groundless, and that the Bank is none the worse for the hammering it has sustained, and the desire to re-deposit the money awakens again within them, there can be little doubt which expression of the two—the smile or the frown—will have the larger effect in attracting the money back to you, or deflecting it to other banks.

When you find that a run has actually set in upon you, you will have to carry yourself at all points without trepidation ; because if those who come first see that you are nervous, or put about, they will conclude that there is ground for their uneasiness, and will not fail to convey the fact to their neighbours,—as soon as they have their own money safe, and can afford to be generous. Your course indeed, will be to meet all demands with an eagerness of despatch ; you will thus prevent, amongst other things, a gathering together of excited persons, three or four deep, outside your counter ; an assembly which cannot be too promptly dispersed. If left too long to simmer, it may boil over, and intensify matters within doors and without.

And you have to take into account, that the persons running for their money will not be limited entirely to those whose deposits or credit balances are payable at call. Others will join in the rush, and demand their money with equal emphasis, although their deposits are subject to notice, and no such notice has been given. The persons who will thus seek to break through their bargain with you may be few in number, or they may be many—it is impossible to say ; so much will depend upon the incidents of the moment. But it will be safe to conclude that the great majority of your depositors, under any circumstances, will honourably abide by the term of notice which they have covenanted to give.

The question remains—how best to deal with the impracticable few. You would refuse point-blank to pay them their money without the stipulated notice. You are aware, you add, that this step will transform some of them into brawling idiots on the spot; but you would not, on that account, suffer the Bank to be bullied. You do not doubt that your firmness will cause the Bank to be vilified up hill and down dale. In every bar parlour in Oxborough, you feel assured, the thing will be discussed to the accompaniment of pipes and beer. The pernicious Bagster will not fail to suggest, that a bank must be hard up, which asks for a month's time to pay old Ricketts his seventy pounds, which the poor old man wants so badly. You are conscious that all this will tend to widen the area of disturbance, intensify the run, and enlarge the ultimate chasm in your deposits; but you know that the position of the Bank is invulnerable, and that it can afford to adhere to principle, and hold all these possibilities in utter contempt and defiance. In short, you would hold every depositor to the letter of his bond, and have no paltering with the sanctity of contract.

But the question at issue is not the stability of the District Union Bank—that goes without saying—nor the sanctity of contract. The question at issue is the simpler one—Is the procedure you propose worth its drawbacks? For the mere sake of holding strictly to their engagements, in respect of notice, a score or two of depositors, under the influence of temporary delirium; is it worth while to give impetus and expansion to a movement, which might be a source of serious loss to the business of your Bank and of grave consequences to many of its constituents? You have to bear in mind that your deposits, taking them all round, yield a profit on their use, and contribute materially to your rate of dividend. It is incumbent upon you, therefore, to avoid causing the withdrawal of any portion of them, by any act of your own. A contract which the other party seeks to break, need surely have no sanctity for you, if it be to your advantage to let him break it? If by refusing payment of his £100, without the required notice, to some panic-stricken creature, you cause him to make an outcry which shall incite other people to run upon you for twenty times the amount; you will have held him, against his will, to the conditions of a contract, which it was twenty times more your interest than his to set aside.

But there is another consideration : a banker employs the bulk of his deposits in discounts and advances, whereby the agricultural, trading, and other interests of his district are daily convenienced and benefited. When his depositors turn upon him, therefore, and withdraw their money, he is obliged to contract his discounts and advances to a corresponding extent. Apart from the contraction of business and shrinkage of profits which this process will entail upon himself, he is bound to consider its effect upon the business arrangements of his customers, and the certain inconvenience and possible loss which it may entail upon them. It follows, I think, that your first and paramount object, when you are menaced with a run, should be to limit the extent of the movement, by all just and available means ; so as to render the ultimate chasm in your deposits as little serious as possible.

But your proposed line of action is not calculated to bring about this result—you would hold a score or two of ignorant and excited people at defiance, on what will appear to them a shallow pretext and trivial point of form ; you will thus transform them into so many firebrands, who will go forth into the highways and by-ways and spread the conflagration. At the first appearance of fire you would drown it out; for a like reason, at the first appearance of a run, do your best to stifle it, because, like fire, it is swift and terrible of growth.

When a depositor demands payment of money which

is not due to him for a month, or whatever the term of notice may be, and it is manifest that for the moment he is beyond reasoning with ; offer to pay him at once, but with such abatement of interest as the circumstances demand.   He has in fact forfeited his claim for interest altogether, because he has violated the condition on which interest was made to run.   In the most liberal view of the matter, he must rest content with such interest as would have accrued on the deposit if placed with you at call.

If he objects to the deduction, he has the remedy in his own hands; he can leave the money where it is, and give the required notice.   The more panic-stricken will agree to the abatement without demur—only too thankful to have the money back again on any terms ; but the less alarmed will probably take another view of the situation.   The fact that you are ready and willing to pay every demand at once, whether due or not due, will satisfy them that you are not going to break after all : and rather than let you have the advantage of them about the interest, they will give the required notice and leave their deposits where they are.

In either case, the minds of bystanders will be favourably impressed.   They will see that so far from being hard up, you are prepared, on reasonable conditions, to pay thousands upon thousands of deposits, not yet due, and unfairly demanded ; and Mr. Bagster will be non-plussed.   The touching incident of old Ricketts and his £70 will not be available as a sensation, because it will never have attained existence as a fact.

One reason for having as large a portion as possible of your deposits put on deposit receipt is this—the receipts are not transferable.   They must be presented for payment by the depositors in person, and the majority of depositors are shy of exhibiting a want of confidence in their banker to his very face, and will not lightly join a run upon him.   But where the money is lying on current account, and can be drawn out by cheque payable to bearer, the depositor is enabled to avoid this hurt to his feelings, by passing the cheque to a friend, who will draw the money for him without pain or scruple. Persons are known to have gone beyond even this method of evasion, by drawing numbers of cheques on their accounts, during the worst hours of a crisis, in payment of fictitious wants and imaginary creditors ; thus hoping to hoodwink their bankers, by a puerile device of transparent meanness. If these men had had the manliness to go to their bankers, when their fears became acute, their anxieties would have been set at rest, and they would have been guiltless of contributing their little utmost to the monetary strain of the time.

In the good old coaching days, before the electric telegraph was thought of, and whilst railways were yet in their infancy, a Branch was sometimes distant from its centre, or Head office, several days even by post. A sudden and unexpected run had then to be differently faced. The object to be gained was time, to tide the Branch over the first rush of depositors, until supplies could arrive from head-quarters. The traditional shifts resorted to for this purpose were varied, and sometimes tinged with humour. The cashier who inscribed ' No funds' on a large cheque, which he had not money enough in his till to meet, must have been a born humorist ; and only thirty years ago, a writer of the name of Bullion is to be found, who calmly recommends a Branch Manager to begin to pay everything during a run in his own notes. The adoption of this course, this cynic observes, will have the effect of gaining time, and obliging each depositor to resort to a series of fictions on the spot, as reasons why he would rather have gold. To go still further back, ' The bankers are so called upon,' writes Pepys in 1667, ' that they will be all broken, hundreds coming to them for money, and they answer, " It is payable at twenty days—when the days are out we will pay you ;" and those that are not so, they will make tell over their money, and make their bags false, on purpose to give cause to re-tell it and so spend time.'

But the necessity for all such shifts now-a-days no

9

longer exists. The railway and the telegraph have practically brought the head office of a bank and its branches under one roof; so that the entire resources of the establishment can now be brought to bear, at a moment's notice, on any point assailed.

If I had been writing the present book only a few years ago, I would have omitted all mention of a run upon a bank, as a thing long since obsolete, and as barbarous in its day as rick-burning or the wilful destruction of machinery. But the events of December 1878, effectually upset this complacent view of things. The country then became the astonished witness of persistent, and in certain cases, concerted runs, directed against some of the largest deposit banks in the kingdom—not headed by the more ignorant classes of depositors, for whom there might have been some excuse; but by persons for whom there was none. Happily for the common weal, the banks run upon were without exception of assured strength ; they were shorn of many millions of deposits in a few weeks, but they passed through the ordeal with untarnished credit, and thus averted a momentary crisis, of which it would be difficult to estimate the range or the consequences.

LETTER XVIII.

INTEREST AND DISCOUNT.

Were it not for this easy borrowing upon interest, men's necessities would draw upon them a most sudden undoing : in that they would be forced to sell their means (be it lands or goods) far under foot ; and so, whereas usury doth but gnaw upon them, bad markets would swallow them quite up. BACON.

IN the great provincial cities, second only to London itself in the magnitude of their commercial and banking operations, the rate of interest will follow more or less closely the London rate, both in respect of interest on deposits and the discount on bills : but in the smaller towns and country districts, a less fluctuating scale of rates is followed and preferred.

INTEREST ON DEPOSITS. In respect of money lying on deposit at their bankers, country people prefer a steady average rate. They do not care to have the interest worked on a scientific scale ranging from 1 per cent. to 5. They could never arrive at a notion of what the interest would come to, with so many jumps from one rate to another.

You could no doubt reconcile them to London rate as long as it stood at 4 or 5 per cent. : but all the King's horses and all the King's men would never bring them back again, with their own wills, to one per cent. You might prove to them beyond cavil, that the condition of things in Lombard Street compelled the reduction; but country people know nothing about Lombard Street, and they have no desire to know. You might as well hope to explain to them the principle of the Integral Calculus, as the mysteries of the exchanges. It suits their ways better to have an arrangement about interest which does not require so much thinking about. They do not approve of a rate that veers about so frequently that they can never rightly know where they are. They dislike bother, and this would bother them exceedingly. They prefer an arrangement with their bankers, which shall continue without change, until they want the money out again; let the value of money in London in the meantime be what it may.

The rate thus agreed upon will vary in accordance, partly with the custom of localities, partly with the usage of individual banks : but mainly with the condition upon which the money is deposited.

You could not, for example, allow the same rate of interest on £1000 repayable at call, and which may be withdrawn at any moment, as upon a like amount which cannot be withdrawn short of a month's notice ; because deposits payable on demand must be invested in banking securities of the highest class, and will consequently yield a low rate of return.

Deposits, on the other hand, which are subject to notice, afford you time to turn in, and could be employed in less available securities and bringing you a somewhat better yield of interest. If your rate for deposits payable on demand were 2 per cent. for example, it might be $2\frac{1}{4}$ on those subject to your usual term of notice, and $2\frac{1}{2}$ on those lodged for longer periods.

Country banks for the most part adhere to their average rate, even when the London banks are only allowing one per cent. : so that if the country rate never mounts so high as that of London, neither does it ever sink so low.

' London rate ' for deposits, rules at one per cent. below the published rate of discount at the Bank of England for the time being. It is never more than this, and it is seldom less.

Now the average of Bank rate, during the ten years ended 31st December, 1884, was £3 3s. 11d. This gives us about 2⅛ per cent. for average London rate. The London banks, therefore, hold their interest bearing deposits on terms which would probably be found in close proximity to those, on which the country banks on the average hold theirs: so that it comes to much the same thing, whether a depositor works by the one scale or the other.

In the course of your business, you will no doubt be assured at times that your rate on deposits is lower than at some other bank: but it will be well to verify such statements in all cases where practicable, because they are not always true. You hear of banks offering in some cases rates for deposit money, sufficient, you protest, to make your hair stand on end. It may not be true: but if it is, let us hope that the cases are few in number and the banks fewer still. That high interest means high risk, is a maxim which has a meaning even for bank depositors, if they would note it.

The average rate which a country bank can prudently allow on its deposits is not an arbitrary thing, which may be safely disregarded and put aside. It is the result of deliberate calculation, resting on experience spread over many years, and is virtually based on the average London rate, which it exceeds only by a small fraction. No country bank, therefore, can habitually purchase the use of money at a price materially in excess of its average value, unless such bank is prepared to do one of two things—it must be prepared, either to employ the money at a loss, which is incredible: or to risk its' employment in forms of advance, which may bring it a high rate of interest, but will not be available in time of need.

The depositor cannot with impunity, as we have said, be requested to call again for his money some other time. It is no concern of his, if his money has been locked up in advances, resting on securities

more or less dubious in character and difficult of realization.   He expects to receive his money when due, and
it will be an evil day for the bank, which has mainly to
look to such securities, to meet the demands of its depositors, should they at any time make an attack in
force upon its immediate resources.   Better a thousand
times let deposits go past you, than accept them on
terms which oblige you to employ them in ways which
will render the money inaccessible, when your need for
money is at its worst.   That time has come before now
to the strongest banks, and may come again : but at its
next coming, it may take a wider and lower range than
in 1878, and assault the weaker and less guarded points,
instead of the Redans and Malakhoffs of our banking
system.

DISCOUNT ON BILLS. Your rate of discount will
vary with the quality of the bills themselves, and to
some extent with the current value of money. A bill,
for example, drawn by a first-class house abroad on a
leading house at home, and bearing the indorsement
of a powerful bank, is a widely different instrument
from the loan bill or promissory note, or even the
trade bill of country banking ; and would command
proportionately easier terms in the matter of discount. 'Bank paper' is in fact the highest form of
banking asset. You can re-discount and turn it into
money, at any moment, in the worst of times : but
in respect of bills of inferior grade, the re-discount
market is uncertain of access and, in a panic, is
sometimes closed altogether. Moreover, you can rely
upon bank bills and their equivalents being met at
their maturities. You may in fact reckon them in
advance, as assured additions to your cash in hand
the day they fall due. They are so many bank notes
in a latent form. When you wish to increase your
reserve of cash, you have merely to restrict your

discount of such bills, and those running off will of themselves turn into money and accomplish your desire.

You might, it is true, restrict your holding of Mr. Bowdler's paper and the like : but this would not serve to replenish your till with the same degree of certainty.   Such bills are not to be reckoned as equal to so many bank notes on the days of their maturity. They will no doubt be paid in time, but not necessarily at your time.   Neither are they negociable—you could not re-discount them if you would; so that financially they are all but valueless.

But betwixt these two classes of bills—betwixt the highest quality of paper and the lowest—comes the inland or trade bill; such as that drawn by Cartridge on Booker & Co. ; which may be regarded as a type of by far the largest class of bills known to provincial banking.

The trade bill is as inferior to bank paper, in point of quality, as it is superior in all other respects to the lower class of bills.   You can rely on its being met when due, and you could re-discount it in any condition of the money market short of panic; although not on the same terms on which you could melt bank paper.   For that and for other reasons, the rate for trade bills, whether in London or the provinces, will necessarily rule at a point higher than that current for bank paper.

Nevertheless, Mr. Nayler expects you to take his bills, 90 per cent. of which consist of trade paper, at London rate all round.   Mr. Nayler is of those who, in the way of a bargain, ' will cavil with you on the ninth part of a hair.'   When the rate for deposits in London is less than your own, Mr. Nayler prefers the good old country rate ; but when the rate in London goes above your average, he holds the metropolitan principle to be the only equitable basis of price, as between man and man. It is true that when Mr. Nayler asks you to take his promiscuous paper at London rate, he freely gives you leave to charge other people what you like: which you hold to be an exasperating suggestion: but, letting that pass, to expect you to work at 'London rate' for ordinary trade paper, is ridiculous. That rate is the quotation for A 1 bank paper, or its equivalents, only— for a class of bill, the percentage of which in your bill casé would be slight in the extreme. A stray one will find its way to Oxborough, at intervals more or less apart, and move you with a mild surprise: but it will be more of a curiosity than an everyday addition to your general holding of bills.

But even on the supposition that your discounts at Oxborough consisted wholly of bank paper—I say that even so, you would not stand on the same platform with London banks and Discount houses, and therefore could not work on their terms. You are established in Oxborough, with all means and appliances for the conduct of a business, larger than you will ever command, perhaps, but which are necessary to work the business which you do. You have brought to the very doors of the Oxborough people an establishment, not much to look at, it may be, in point of appearance, being but a Branch; but equal in all other respects to a bank of the first magnitude. You are prepared to entertain and to carry through any transaction, whatever its nature or amount, that any other bank out of London can.

But whilst your discount transactions are reckoned by fifties and hundreds of pounds, the operations of the great London banks and bill brokers are measured by tens and hundreds of thousands. And the same extent of book-entry and calculation is required to pass a bill for £50 through the books of a bank, as if it were one for £5000. Your business, therefore, is worked at greatly heavier cost, relatively to income, than a great London business is. The enormous volume of their transactions enables the London banks and discount houses to work on terms of dis-

count at which your business would starve. If you
are to transact a discount business at all in Oxborough,
and pay your expenses, and leave something towards
dividend; it must be on terms necessarily above those
of London, whether for first. class bills or for ordinary
trade paper.

If your customers generally were to adopt Mr. Nayler's
views, Oxborough Branch would cease to pay its expenses, and would have to be shut up.

It has also to be considered, that if your discount rate
never sinks to the low level which sometimes rules in
Lombard Street, neither does it on the other hand ever
mount to 10 or 12 per cent. Your clients are accustomed
to a less spasmodic scale, and would rather work upon
one that seldom lost sight of 5 per cent. very far either
way, as a rallying point. In fact, your terms of discount must be governed, more by the expenses of
your Branch, than by the movements of bank rate, with
which the daily business of Oxborough has no visible
connection.

Your milliners and grocers, your butchers and bakers,
do not regulate their transactions, with one eye upon
the foreign exchanges and another upon the reserve in
the Banking Department. They require certain produce and commodities to replenish their stocks, in
order to supply the daily wants of their customers,
and they do not understand what a million of bullion
more or less in the Issue Department has to do with
the matter.

Your customers hear, no doubt, of a tightness in the
money market and a heavy drop in the exchanges : but
as they have not contributed to bring about the one, and
do not understand the other, they object to being incom-
moded by either. Let those, they say, bear it who have
brought the trouble. Because the Bouncers and Plungers
of commerce all over the world have been speculating in
this, or 'cornering' in that, and brought about a commercial crisis and a money panic—that appears an

insufficient reason to Mr. Cartridge why his usual discount facilities should be curtailed, or to Mr. Wheeler why half his overdraft should be called up. They have had no hand in producing the crisis, and will deem it hard if their convenience is sacrificed to set it right.

INTEREST ON OVERDRAFTS. The £1000 advanced on overdrawn account, and the same amount invested in the discount of a negociable bill of exchange, are widely opposed transactions, and will involve different conditions of charge. When a country bank covenants with a customer that he may overdraw his account at any time to the extent of £1000, it virtually grants him the loan of that amount so long as the account shall continue; but with this important concession in favour of the borrower, that interest shall be charged only on the balance owing from day to day. The lodgments on such accounts are credited with the same rate of interest as is charged on the payments.

The balance owing on an overdrawn account, therefore, being of the nature of a permanent loan, will not follow the ups and downs of London rate, except at a respectful distance. It will never touch a very low point, but neither will it rise to a very high one. Moreover, as in bills of exchange, so also in overdrawn accounts—there are degrees of quality; hence some difference in the terms of charge. The overdraft which is constantly being paid off and drawn out again, is entitled to easier terms, in respect of interest, than the account which is never turned creditor. The one enables you to make frequent use of the money in other directions, the other never.

The overdrafts on which you will levy your highest rate, will be those which have assumed the character of dead loans, but in respect of which, for special reasons, you may be reluctant to take the extreme course of calling them up. The imposition of an extra rate will pro-

bably have the result you desire, without touching the
susceptibilities of this class of borrowers, who will consist
for the most part of persons ignorant of business, and
who look upon 5 per cent. as the furthest limit of legal
interest—beyond which lies perdition to the man who
borrows.

LETTER XIX.

BANK CHARGES.

Hence it is, that though prejudice is so far softened, as to acquiesce in the lender's making some advantage, lest the borrower should lose altogether the benefit of his assistance; yet still the borrower is to have all the favour; and the lender's advantage is for ever to be clipped and pared down as low as it will bear.

DEFENCE OF USURY.

ON a certain portion of your accounts you make a charge for commission: the rate of charge being governed by the nature of the account itself and the description, number, and amount of the transactions passing through it.

There are accounts in England, the lodgments on which are all in Bank of England notes, or gold of standard weight; the balances are always in favour of the customer, and the cheques drawn upon them are all paid across the Bank's own counter. On such accounts no commission is charged; but on the other hand, no interest is allowed on the balances in hand of the Bank.

If one had to picture to himself a banking Eutopia, it would be ledgers teeming with such accounts and none other; with Treasury bills his only discounts, and Consols his only form of overdraft. His sole debtor being the British Government, his income, if restricted, would at least be assured, and the haunting fear of loss would cease to trouble him.

But although the class of account we here speak of is known to some extent to London banking, and here and there perhaps in our larger commercial centres, it is rarely met with in rural parts. There is probably no such account on your books at Oxborough.　If there were, you would be ready and willing to conduct it on London terms.　That is to say, you would charge no commission upon it: but you would expect a certain balance to be kept at the credit of the account, and on this balance you would allow no interest;—you would accept the use of the money in lieu of commission.

The balance thus left in your hands would be governed in amount by the nature and working of the account. You would, for example, require a larger balance with an account turning over £10,000 a year, than with one on which the turn-over was only half that amount. Again, if the cheques drawn upon the account should average £20 each, you would require a larger balance to be kept at its credit, than if the cheques averaged £100 each; because in the one case, you would have 500 different payments to make on the account; in the other only 100.　The extent of book entry alone would be as five to one.　It would require five times as many ledgers to hold the one class of accounts, as would suffice to contain the other; and five times the staff of book keepers to write them up.

But, as already stated, this class of account is practically unknown in rural districts.　The payments to the credit of a country bank account will not consist exclusively of Bank of England notes or gold of standard weight.　On the contrary, these will form as a rule but a slight percentage of the lodgments.　The circulating medium of the provinces is not of uniform quality, and the par of most of its components is nominal.　Some three-fourths of the provincial circulation consist of sovereigns and half-sovereigns, of which over fifty per cent. are below standard weight.　Side by side with these, circulate the four millions of country bank notes, which have the defect of not being legal tender, and have for the most part to be remitted to London to be converted into that medium.　Then come cheques and drafts on other banks, dividend warrants, interest coupons, post office orders and bills, for collection, wherever these articles may be payable within the limits of the United Kingdom. Last, but not least, you have to take into account the silver in circulation. This will come to you plenteously, in packets of £5 or £10 each, or direct from your customers' pockets in promiscuous handfuls, embracing specimens of our silver coinage from a three-penny bit to a crown piece.

The items here enumerated, with a sprinkling of Bank of England notes and heavy gold, constitute, in varying proportions, the ordinary payment to the credit of your customers' accounts.

Nevertheless, Mr. Bagster would have you treat the whole as ready cash. He would expect you to pass this miscellany of currency, without charge or abatement, straightway to a man's credit; just as if the entire lodgments were in crisp Bank of England notes, or gold fresh from the Mint.

But it is manifest that before such media can be regarded or treated as 'cash,' they must undergo transmutation; they must be realized, before they become usable money. You must send all country notes, for example, which are not redeemable in Oxborough, to your London agents for collection. You must despatch the cheques, bills, coupons, and the like to every point of the compass at which they are payable, and await their payment in London, before they can become cash to you. You must send your gold and silver, at your own risk and charge, to the wage-paying districts where it is wanted; or it will accumulate on your hands at still greater cost and sacrifice. It will be seen, therefore, that almost every lodgment to the credit of a Country bank account, involves the Bank itself in expense, before the items of the lodgment can be turned into actual money or legal tender.

It is different with the currency of Scotland. The circulating medium of that part of the Kingdom consists almost exclusively of bank notes, which, although not legal tender by Act of Parliament, are universally accepted as such, which amounts to much the same thing. They require no process of conversion to turn them into money, because, to all intents and purposes, they are already money, and have as great circulative capacity North of the Tweed as Bank of England notes have on this side of it.

PAYMENTS TO DEBIT. Turning now to the debit side of a country bank account, it also has features of its own. The outdrawings upon it do not consist exclusively of cheques presented at your counter and cashed out of your till. On the contrary, transactions of this nature are the exception and not the rule. The items debited to the account will consist partly, often largely, of the customer's acceptances payable in London, which you have retired for him: partly of his cheques which he has sent to various parts of the kingdom, and which you have redeemed for him directly through other banks, or indirectly through the Clearing: partly of drafts or letters of credit, which you have drawn upon your London or other agents to his order: and partly in cheques paid in cash across your counter.

On each of these transactions, with the exception of the last, you have yourselves to pay a commission, either to your London agents or to other banks. They cannot afford to transact your business, without some charge for the doing of it. They have the salaries of their Managers and clerks, their rents and taxes and other expenses to pay, which they would find an obvious difficulty in doing, if they conducted their business for nothing.

The working of every account in his books, therefore, subjects a country banker to expense on both sides of it,— the expense of converting miscellaneous lodgments into legal tender on the one side, and the remuneration of its London and other agents for services rendered by them, on the other.

It is the practice of some banks to make a separate charge on each transaction, debtor or creditor, as it arises, which is subject to commission. The banks in Scotland do so, and work upon a scale which indicates some sixty varieties of charge.

The usage of most English country banks is different. Instead of a separate levy on each transaction as it arises, the banks make one charge at the end of the half year; and this is usually in the form of a percentage on the total outdrawings on the account for the six months, whatever they may consist of. The process is admittedly less exact than the Scotch method, but it comes to much the same thing in the end, as far as the customer is concerned, and it has the merit of simplicity.

It is true that no two banking accounts are alike in every particular. There is not a single account on your books which is the exact counterpart of another: but you know what the working of your accounts costs you as a whole, and can therefore arrive at a rate of commission which will be a fair average charge all round.

No doubt there are exceptional accounts which no average will fit. In respect of these you may have to exceed your average in some cases, and to go below it in others. Other accounts, again, the operations on which consist of transactions which put you to little cost and less trouble, it may suit you to conduct for a fixed sum per annum, based on the number of cheques and magnitude of turn-over.

Let us say then that your average rate of commission is one-eighth per cent. on the outdrawings of a current account. That will be equal to a charge of fifteen pence per hundred pounds on both sides of it. That will be the rate of charge, out of which you have to provide for agents' commission, expense of transmission of notes and specie, loss on light gold, and all risks of forgery, fraud, miscarriage, burglary, or embezzlement. You have to make provision for all these out of your one shilling and three-pence per hundred pounds: and, if there is anything over, it can hardly amount to an extravagant recognition of the services of yourself and staff

But as against your charge for commission, your customer has a substantial set-off. You allow him interest from day to day, on the balance at his credit, however much it may fluctuate. But, under the London system, no interest is allowed on the fluctuating balance of a current account; so that practically it comes to much the same thing, whether, as a question of loss or gain, a running account is kept on the one system or the other.

But there is one material point of difference. Under the London system a man is expected never to reduce his balance below a certain agreed-on figure. He has thus practically to lock up a portion of his capital in his bank account, and lose the use of it in his business; whereas, under the provincial system, he can at any time withdraw his balance to the last sixpence, without incurring the penalty of having to close the account.

Let us take the case of your customer L. S. D., the over-turn, debtor and creditor, on whose account is £8000 a year, and your commission on which is £5. There is no set-off against this charge, because L. S. D. leaves no money in your hands at the credit of the account: he prefers to employ the whole of his means in his own business. But let us suppose that he shall elect to work on the London principle; and, instead of paying commission, shall leave a balance in your hands not bearing interest, and that the balance thus left is £200.

What the annual return on his capital may be will depend on circumstances; but it must be an indifferent sort of trading, that will not yield an annual return of 10 per cent.

By locking the £200 up in his bank account, therefore, he loses £20 a year of profit on his capital : in other words, the working of his account on the London principle costs him £20 a year : whereas under yours, the cost to him is £5 only.

COMMISSION ON OVERDRAFTS. We have thus far

10

dealt with the ordinary charges on accounts, the balances
of which are always at the credit of customers. We now
turn to the commission on accounts, the balances of
which are always overdrawn.

An average sample of the overdrawn account of
country banking will be found in that of your customer
Mr. Silas Wheeler. The authorised limit of advance is
£1000 of which he steadily avails himself, and the outdrawings amount to £10,000 a year. The lodgments to
the credit of the account are of the usual mixed character of the provincial currency; whilst the outdrawings
are akin to those on other accounts, except that they
consist for the most part of Wheeler's acceptances payable in London. The cash transactions to the debit are
few and of limited amount.

If the balance of the account were always in his
favour, your charge upon it would be an eighth per
cent. on the outdrawings, as in the case of other creditor
accounts; but inasmuch as the balance is always at
his debit, you charge him an additional eighth per
cent.

One-half your charge, therefore, is virtually a *del
credere* commission, or provision against loss; and
amounts, in the case of Mr. Wheeler, to threepence in
the pound on the amount of advance. Adopting his
account as an average, and taking the overdrafts at
your Branch at £20,000, this annual provision against
loss would amount to £250; and if you will cast up
your losses on this form of account for any given
number of years back, you will find that a fund thus
set apart and frugally nourished, will never have much
of a balance at its credit; if indeed the balance shall not
at times emphatically incline the other way.

Your extra charge then on Mr. Wheeler's account,
by reason of its being overdrawn, amounts to £12 10s.
a year: but against this there is likewise a set-off:
because you sanction repayments in reduction of the
balance, in dribblets day by day; and on these dribblets
you allow the same rate of interest that you charge on

the account.   If the rate is 5 per cent., you allow him
to bank his money with you at that rate from day to day,
in anticipation of his acceptances or other payments
coming due; and the interest on these fugitive lodgments goes far to extinguish the extra charge of commission on the account.

There is one other point of view from which to regard
the overdrawn account of English country banking. Mr.
Wheeler pays for the bulk of his purchases by acceptance
at three months' date.   But if he paid in cash instead, he
would be allowed the usual trade discount of $2\frac{1}{2}$ per
cent.   The £1000 you lend him enables him to pay in
cash, instead of by acceptance, for £4000 worth of goods
within the year, on which the trade discount would be
£100.   He has this to set against your charge for interest
and commission upon his account, which amounts at the
outside to £75.   So far then from his dealings with you
putting him to expense, they leave him with some five
and twenty pounds annually in pocket.

But Mr. Bagster remains unconvinced, and still in-
veighs against commission in the abstract.   It is looked
upon indeed as his strongest point, and he is reluctant
to give it up.   When he desires therefore, in a general
way, to be informed on what pretence a bank makes a
charge for paying a man his own money back again, he
has the bar parlour with him, you tell me, to a man.

But it is not his own money back again which a
customer gets from a country bank.   His own money,
for the most part, would have consisted, as we have
seen, of gold light of weight, loose silver, cheques on
distant banks, and so forth: in exchange for all which
he expects to receive, and does receive from the Bank,
actual money of account, or legal tender.

It is unfortunate also for Mr. Bagster's point, that you
charge no commission on the greater number of your
accounts.   You make no charge on the withdrawal of
sums which have been placed with you on deposit
receipt or deposit account, no matter how mixed the

monetarial value which created the deposits may have
been.   You thus make a distinction betwixt accounts,
the balances of which you can make use of, and those,
the balances of which are here to-day and gone to-
morrow.   If Mr. Bagster worked his own business on the
terms on which he would have you conduct yours, he
and his family would soon be on the parish.

Without indorsing the strong language which you
apply to the whole tribe of 'screws;' one can understand
your inward enjoyment when you had to inform Mr.
Nayler, that the large advance on overdraft for which
he had applied to the Directors, had been refused; for
the sufficient reason that the unprofitable nature of his
account did not warrant the advance.   The loan of the
money at the time, and for the purpose to which Mr.
Nayler meant to apply it, would have yielded him a
profit many times greater, you affirm, than all his
cheese-parings in discount and commission for twenty
years put together.

A banker, after all, is only an average human being.
He is not influenced by the emotions in his dealings, it
is true : but he has a just perception of the principle of
'give and take,' in business.

He is naturally disposed, therefore, to deal liberally
with those who deal liberally with him.   He does not
relish habitual attempts to beat down his current rates
of charge, as if he were a cheap Jack, with half a dozen
prices for the same thing.   His rates are not arrived at
hap-hazard, but are based on observation and experience ;
and he dislikes to huckster with meanness, or capitulate
to greed.   A man loses nothing in the long run, by
leaving the charges on his account and bills to his
banker's sense of fairness and right.   It would be strange
if, in the course of events, an opportunity did not arise,
which would enable a banker, in one way or another,
to repay such confidence with usury.   But neither
does Mr. Nayler, nor Mr. Bagster, see this.   The man
who never troubles his head nor tries his banker's
patience about the charges on his account, betrays, in

their estimation, something like softening of the brain; and they have yet to learn that in dealing with one's banker, a penny saved is not always a penny gained.

And whilst you are jealous to guard and uphold your own terms of business, do not begrudge their proper charges to others. Do not chaffer with a man about his customary commission and try to beat it down, especially if he is poor and must submit to your fiat, whatever it may be. The Bank which shall acquire a reputation for meanness will find itself put to the screw whenever occasion offers: whereas if it shall act in a liberal spirit in all its dealings, its liberality will bear fruit. It will secure to the institution the breath of popular favour; and that has a perceptible influence in directing fresh business to a bank.

LETTER XX.

CIRCULATION.

The banks, these traders seem to have thought, could extend their credit to whatever sum might be wanted, without incurring any expense besides that of a few reams of paper.
WEALTH OF NATIONS.

ONE of the customary services which a bank renders to the community, and for which it is but poorly recompensed, is the transmission of money to other places on behalf of its clients; whereby they are enabled to make payments in all parts of the Kingdom, and are saved the risk, expense, and trouble of taking the money to such places themselves.

DRAFTS. When one of your customers, or the traveller for a commercial house, wishes to make a payment in London, Manchester, or elsewhere; the medium usually employed is the draft of your Bank on its London agents, in favour of the person or firm to whom the money has to be paid.

This draft will be drawn payable either on demand or at a certain number of days after date, according to the wishes of the remitter. On a draft payable so many days after date, you make no charge, because the use of the money during the currency of the draft is supposed to yield you a sufficient profit on the transaction. If instead of a draft after date, one on demand is preferred, you charge a commission upon it which will be governed in rate by the description of currency which you receive

150

in exchange. A rate that would be remunerative when the value received was in Bank of England notes, or heavy gold, might be the reverse of profitable, when the value received was mainly in unconverted media, such as cheques on distant banks, gold of dubious weight, and a heavy percentage of silver.

When you issue a draft after date, your usage is to draw at fourteen days : but you hear of other banks drawing at shorter dates ; for which, however, there may be adequate reason.

If Oxborough were in a large wage-paying district, for example, and you required constant remittances of specie from your other Branches to supply the demand for wage money; it might suit you to take gold and silver from commercial men, or anybody else, against drafts at less than 14 days' date ; for the obvious reason that by thus receiving money on the spot, you save the expense and risk of bringing it from elsewhere. But if your position at Oxborough is that of most agricultural towns, and you have constantly to remit to your Head Office specie for which you have no use at the Branch, then clearly the issue of drafts at seven or ten, or even fourteen days' date, is not a description of business to make a fortune by.

On drafts payable on demand, you quote your ordinary rate of charge at one-eighth per cent. This half-crown per hundred pounds has to cover the cost of converting the circulative media of the provinces into cash, commission to London agents, and the risk of transmission.

What would be the proportion of the half-crown, to set aside to cover this last item alone, is easy of estimate. The leading railway companies put it at one shilling per £100. They will guarantee the safe carriage and delivery of a remittance of specie at that rate. You have therefore to part with 40 per cent. of your commission to the railway companies, or adopt the risk of transmission yourselves.

Supposing, then, that your messenger, in conveying your weekly parcel of specie to Head Office, gets robbed by the way, on some unhappy occasion; and that the parcel contains £1000. If it were made the penalty for his carelessness that he should redeem the loss by greater care in future acts of transmission, he would have to convey two thousand parcels of £1000 each without loss or mischance; a penance, which, reduced to figures, would take him eight and thirty years to accomplish.

There are people, nevertheless, who prefer to be their own transmitters of money, and who carry sometimes large amounts in bank notes or gold about with them from place to place, to make purchases or settle accounts, whereby the cost of a draft or letter of credit is avoided. The saving, as we have seen, can only be put at half-a-crown, at the outside, on every hundred pounds thus carried about.

For this charge, you will open a credit for a man at any of your Branches or agents, against which he may draw in the town where his payments have to be made, to the exact amount he has to.disburse: so that he need have no balance to bring back with him after dark, from fair or market, at the risk of being robbed by the way; or by a worse chance, knocked on the head.

On the other hand, if a customer has to collect or receive money in other towns, the money has simply to be paid to your Branch or agents at the place; and you will pass it to his account, on exactly the same conditions as if the money had been paid to his credit across your counter.

OWN NOTES. You are entitled, under the Act of 1844, to issue these to a limited extent.

You take from customers the notes of distant banks, or cheques upon them, or gold of average lightness, or silver, or anything else in the shape of monetarial value, and give them your own notes in exchange, free of charge.   For every £100 in mixed value, you are always prepared to give £100 in your own notes to a regular holder, without abatement or charge of any kind.   And you do this for the simple reason, that your notes thus issued will, on the average, remain in circulation a sufficient length of time to more than cover their own expense, as well as the cost of turning into cash the miscellaneous value received by you in exchange for them.   I use the term regular holder, because you would not give your own notes free of charge, in exchange for light gold or its equivalents, to anyone who, you have reason to suspect, would straightway cut them in halves, and dispatch them by the first post as a remittance to London or somewhere else.   The notes, thus mutilated, will go to your debit at your London agents, where they are redeemable, possibly next day: and you will have to pay a commission for their redemption.   The notes will then be sent back to you at the risk and cost of a double transmission by post.   They will be sent from London to your Head Office, and then by your Head Office to you : and when the notes come to hand, your junior apprentice will have the hateful task of re-uniting the severed halves with gum-plaster.   It is needless to observe, that the issue of your own notes under these conditions, would be more fertile of loss and irritation than of profit or satisfaction.

You issue them free of charge, in exchange for notes of other country banks, to cattle-dealers and others from a distance, who visit your fairs and markets as buyers, and who find your notes the popular means of purchase in your neighbourhood, and will thus give them legitimate circulation.

It would no doubt amaze the Governor and Company of the Bank of England, if they were informed that their notes are in less favour and request than your own, with certain classes in your district ; and that to ease the minds of ignorant holders, you have sometimes had to indorse the notes of that august issuer, or give your own notes in exchange.   This preference for local notes prevails more or less in rural parts. The people who get your own notes, from your own hands, know at all events that they are genuine : but they are not judges of Bank of England notes. They have seen notes of the Bank of Elegance, which to their eyes looked every whit as good. When they receive at fairs or markets the notes of the great issuer, therefore, they not seldom prefer to have your notes instead ; because they know where they are, then, and are freed from all qualms about forgeries.

The chief circulators of your notes will be found amongst your ordinary customers, who receive and pay them away in preference to other forms of currency, in settlement of accounts, or the payment of rents, or the adjustment of any kind of transaction which involves the use of money.

The right of private issue has therefore this to recommend it. It is an advantage to the issuer himself : but he at least shares the advantage with the community, by extending to it many facilities gratuitously, which otherwise would be subject to charge.

But Mr. Bagster has views of his own as to the right use of your circulation. He holds that when the trading interests of Oxborough are at stake—that is to say, in plainer English, when certain of its burgesses are hard up for money—it is mean in a bank like the District Union, holding nearly three millions of deposits, to boggle at the risk of a few thousands. A concern paying an annual 15 per cent. to its proprietors, ought not to betray this narrowness of view and sordid fear of loss. Moreover, if a loss does arise, he contends that you can fill the gap up with your own notes, which cost you nothing. It is but just to add that Mr. Bagster would deal with the National Debt in the same way : he would pay it off by the issue of 750 millions of one-pound notes payable to bearer on demand.

There is a character in one of Mr. Dickens' novels who, when he gives his acceptance for an account, regards the debt as thereby satisfied and discharged.

Mr. Bagster obviously looks upon the private issuer of notes as a species of banking Micawber.

If you cannot satisfy Mr. Bagster and his disciples that you do not possess the gift of Midas, you will at least be able to convince them, when occasion offers, that you are not furnished with his ears as well.

LETTER XXI.

THE USE OF A BANKER.

Both are equally absurd, he that will burn his taper while the sun shines, and he that will go to bed in the dark to save the expense of light. FELTHAM.

WHERE commission is charged upon the outdrawings of an active creditor account, the charge has to cover a variety of services to the customer, besides the mere conversion of promiscuous money's worth into money.

In evidence of this, let us take the account of your client Mr. Basil Crofton ; which affords a fair average example of the working of a country gentleman's bank account. Mr. Crofton's income is £4000 a year, and consists chiefly of rents, but partly of dividends on railway stock, interest on money lent, and other items. He passes the whole through his account, the lodgments on which are therefore of the usual miscellaneous description.

On the debit side, you find recorded every payment he has made by cheque throughout the year. The cheques vary in amount, from actual subscriptions to charities, to the larger payments to tradesmen and others : but the average is £20 a cheque, and you have cashed 200 of them in the twelve months. You have received £4000 in miscellaneous value, which you have disbursed for him in the form of ready money ; and your charge on the account, to cover all, is one-eighth per cent. on the debit side, or £5 altogether.

But the balance at Mr. Crofton's credit, which fluctuates from day to day, sometimes touching £500, sometimes approaching vanishing point, but averaging £150 for the twelve months, yields a material set-off against this charge. On this most unstable and capricious deposit, or rather series of fluctuating balances, you allow interest at 2½ per cent. from day to day: this comes to £3 15s. and reduces your charge on Mr. Crofton's account to five and twenty shillings a year.

In return for this attenuated allowance and humble rate of pay, what services have you rendered to Mr. Crofton? You have, for one thing, protected his loose money, or money's worth, amounting as we have seen to a good many hundreds at times, against destruction by fire or abstraction by theft. These risks, such as they are, you have adopted. If you were personally attacked and overcome by burglars, and your safe looted: or if its contents were reduced to tinder by fire, neither event need cost Mr. Crofton the loss of an hour's sleep. His money would be safe, whatever evil stroke of fortune might light upon you or the Bank.

In the second place, you have made 200 payments for him in the course of the year, and taken your risk of over payments, or payments to wrong parties, through fraudulent possession or successful forgery.

In the third place, you keep Mr. Crofton's accounts for him. Every sum paid into or drawn out of the account, is duly entered on one side or the other of the pass-book with which you furnish him; and which thus becomes to him a cash-book so complete, that he has no need to keep any other.

If he requires to know how his rents and other revenues have come in, he has merely to consult the credit side of his pass-book, where he will find them recorded, item by item, as they reached your hands, with detailed exactitude. If he requires to know what portion of his income he has spent, and how; the debit side of his pass-book will, with equal clearness and simplicity, afford the required information. Mr. Crofton does not draw his cheques in favour of persons under the mask of numbers, as if his payees were limited to members of the Police Force. He finds it more useful in every way to name on every cheque, the person to whom he wishes the money paid, or the purpose to which he desires the money to be applied. Every cheque he draws becomes thus a supplemental voucher and legal acquittance of debt. In the event of his receipted accounts perishing by fire, or being mislaid or lost, and a dispute arising as to the payment of some particular account, and its payment is demanded a second time; the cheque wherewith the debt was discharged will put the claimant out of Court with ignominy, and righteously saddled with costs on both sides.

By thus dealing with his money matters, that is by passing the whole of his income through his bank account, and paying for everything by cheque, Mr. Crofton makes you his private treasurer and accountant.

His drawings upon you during the twelve months, although only two hundred in number, have involved twelve hundred different entries and calculations in your various books—a matter which, although it does not concern Mr. Crofton, is of some importance to those who have the entries to post, and the interest on the ever-changing balance to work out day by day. In requital for services to Mr. Crofton, in the performance of which you become his clerk and almoner, he has to put his hand into his pocket once a year for the net douceur of five and twenty shillings,—say sixpence a week. Surely nowhere in the world will you find a larger service for a lower wage?

You are persuaded, nevertheless, that many persons do not pass the whole of their cash transactions through their bank accounts: the temptation to avoid the payment of a small commission being too great for them to withstand. You know that many persons habitually keep money at home, in order to use it direct, in the payment of wages, or the settlement of purchases or debts.

There are those amongst your customers, no doubt, as you allege, who will spend precious time in scheming how to save a shilling in the commission on their bank accounts. To gain the weather side of their bankers in this direction, charms some natures with a sense of superior tact, and a pleasing experience of the penny saved.

There are others, to whom such indulgence in the intricacies of vulgar fractions would be a source of cerebral irritation, and who prefer to work their accounts on the principle of an arbitrated sum per annum. To a man of this temperament, the taxing each transaction as it arose, with the commission upon it, would be intolerable. To find the £100 which he has lodged to his credit recorded in his pass-book as £99 18s. 9d. net : or his cheque, let us say, for £6 13s. 4d. charged against him as £6 13s. 5d. would drive him crazy. His books and yours would never balance. The discrepancies, it is true, would be of trivial amount, but that would only render them the more harassing. His wound would be great because it was so small.

But the great bulk of your customers are people absorbed in business or trade, to whom time is money, and who incline to the principle of payment, in ratio to the service rendered. They desire to pay neither too little nor too much. If the transactions on their accounts amount to ten thousand a year, they pay on that sum ; if they amount to twenty, they pay on twenty, and so forth. They go on the principle of value received ; and thus adjust the cost of their accounts to the necessities of their business.

After all, this matter of commission is merely a question of expediency. We have seen that a gentleman with an annual income of £4000 and an outlay to match, can have his floating cash insured against fire or theft, the whole of his disbursements made and duly vouched for, and a private cash-book supplied, and duly posted for him, from day to day, for a charge per annum hardly exceeding the price of a stall ticket for the opera.

If a man prefers nevertheless to act as his own banker, and be the custodian and disburser of his own money, there is no law to the contrary. He will, in that case, have to act as his own cashier, and make all his payments personally, or by post. He will have to keep his own cash-book, if he is to have anything beyond a hazy notion of how his money matters stand; and the science of book-keeping is not a pleasing study to most people, nor its practice a favourite pastime. If he mislay a paid account or receipt, he will have no cheque to fall back upon as its legal substitute. Instead of keeping his loose money at the Bank, he must keep it at home of nights—possibly under his pillow, if he is a nervous man ; and thus instead of receiving interest upon it, will lay it out at usury in nightly fears of burglary and outrage.

When he can avoid such disturbing fancies, shirk private book-keeping, and save himself all risk and trouble in the receipt and disbursement of his money, by simply passing the whole of it through a bank account, it is difficult to understand why anyone should hesitate to do so; unless he has still to read Gilbart's ' Ten minutes' advice about keeping a banker' of which, in some points, this letter is an unavoidable paraphrase.

LETTER XXII.

SALARIES.

All things have their bounds and measures, and so must liberality amongst the rest, that it be neither too much for the giver, nor too little for the receiver, the excess being every jot as bad as the defect. L'ESTRANGE'S SENECA.

You ask whether it would not be possible to attach a fixed salary to each Branch, proportioned to its profits, and to appoint the Managers in the order of merit, placing the best man in charge of the best Branch, the next best man in charge of the second best Branch and so on.

But a fixed salary to each Branch, on the principle proposed, might become a fixed injustice; because the profits of a Branch fluctuate from causes over which the Manager may have no control. If your scale is to be governed by these fluctuations, its fixity is gone: if not, then its equity is destroyed.

But let us follow the scheme out to its consequences, and when Manager A. dies, or retires, then as a matter of right B. takes his place, making room for C. who is replaced by D. and so downwards; until your entire managerial force is re-shuffled and you start a new game with fresh hands.

Have you counted the mere cost of removing your thirty Managers, their wives, families and servants, their goods and chattels, from one Branch to another every now and then, like children of the desert? Even on the supposition that the members of your provincial staff should come to relish this nomadic form of existence, there is no reason to believe that your customers would long submit to it. They will hardly care to establish

11

permanent relations with Managers who will be as migratory as so many Bedouins.

The confidence placed in the Manager of a bank by its customers is usually great and frequently intimate; and this confidence is not willingly transferred to a stranger. A man, as a rule, is as averse to changing his banker as he is to changing his lawyer or his physician : he is still more opposed to having his banker changed for him, whether he will or not.

It is not sufficient to reply that the change does not involve the change of one's banker, because virtually it amounts to that. It is not to the Directors and Company, but to the Manager personally, that the customer unbosoms himself, and seeks for friendly counsel as to his money matters.

Moreover, it is undesirable and a waste of power, to remove a Manager from a district with which he is familiar, to one to which he is a stranger; because a knowledge of the persons with whom he has to deal is manifestly one of the most important acquisitions which a Bank Manager can possess, and ought not lightly to be set aside and sacrificed.

Such a removal, it is true, may at times be unavoidable. The management of an important Branch may become vacant, and the fittest man to fill the vacancy may be the Manager of a Branch in a different part of the country. The point to be arrived at is,—not the perpetual fixity of every Manager to a particular Branch, whatever may come to pass ; but the greatest possible avoidance of change.

You cannot regulate promotion in a bank by any arbitrary scheme of precedency and succession. The services required from the officers and clerks of a bank are not altogether automatic. These men are something more than hewers of wood and drawers of water. They are not a mere combination of wheels and movements in a complicated machine, bound to revolve blindly, each on its own axis, without thought or care or responsibility. A certain uniformity is no doubt indispensable in the routine work of a bank : but banking is not all routine; it is not all a matter of red tape. It gives scope for the exercise of qualities, ranging from those of the mere drudge to abilities of the highest order. Its salaries therefore must be measured by the mental capacities of its officers, as well as by their grades of seniority.

Other things being equal, the officer of senior standing has the prior claim to advancement : but if other things are not equal—if he has allowed a junior in the service to outstrip him in the race for distinction, it is but just that the better man, although the younger, should take the better place.

This may seem hard on the less capable amongst the officers : but any other course would be still harder upon the Bank. It is bound to place its ablest hands where ability is wanted; and ability does not always ripen with the years.

No doubt, among the rank and file of every bank, there are those who deem themselves qualified for higher things than figuring, or the casting up and balancing of cash books and ledgers : but, even so, it is clear that all cannot be Managers, or Secretaries, or Chief-accountants. Banking may have its mute inglorious Miltons; but this is certain, that Boards of Directors have no object in making choice of their higher range of officials, other than the selection of the fittest. This being so, it need no more be a reproach to a subordinate officer, that he has not the special capacities required for high office in banking, than that he was not born to command the Channel Fleet or lead the House of Commons. It is his misfortune, if misfortune it be : but one has heard of men in the foremost ranks of banking, looking back almost with regret, to those early days, when their salaries were light and their cares in proportion.

There are those in the service of every bank who would no doubt prefer the system of promotion by seniority ; a method of choice which recognises but one standard of intellectual value—the weight of years. Weighed in such a balance, seniority preponderates as a law; and judgment, thought and aptitude, if linked with youth, inevitably kick the beam. It would be an untold relief to your Directors and Chief Manager, if they could adopt this system. The lengthened and earnest consideration which they now give to every case, as it arises, in order to place the right man in the right place, and measure out justice impartially to all, would be spared them. The law of seniority requires no thought and no supervision; it is self-acting. It reduces promotion to a question not of merit, but of mortality amongst the seniors. It robs the service of all interest, except in dead men's shoes. If promotion is not to be the reward of active brains and willing hands, why disquiet themselves in vain? and why ought we, the lookers on, to feel surprised at the do-nothing apathy, and the official insolence, which are too often the outcome of the system?

A bank cannot give high salaries to all its officers; but if its highest offices are open to every one in its employment, who shall prove his fitness for the same, there will be no apathy in its staff. It will be the object of every one to devote his best abilities to the practice and study of his profession; and thus an able, zealous and loyal staff will be developed.

But although a bank cannot give high salaries to all, it is not a wise policy to give insufficient salaries to any. A bank ought not to appraise the value of an officer's services merely by what they would fetch in the clerk market. He may not be a man of capacity: he may be even little more than an honest and willing drudge; but when it is considered how much the Directors of a bank have to trust to the honesty, integrity and honour of its staff, they will not lightly part with those who have proved themselves, by long service, the possessors of those essential qualifications, even if they have little else to recommend them to consideration. In the best interests of the Bank, its Directors will rather give an officer they have known and trusted for years, a trifle more to stay, than a stranger, however highly commended, a trifle less to come.

If the system of promotion followed by your Bank gives rise to occasional heartburnings, such feelings are probably the monopoly of the few, who cannot, without envy and bitterness, see better men passed over their heads. But the system is not in fault. It is reasonable in its requirements and just in its action. It has no favourites, except that it favours superior talent, energy and desert. It holds forth the inducement to all alike to press forward: and impartially assigns its prizes to the winners in the race.

There are grumblers to be found in every staff. There would be such even if a second Daniel came to judgment. There are some in every bank possessed with a conceit of themselves which no salary will ever rise to the height of.

Your teller Mr. Coigne is not exactly one of these, but he looks upon his services as grievously underpaid. He gives his mind over rather to speculation than to practice, and could pass a searching examination on the abstrusest theories of the currency; on which he delights to cross an occasional sword with a certain H. B. in the columns of your local paper, to the bewilderment of its readers, if not to the surrender of his antagonist. Mr. Coigne has all the qualities requisite in a good subaltern, but is deficient in those which are essential for command: Wherefore, he is still only a Branch Cashier, although he has applied for the management of every Branch which has become vacant during the last ten years.

Your Accountant has likewise a grievance. He has applied annually for an increase in his salary for some time past, on the ground that he has married a wife and has a young and increasing family: but if a man persists in marrying on a salary only sufficient to maintain himself in comfort, that is his own affair. The Directors cannot make every increase in a man's family the occasion of an addition to his salary.

You have a slight grievance yourself. You have less salary than your predecessor had, and you have heavier work to do, and you have to carry some of his burdens as well. But Mr. Littleworth was one of the oldest officers in the service, and numbered twice your years. If you look at the salary he received, when he was of your age, you will probably find that your present stipend is munificent by comparison.

There are those who persistently remind the Directors of their services and aspirations, whenever the time comes round for the revision of salaries. Whether this course has the effect of furthering their wishes, is, to say the least, doubtful. The officer who is content to leave the question of his salary to the judgment and justice of the Directors, and abstains from worrying them about it, is not likely to suffer by reason of his abstention. The merits of every individual in the service are perfectly known to the authorities at head quarters ; and an officer. will not enhance the value of his services by the continual blowing of his own trumpet.

LETTER XXIII.

OFFICE EXPENSES.

In expenses I would be neither pinching nor prodigal; yet, if my means allow it not, I would rather be thought too sparing than a little profuse. FELTHAM.

THE great item of your expenditure will consist of the interest paid half-yearly on your deposits and credit balances.

Next in amount come salaries, with which we have just dealt: then sundry less important items, which have nevertheless to be glanced at as we pass on. And first as regards the item of

PREMISES. Your premises in Oxborough, you state, are of moderate rent, but they are old and mean-looking, and rather out of sight: whereas the premises of your competitors are the architectural glory of Oxborough, and the admiration of the county. They occupy an imposing site on the South side of Market Square, and are conspicuous from every point of it: whereas you command that important centre only by the word BANK in colossal capitals, on a dead wall; and your front door is round a corner.

You believe that Messrs. Yewtrey & Co. sit at a rent some five times greater than your own; but you are doubtful whether the impression made upon the public mind by their superb building, may not compensate for this; by attracting business to them, of which you would have an equal chance, if you were housed with equal splendour.

167

No doubt, there are those who judge of a bank to a certain extent by its externals. A large and costly building is an assurance to some minds of corresponding wealth and stability within. A massive structure, guarded at all points with arrangements in iron, crowned with javelin tops, for the impalement as it might seem of incautious burglars, will appear to many persons a more secure place to deposit money, than a building like yours, of humbler pretensions; which was somebody else's shop and dwelling-house in the last generation, and would seem designed rather to invite burglarious attack than to defy it.

There are those again, who experience a sense of reflected dignity, as they pass under the Grecian portico of your rivals, with the eyes of Market Square upon them. This is the style of thing, they seem to say, that corresponds with our business position, and commends itself to our approval.

On the other hand, in a small town where everyone knows what everybody else is doing, it is certain that many persons would rather their banking were transacted with a greater regard to privacy, and less in the glare and focus of the public eye.

A man visits his bankers ordinarily to do one of two things. He goes either to borrow or to deposit money. If to borrow, he would rather the eyes of Market Square were not upon him. The nature of his errand it is true, is not written across his back : but he will have an uneasy feeling, that its object will be shrewdly guessed at by observant neighbours. On the whole, he will prefer to turn your corner quietly and do his borrowing with you. If his business, on the other hand, is to deposit money, he may desire to be equally circumspect. He does not wish it to be popularly known that he has money in the Bank : because this may expose him to solicitations for loans by needy neighbours, and deprive him of the unanswerable excuse that he has not the money to lend. Mr. Nayler was never known to lodge money to his credit when anyone was looking on.

It is at least open to question, therefore, whether your premises are not as desirable, in point of situation, as those of the old bank.   A site such as yours, which is at once public and private, central and yet retired, will commend itself to at least as many people as it will repel.

It may be that your constituents in Oxborough shall so increase and multiply, as to oblige your Directors to construct a building of their own, some day, which shall rival even the structure of Messrs. Yewtrey & Co. in commodious arrangement and architectural magnificence.   In the meantime, you can rest well content with your present housing, and keep your expenses down. A large building will involve a serious increase in rent, rates and taxes, and in various other ways.

INCIDENTAL EXPENSES.   It would be well to accustom yourself to reflect, that the example of any one Branch, in the direction of increased expenditure, is apt to spread.   If you are inclined to be lavish, you have no right to assume that your nine and twenty fellow-Managers are models of thrift.   If Oxborough shall spend money, let us say, in replacing the shabby old office clock, by a new and gorgeous instrument, the other Branches may be stirred more or less by a desire to follow suit.   There will be a perceptible touch of clock fever throughout the establishment.   When you experience an inclination, therefore, to add to the existing expenses of your Branch, whatever form the inclination may take, multiply the cost of the proposed addition by thirty; because what may be deemed a proper outlay at your Branch, may be looked upon as a thing equally to be desired at all your other Branches.

And whilst you thus keep in subjection any leanings of your own towards an increased expenditure, there is a tendency to waste in small things, in the daily working of a bank, which you will do well to check, if you find that it exists at Oxborough Branch.

It is related of a youth in the staff of a certain bank that when he travels in its service, he does so 'like a gentleman,' has tawny port with dinner every day, and rewards the attendants with princely munificence : all which he will placidly assure you, he does for the credit of the Bank as its representative. His taste in pens is said to be so fastidious, that in finding one to suit· him, he throws two others away. In the intervals of business, he carries on a large private correspondence, making free use of paper, envelopes, and sealing-wax, not his own : but what Board of Directors, as he demands with scorn, would condescend to notice such trifles, or chronicle such small beer ? We shall have the inspector counting the dusters next, proceeds this malapert : and putting our charwoman on a reduced allowance for soap.

This young man flatters himself that amongst other accomplishments he has a pretty turn for satire. When the Directors made the last disappointing advance in his salary, he thanked them with such polite mockery and elaborate sarcasm, that he had well-nigh forfeited both salary and situation.

I do not introduce this youth to your notice as a representative bank clerk. On the contrary, it is to be hoped that in his all round capacity for waste in little things, he is without a rival. But if others have not his many-sidedness, they sometimes have tendencies of their own towards waste, which you may have to check. A reckless consumption of coal and gas, for example, is a conspicuous and somewhat dangerous form of extravagance. I have heard an experienced bank Inspector declare his wonder, in a sardonic way which he had, that there are not as many bank offices set on fire every year in England, as there were huts in China, whenever, according to Elia, a certain process in primeval cookery was resorted to by the inhabitants.

It is not necessary that you should push economy to the verge of meanness : there is a degree of parsimony which defeats itself. What you have to fight against, if you find it to exist, is thoughtless waste, not reasonable consumption. If you would not have the office ink smearing your walls, desks, and floor with indelible arrangements in black, neither would you measure it out by the gill. You would not stint the office to so many sticks of sealing-wax a week, but you might interdict a wasteful apprentice from sealing the day's letters in discs of wax, sufficient to take off the Great Seal itself.

Acts of unthrift like these flow less from want of principle, than from want of supervision. 'They care not what they spend,' says Fuller, 'who are never brought to an audit.'

Waste in small things, where it prevails and is left to itself, is continuous, and may be reckoned by the hour. Now there are six hours in your working day, and some three hundred days in your working year, and you number one hundred and fifty officers and clerks all told.

These figures—6 × 300 × 150 yield a formidable total. They indicate 270,000 opportunities for unthrift, of one hour each, in the course of a year. Even farthings, with such a multiplier, would come to something. But whatever the amount may be, it will be well to note that it has to be charged to the same fund out of which salaries are paid. The Executive of a bank, therefore, from the Manager to the youngest apprentice, have a direct personal interest in keeping expenses down.

SUBSCRIPTIONS AND CHARITIES. You are dunned once a year for a subscription by the Bank to Oxborough Races. There are many of your best clients on the Race Committee, and you are doubtful whether the persistent refusal of your Directors to subscribe is sound policy.

Their difficulty is no doubt this. Amongst a proprietary so mixed as that of a joint stock bank, there may be those who entertain the strongest objections to horse-racing, on religious grounds. It matters not whether horse-racing morally speaking be good, bad, or indifferent: it is enough that objections to it exist among your share-holders, to render inexpedient any application of the Bank's funds to its support.

The same difficulty stands in the way of the Bank subscribing to any object, concerning the merits of which your proprietors may be divided in opinion, on political or religious grounds. You cannot subscribe to the erec-tion of a church, and refuse to contribute to the building of a chapel. You cannot support Church of England Schools, and turn your backs upon all others. Not to speak it profanely, a Joint Stock Bank is virtually of no religion. It looks with the balanced eye of business upon Christians and Jews, Infidels and Heretics, with impartial recognition.

But as regards dispensaries, hospitals, asylums, and other institutions, to which all creeds and parties may contribute on the broad basis of common charity, your Bank will no doubt be ready at all times with its proper share.

In estimating, however, what this should be, you have to take into account that your shareholders in Oxborough may have already subscribed individually towards the object in view. Not that this circumstance will absolve the Bank from giving, in its capacity as a householder, as well: but it may serve to modify the views of those who appear to think that a bank has a limitless power of giving, and the unrestricted run of its shareholders' pockets.

Your Directors, nevertheless, will not regulate the cha-rities of the Bank, by calculating how little, but rather how much they can rightly give to all good works : because they know that money thus given, is not always money. wasted. Such giving is not always a sterile form of in-vestment, even from a business point of view.

It troubles you that your subscription to the funds of your Infirmary is only two guineas a year, whilst Messrs. Yewtrey & Co. give ten. The fact, you observe, gives occasion to certain people for contemptuous remark and injurious comparison. But such persons must either forget or ignore the fact that Messrs. Yewtrey & Co. have no Branches. Their sole office is at Oxborough: whereas your Bank has to contribute at thirty different points. You subscribe to thirty Infirmaries, therefore, as against their one; and contribute sixty guineas a year to their ten.

LETTER XXIV.

ROUTINE DUTIES.

The every-day cares and duties, which men call drudgery, are the weights and counterpoises of the clock of time, giving its pendulum a true vibration and its hands a regular motion.

LONGFELLOW.

You take exception to certain of your routine duties as you find them set forth in your code of instructions.

ATTENDANCE. If your printed regulations are to be strictly observed, in the matter of attendance, for example, you submit that they would tie you to your counter from day to day, without respite, from one year's end to another, except during your annual holidays. But if there is a grievance in this, it is a penalty which you pay to your profession. It is a regulation common to every Bank. In banking, more than in any other business, the customer elects to deal with the principal. However qualified your second in command may be to represent you, he is not the Manager, and will not be accepted by the customers as your second self or human equivalent. If it be the first necessity of banking that your office doors should be open during the usual hours of business, the second is that you should be inside of them. If your clients find that there is an uncertainty as to this, and that transactions, of vital moment to them, have every now and then to be submitted to a subordinate, or delayed a post, in order that you may have a day's fishing, or a day's shooting, or a day's some-

174

thing else; they will consider themselves ill-used and begin to calculate how long they will put up with it. A medical man of sporting habits, who should leave his patients every now and then to the care of his surgery assistant, would soon experience a sensible falling off in the demands upon his skill.

Neither is this matter of relaxation an obvious necessity. Mr. Coigne, it is true, exclaims against 'the thraldom of the desk,' and protests that in all Oxborough, there is not a journeyman shoemaker, nor a draper's apprentice, so tied by the heels to his work, day after day, and every day, as the officials in banks are. But if Mr. Coigne's work is continuous, it is of the briefest in point of duration. The inscription on the brass plate of your office door is,—'Open from 10 till 3;' and even out of this brief period of time, Mr. Coigne takes little less than an hour for his mid-day meal. His daily work, therefore, cannot be put at much more than five hours out of the four and twenty; whereas the working hours of those whose happier lot he appears to covet, are nearer ten than five. Their work absorbs twenty weeks out of the fifty-two—his only ten. His workaday life therefore, his daily labour under the sun, compared with theirs, is a perpetual half-holiday.

You suggest whether it might not be expedient, on the occasion of fairs and markets, that you should go about amongst your country clients, were it merely to shake hands and have a talk about the weather and the crops. You believe that in this way, you might pick up a useful hint here and there, as to how some of your agricultural friends, particularly those on the debit side of your ledgers, were getting on. But to discuss the position and prospects of people in the publicity of a market place, even in whispers, is clearly undesirable. These subjects of inquiry ought never to be attempted except in the privacy of your own office; whilst the weather and the crops might be sufficiently gone into at any time across your counter.

The business of a banker does not lead him to the

public, but the public to him. He does not cross the street to Brown to beseech him for a deposit, nor to Jones to implore him to overdraw his account. As we sought in a former letter to render manifest, it is for its customers to come to a bank, and not for the bank to go to them; for the simple reason that banking would otherwise be impossible and come to an end. But this being so, the community have a right to demand that the Bank shall at all times be in complete working order; and to insure this, the Manager has to be as much a fixture in the office, during the business hours of every business day, as the office desks or the bank counter.

You ask, if you are thus to pass the remainder of your days inside your office, how you are to push the business? But banking is a · business to which the process of pushing must be applied, if at all, with the utmost circumspection.

To entice the customer of another bank, for example, to bring his account to you, would be, to say the least, an unneighbourly act: but what is worse, it would be a blunder: because, for one reason, the other bank could play at the same game. It would be pawn for pawn, and piece for piece, and at the best a drawn battle, which would leave mutual and angry wounds behind it. The advice to those who live in glass houses to beware of throwing stones, has many applications.

Those of your customers whose good will you have won, backed by your detachment of local shareholders, constitute an auxiliary force, which will bring fresh business to the Bank, when there is fresh business to bring, without your moving in the matter, or getting yourself into unpleasant relations with neighbouring banks.

And there is a further objection. If at your personal solicitation, a man brings his account to you from another bank, he will naturally expect not only the same facilities from you, which he has just surrendered, but something in addition, by way of consideration for his having made the change: and it will be ungracious to refuse him, however much his expectations may exceed your own idea of the fitness of things in his case.

So far from frequenting fairs and markets, let no one entice you to talk about or transact business outside the Bank. When you lock your cash up at the close of the day's business, lock the doors of your mind upon banking at the same time, and let them continue locked, until the next day. Do not let a few troublesome accounts even, if you have any, accompany you to your pillow and trouble you in the night season. You will not render them less troublesome by losing your night's rest over them. 'Put off thy care with thy clothes,' says Quarles, 'so shall thy rest strengthen thy labour: and so shall thy labour sweeten thy rest.'

PRIVATE CONDUCT. The espionage upon the private conduct of their officials, throughout the establishment, which your Directors countenance and encourage, is gall and wormwood to certain of your staff, and appears to be regarded with some disfavour even by yourself: not that you fear the closest watching, you remark, but because it is rather humiliating to be suspected.

But is not this putting too fine a point upon it? Watchfulness is not synonymous with suspicion. When, for example, a stranger presents for payment a letter of credit in his favour, and you require a reference as to his identity, you do not thereby entitle him to assume that you look upon him as an impostor? You make the requisition purely as a matter of business. Or when your Inspector of Branches comes round and counts your cash, to see that it tallies with your returns, he does not thereby impute that he suspects your honesty. He does not count it with the slightest suspicion that he will find it deficient. He checks it purely as a matter of routine. To watch, is not necessarily to suspect. It is simply to keep one's ears and eyes open. You would not have your Directors to seal both these organs up, or your

12

Inspector to make his rounds blindfolded? There are limits, well defined, within which even the inquiring gaze of your Inspector may not penetrate : but beyond these the conduct of every officer in a bank is justly open to the supervision of its Directors.

With your private convictions in religion or politics you will have no interference, provided you keep them in reasonable measure to yourself The Directors will not require to know what communion of Christians you belong to, nor to which party you give your vote at elections. But it is one thing to entertain an opinion, and quite another to seek its propagation. When a Bank Manager therefore becomes either a prominent political partisan, or a pronounced religious zealot, his Directors have the right to admonish him, that such outbreaks of zeal are incompatible with his duties to the Bank, and are not included in the services for which they pay him a salary.

Banking, as we have said more than once, does not lean to any sect in religion, nor incline to any side in politics. It deals alike with all sorts and conditions of men. Identify yourself, therefore, conspicuously with any sect or party, and succeed in setting half Oxborough, every now and then, by the ears,—and defections from the number of your constituents will assuredly follow.

His Directors have no concern with a Manager's tastes, habits, or pursuits, so long as they do not interfere with the efficient discharge of his duties : but should he overstep the lines of prudence or propriety, they are bound to interfere. If his style of living, for example, becomes extravagant, and obviously in excess of his income, the Directors are bound to call him to account; because he cannot live beyond his means for long without one of two things happening: either he will meet the growing deficit in his finances with borrowings from the cash—no doubt with a confident trust in his ability to make all square again in time: or he will run into debt with customers of the Bank, and thus bring undeserved .odium upon it, when the inevitable crash comes.

INSTRUCTIONS FROM HEAD OFFICE. The feelings of your staff are frequently outraged, it would seem, by the circulars sent from time to time by the Head Office to its Branches on matters touching the business and regulations of the Bank.

It may seem unjust to the executive of your Branch to be severely cautioned against the repetition of irregularities which they have never been guilty of But the circular is an impersonal missive. The irregularities to which it refers have arisen at one or other of the Branches, and the caution is for those whom it may concern. But it will not be wise in the members of your staff to treat every circular from head-quarters as designed for the edification of somebody else. It may be taken for granted that the parent establishment will not issue a single order that is superfluous. Your subordinates at Oxborough will best study their own interest, therefore, by a prompt compliance with such instructions as may reach the Branch from Head Office.

A bank, in the working of its routine, partakes in a great measure of the movements of a complicated piece of mechanism : and the Manager or clerk who shall cause a hitch at any point, by disobedience or neglect, may throw the whole machinery out of gear. To have the great semi-annual balance of the Bank, for instance, held in suspense, even for a day, by the default or stupidity of a single officer, which is a possible thing, need well be a serious matter for the delinquent.

The routine of a bank, to a large extent, is automatic, and is usually framed on the simplest and most direct methods of doing those things which have to be done swiftly and effectually. In office work, you prefer to reach an object by the line of its diameter, rather than by that of its circumference. Here and there, no doubt, a bank may still be found with leanings to old ways—to methods of reckoning and account which would seem to add needlessly to human labour. If the man is a benefactor to his species, who causes a blade of grass to grow where one never grew before, the man who renders one book entry out of three to be for ever needless, deserves the lasting gratitude of the clerkhood of banking. Superfluity of record, and excess of books and book-entry only puzzle the brain, lengthen the hours of office work, and multiply the chances of error.

MANAGERIAL RESPONSIBILITY. You take exception to certain articles in your code of instructions, the disregard of which exposes you to personal responsibility.

'If we let a customer overdraw his account without authority,' you write, 'we are responsible. If we discount bills beyond a certain amount without leave, we are responsible. If we cash a cheque upon another Branch or bank, and it is dishonoured and becomes a loss, the loss is ours. If we discount a forged bill, or cash a forged cheque, and become the victims of the fraud, we have to make good the loss.'

You hold it to be unjust and impolitic, thus to tie a Manager neck and heels with the cords of liability, and that much of all this might with advantage be left to his discretion. But to give a Bank Manager or anyone else a discretion to follow certain rules, or to set them aside, would virtually be to cancel the rules themselves.

When you cash a cheque drawn upon another bank or Branch, in ignorance of the state of the account drawn upon, and the cheque is dishonoured, the risk is self-taken, and the loss ought to be self-borne. That you should be held responsible for the cashing of forged bills, or cheques, is only consistent with all usage. It is one of the special functions of a Bank Manager, or his cashier, to see that every cheque or document, against which he parts with the funds of the Bank, bears the genuine signature of the party entitled to the money, or that of his duly accredited agent. In all conditions of life, he who pays money to the wrong person has to bear the loss; just as it is the common lot that he who burns his fingers has to bear the smart.

But Boards of Directors are not all of flint and adamant compounded. Forgeries which would have imposed upon any one; errors in the cash on busy days; transactions undertaken in the interest of the Bank, under circumstances calculated to deceive even the wariest;— lapses like these from the written law of your instructions, if not entirely condoned, will at least be leniently dealt with. It is the violation of the code, in clearly specified cases, either from carelessness or conceit, which will be visited by the Board with their worst displeasure.

In respect of the limitations put upon your action in the matter of advances and discounts, you hold that they leave little or nothing to the discretion of a Manager, and reduce him to an automaton. You desire to be more of a man and less of a contrivance.

But in a large establishment like yours, there are Managers and Managers. There are those with diseretion largely developed: but there are others in which that quality is not so conspicuous. Based on the axiom that the strength of a chain is its weakest link, the regulations of a bank are necessarily adapted to the capacities of its least capable functionaries.

LETTER XXV.

CORRESPONDENCE.

When thou communicatest thyself with letters, heighten or depress thy stile according to the quality of the party and business: that which thy tongue would present to any, if present, let thy pen present to him absent; the tongue is the mind's interpreter and the pen is the tongue's secretary. QUARLES.

YOUR principal correspondent will be the chief Manager of the Bank. You may have to write to him several times a week on various matters, and it will be well to bear in mind that the nine and twenty Managers at your other Branches have to do the same. In dealing with this extensive correspondence and its miscellany of contents, he has to take counsel with 'the Board.' Every letter addressed to him, has more or less to engage the attention and exercise the judgment of a body of gentlemen, to whom, for the most part, time is money, and by whom it is appraised, not by the hour but by the minute. When you write to your Manager in chief, therefore, you are addressing your six Directors as well.

Your virtual correspondent, then, being a species of modified Briaræus, with seven heads and twice that number of ears, it is unnecessary to suggest that your communications to this formidable being had best be featured by lucid statement and legible penmanship. The clearest statement becomes blurred to the mind of the reader, if it is conveyed in a hand-writing so obscure as to require an effort and strain of the mental powers to worm the meaning out of it. If the Manager who gives away to an inscrutable penmanship, had an ink-

182

ling of the angry impatience of the Board, whilst his
meaning is puzzled over and painfully extracted, he
would promptly 'take a thought and mend,' and never
cease to mend, until he had achieved a style which should
at least be readable.   Better a hand of even extra
uncouthness which is legible, than one with the beauty of
copper-plate from which no man can extract a meaning.
'Better,' the Spaniards say, 'ride an ass that carries
you than a horse that throws you.'

And next to clearness of statement, a Manager should
study brevity, which is no less the soul of business than
of wit.   The limited time during which committees of
Bank Directors usually sit, and the variety of matters
which they must dispose of at each sitting, do not
afford the time to read a roundabout epistle: it has to
be abstracted.   The official, whose business it is to
operate upon verbosity, mentally applies the knife, and
fluent pages are thus cut down sometimes to as many
lines.   If the exactitude of a Manager's views is impaired by this process, he has himself to blame: the
writer 'who draweth out the thread of his verbosity
finer than the staple of his argument' has to undergo
compression; his sentiments have to undergo the operation of being 'limited and reduced.'

And in your correspondence with Head Office, whilst
you seek to express your views upon the matters in
hand with respectful firmness, it will be wise to avoid
argument; it is for you to place the facts before the
Directors, not to guide them to a decision.   Nor is
'tone' a quality to be slighted in your letters to head-
quarters.   When you wrote the letter of which you
speak, on behalf of a deserving charity, and enforced
your appeal with an apt quotation from the Greek, it is
hardly matter for surprise that, although your appeal
was handsomely responded to, you had a gentle hint
to confine yourself to the English language in your
future communications to the Head Office.   A business
communication has no place in it for the classics; a
Greek quantity is not suggestive of a sum total:

in matters so peculiarly British as pounds, shillings, and pence, the English language is the natural vehicle for the conveyance of thought.

When upon another occasion you suggested that one Brown by name, an obstinate debtor, should be handed over to your solicitors, with the expression of a hope that they would make him look Blue, it is even less matter for surprise that you were invited, in reply, to abstain in future from jocosity in matters of business. Even if your little joke had been feebler than it was, which is impossible, your whole Board of Directors, remember, had to sit upon it. No wonder that the Manager was instructed to sit upon you instead. A bank Board is not given to exchanges of drollery with its officers; its business is with realities, some of them stern enough, but none of them so trivial as to be dismissed with a jest.

LETTERS TO CUSTOMERS. In your intercourse with your clients, you will find it a safe observance, never to discuss with a customer the position of his account by letter, if you can by any means arrange to do so by word of mouth. If the discussion has to be of an unpleasant cast, the mere putting it in writing will give to your missive a formality and bite of their own.

Let us say that you have written to a man to reduce or pay off his account; you have probably heard something to his disadvantage, but you cannot well say so in writing, or give your authority. He has no chance therefore of confuting the charge, because you do not give it him to confute ; whereas, if you had a friendly talk with him, freed from the constraint of putting everything into writing, he might be able to disabuse your mind of what may be rankling there to his prejudice. It is at least certain that a man will reveal more of his mind to you, in ten minutes' talk, in the seclusion of your private office, than he will ever be able to express or put his hand to in writing.

It is a further objection to your conveying to a customer wishes of an unpleasant nature by letter, that he may be from home at the time, and your missive be opened by some one in his absence. If this some one should happen to be a nervous wife or a loose-tongued clerk, your client will have a right to ask why you sent this epistolary bombshell after him without a word of notice. Rather than be thus brought to book, he would have endured an hour's warming in your sweating-room, at any degree of managerial heat. Your customers, without exception, will prefer to discuss the delicate questions of their overdrafts and bills *in camera;* and you will do wisely to humour them in this preference.

A BANKER'S OPINION IN CONFIDENCE. There is perhaps no more difficult or delicate task which the Manager of a bank has constantly to perform, than to give expression to his opinion, in confidence, of the position and trustworthiness of a customer. When that position is intimately known to the Bank, either by the evidence of the man's balance-sheet, or the possession of his deeds, or bonds, or shares, for safe custody, there is no difficulty; and the Manager has no hesitation in giving his opinion in confident terms and in the plainest English.

But occasions continually arise where the facts required are not so clear. Your knowledge of the person enquired about, for example, may be at second hand. If so, you have equally to guard against doing an injury to the man's credit, and leading the enquirer into a false security. But whatever shape your answer may take in such a case, you must make it clear that it is based on hearsay only, and that you have no personal knowledge of the party's means. There is no reason why you should assume the responsibility of giving as your own the opinion of others, which, however honest, may nevertheless be fallacious and misleading. You may, on your own responsibility, report the man enquired about to be respectable, or a shrewd man of business, or a man who appears to have credit in the trade for the amount named; or even that you yourselves occasionally trust him for such a sum without security: all this you may properly and prudently say, if you can do so in accordance with the facts. Such statements will not prejudice your customer, and they will put it upon the enquirer to judge for himself and draw his own conclusions.

If, on the other hand, the individual enquired about is neither respectable nor shrewd; if he is short of capital and of small credit with the trade, you must say so; but you will say so 'on report.' You will state the facts, so far as they have reached you, without indorsing them as your own. If you neglect this precaution, the person thus adversely reported upon may take proceedings against your Bank for defamation, if your report should reach his ears, which it may possibly do; because the absolute confidence with which a Banker imparts such information, although widely respected, is violated at times. But in such event, if it is apparent to the Court that you have simply stated the truth, as far as it was known to you, without malice, you have no cause to fear the result. Proceedings which have their inception in a thirst for something like blood-money, are more likely to end in a verdict, which shall be in closer neighbourhood to a farthing than a thousand pounds.

The action brought against your Bank by Grindley & Co. for misrepresentation was of an opposite kind: they sued you, not for giving too bad, but for giving too good an opinion of your then customer, Gabriel White. Your Manager, in reply to an enquiry from the bankers of the Grindleys, had given it as his opinion that White was undoubted for the amount named; but White unfortunately failed a few weeks afterwards; whereupon Grindley & Co. brought their action, on the ground that they had trusted White with many hundred pounds' worth of goods, on the strength of the Bank's opinion. In their declaration they went a step beyond this, and roundly charged the Bank with having given this

opinion, with the nefarious object of compassing a reduction of its own debt. It happened, however, that
when White failed, he owed the Bank rather more than
when your Manager gave his opinion, and the plaintiffs
were non-suited. If your Manager had given a less
unqualified opinion as to the position of White—if he
had put it more upon current report and less upon his
own assertion—White would have had no ground for
complaint; the Grindleys would have had no ground
for an action; and the Bank would have been spared
the annoyance of being charged with an act of baseness
of which it was entirely guiltless.

LETTER XXVI.

COMPETITION IN BANKING.

Sometimes our neighbours want the things which we have, or have the things which we want; and we both fight, till they take ours, or give us theirs. SWIFT.

THE opening of a Branch of the Bolchester Bank in Oxborough has filled you with resentment and something like dismay. 'They are pushing themselves here, there, and everywhere,' you state, 'in search of deposits, and care not what interest they allow, provided they get the money. Their terms for discounts and advances are more liberal and less exacting than ours, and scores of our accounts will be sure to go over to them.'

To add to their offences, they have taken into their service one of the clerks in Messrs. Yewtrey & Co.'s Bank, purposing through him, you suggest, to ascertain where the Old Bank's deposits lie. But it is possible that in this indictment you accuse the new comers unjustly. Although the taking into their employment a clerk from either of the existing banks, under the circumstances, may expose their motives to suspicion, no respectable institution would seek in this way to hunt up and prey upon the business of another bank.

The report that the new comers enticed the clerk from Yewtrey & Co. into their service is probably untrue. It is at least equally probable that he applied for the appointment in the first instance, with a view to bettering his position; against which there is no law. Every clerk in a bank has a right to seek an appointment in another bank, if he sees fit,—but always with this proviso, that he does not betray to his new, the secrets of his late

188

employers.   He has signed a solemn declaration to this
effect; and if he is capable of violating this covenant, he
may prove a bad bargain to his new masters.   A clerk
capable of an act of perfidy like this, is not morally fitted
for the service of any bank.   If he has proved false to
one employer, it is a reasonable assumption that he may
prove false to the other, whenever the occasion offers,
and a second act of treason shall appear to be worth the
doing.

Your fear that the new comers will offer more than the
market rate of interest, and thus drain away thousands
of your deposits, may be equally groundless.   The Bolchester Bank is a respectable institution, and is unlikely
to give more than the current rate for deposits: but, if
otherwise, and its rates are what you are informed and
believe them to be, the Bolchester Bank will not trouble
Oxborough or any other place for long.   The first money
panic will bring it to book.

If the alleged munificence of the Bolchester Bank in
advances and discounts should enmesh, as you seem to
fear, and draw away a portion of your business, the haul
will consist of customers who find themselves cramped,
by what they consider your antediluvian views about
security, and who will ardently embrace any less exacting system of banking.   It may be that other accounts,
which you are unwilling to lose, may be included in the
haul;   nevertheless the ultimate balance of advantage
may not rest with the aggressors.   Against the few good
accounts which you may lose, you have to set the more
than doubtful ones which they may gain.

Such being the situation, would it not be a wiser policy,
as soon as you can subdue your present sense of injury
and repugnance, to place yourself, let us say, on speaking
terms with the intruders; rather than hold yourself scorn-
fully aloof and regard them with a bootless resentment?
Instead of ignoring their existence, it might be better to
come to an early understanding with them as to rates:
otherwise you may find yourselves speedily at work,
inflicting lasting injury on each other's business with

mutual diligence and fervour.   If you do not so arrange, Mr. Nayler will hardly be himself, if he fails to play one bank off against the other, to the detriment of both; and his example will spread.

But whatever course your action may take, this is certain—the new comers have planted themselves in Oxborough, and no unfriendliness on your part will of itself cause them to budge out again : on the contrary, the greater your obvious dislike, which they will ascribe to fear, the higher will mount their estimate of the business, which they hope to share with you, and the less their inclination will become to retire from the field.

Let us suppose that you decline to put yourselves on amicable relations with the intruders, and that your intolerant attitude, and the scornful terms in which you openly speak of that 'filibustering concern from Bol- chester,' have reached the ears of its Directors, and inflamed them with an animosity equal to your own, and that war to the knife is the consequence.

Whilst the contest lasts, Oxborough will have 'a good time' in banking: unheard-of rates of interest for deposits; discounts at less than bank rate, and overdrafts for the asking ! It will be a monetary carnival, and Oxborough will be financially debauched.

No doubt, during the contest, you will have punished the enemy severely and done enough for glory, although you have failed to dislodge him ; but what of your own scars ? What of the rents and fissures made in the profits of Oxborough Branch, which it will take years to repair, if indeed your profits shall ever regain their former scale and level ? For Oxborough will monetarially have tasted blood ; and it will not be an easy or a pleasant task, to bring its people back again to the condition of things which prevailed before the war.

The opening of an additional bank in a town may not be in every sense an unmitigated injury to the existing banks.   The new comers have their way to make, and as new brooms sweep clean, they will search out, by means of their friends and connections, those who have not as yet kept any bank account—a less numerous class than formerly, but a class by no means extinct as yet in rural parts. The new comers from Bolchester will give the banking soil of your district a fresh turn-over, so to speak, and this may serve indirectly to fertilize your business as well as theirs. They will have awakened certain people for the first time to the advantage of keeping a bank account, but not necessarily with their establishment. The converts, before acting upon their conversion, will naturally talk the matter over with their friends and be guided by them as to the bank to which they will take their business.

Now Messrs. Yewtrey & Co. have been established in Oxborough for over a century, and your own Bank has had its Branch there for half that time : whereas the Bolchester Bank is to the traders and householders of Oxborough a thing of yesterday, of which they know nothing. Moreover, for one shareholder which it has in your district, your own Bank has at least a score ; so that altogether, the invaders will be heavily handicapped, and will have to compete for fresh business with the Old Bank and yourselves at serious odds.

You would plant a Branch in the Bolchester district forthwith, by way of counterslap. But in banking, you do not levy war on the territory of a neighbour, merely because you have a spite against him. Questions of larger concern than the condition of your spleen have to go to the consideration of that matter. For one thing, an aggressive policy may provoke reprisals : but of this more hereafter.

On the whole, it would seem to be the wiser course to be on terms of amity with your new rivals. Under the most favourable circumstances, they have long years of uphill work ahead of them, before they can do much more than cover expenses. It may happen that they have over estimated their chances of success in Oxborough, and after a time may feel so dissatisfied

with the result as to close their Branch.   In this event,
they will have something to give away.   But, if up
to the date of this determination of theirs, **you** are still
at daggers-drawn with them, it is needless to remark
that they will have no desire that a single account of
theirs shall come to you, which they can by possibility
send elsewhere.

LETTER XXVII.

A NEW BANK FOR OXBOROUGH.

'Tell me, see'st thou not yon knight coming towards us on a dapple grey steed, with a helmet of gold on his head?' 'What I see and perceive,' answered Sancho, ' is only a man on a grey ass, like mine, with something on his head that glitters.'
DON QUIXOTE.

THE material progress of Oxborough must be considerable, seeing that you have hardly recovered from the shock of the invasion from Bolchester, before you are threatened with a new bank—'The Oxborough Mutual Benefit Banking Company, Limited.'

The promoter is our old acquaintance, Mr. Howard Bagster, and the prospectus sets forth among other things the enormous profits of banking. It gives an attractive list of banks whose dividends range from 10 to 20 per cent., with an average of 15 ; and whose shares stand at premiums ranging from 100 to 300 per cent. Mr. Bagster, it will be observed, selects only the best paying banks for his basis. He makes no mention of banks paying less than 10 per cent. That would have fatally affected his average of 15 per cent., and broken the back of his design.

Neither does he allude to the fact that the banks now paying high dividends were established for the most part some half century ago. They did not pay 15 per cent. then. In the earlier stages of their history, some of the greatest and most successful of our existing banks paid dividends not exceeding 4 or 5 per cent. for years— sometimes none at all. Some few had to write off a third or fourth of their paid-up capitals. Others again of our aboriginal Joint Stock Banks did even worse—they lost their all, and are long since dead and buried. But their record was not buried with them, although there is no mention of it in the prospectus : the framers of that document would not have its radiant view of things clouded by unpleasant memories.

Bank dividends ranging from 10 to 20 per cent. are not reached at a bound. They never have been in the past, and in the nature of things they never can be in the years to come. The dividends of the future will necessarily be more tardy of growth than those of the past, if, indeed, they are not retrogressive. When our existing banks were constituted, there was a magnificent area of virgin soil for them to occupy and till. But such a superficies no longer exists. It has been gradually occupied, point after point, by the present banks; so that there is no unreclaimed territory for fresh banks to squat upon. They cannot, therefore, hope to achieve the splendid successes of their forerunners. The banking crop has been already gathered, and they can only follow as gleaners in the footsteps of the reapers. For anything beyond this, new banks must fight the old ones ; or be content for years to come with a rate of annual dividend which will not excite their proprietors to enthusiasm.

It is true they can fight the old banks, by offering more liberal terms to the public; although competition has already reduced those terms to a degree of fineness, which it will be difficult to attenuate further, if any reasonable margin is to be left for dividends. You cannot purchase first-class country bank shares even now, to yield you more than 5 per cent.—far less 15.

But in any event, the game of competition is one at which the old banks can play, and doubtless will play, equally with their assailants, at every point where they are attacked. They will not, without a struggle, part with business which has cost them the labour and contention—the losses and anxieties of half a century to build up. They will object to promoters seeking to reap

where they have not sown, and in a war of rates will
fool them to the top of their bent. But that is a pastime at which the new banks would play at fatal
disadvantage. A course of banking, pursued for a time
at certain points at a loss, would make but a slight
impression on the large reserve funds of the old
banks: but such a course would be ruinous to the
new ones, because they would have no such funds
to fall back upon: neither would they have much to
look forward to. They will have damaged their rivals
to a certain extent: but, in doing so, they will have
cut the ground from under their own feet, and rendered
banking, at any reasonable profit to themselves, an
impossible business.

A new bank, if it shall survive the period of its early
youth, will do well if it pays its expenses and divides
nothing among its shareholders for the first few years:
but this fact, although a part of banking history,
finds no place in Mr. Bagster's prospectus. It might
cool the ardour of applicants, and abate the rush for
shares.

Mr. Bagster does not suggest to subscribers that high
dividends are only reached after an ascent which is
always long, often difficult, and sometimes dangerous.
He does not invite them to put their feet on the lowest
rung of the ladder, to work their gradual way upwards:
he places them, by suggestion, on the top rung at start-
ing. He makes no mention of the fact, that the large
dividends now paid by some of our banks, only yield in
reality something like 5 per cent. to their existing
proprietors.

The Mutual Benefit Banking Company of Oxborough,
is to be worked on principles new to English banking,
and is to bring light and joy to depositors and
borrowers alike, whatever hap of fortune it may bring
to its proprietors. Bank commission is to become a
thing of the past; depositors are to be paid rates of
interest unparalleled in banking history; and profits are
to be rateably divided betwixt shareholders and cus-

tomers.   How this remarkable equation is to be worked
out is not explained: it is discreetly left to the imagination.   But as the Mutual Benefit Bank, conducted on
the lines proposed by the prospectus, can never, by
human effort, make any profit at all, its method for the
division of nothing ceases to be of human interest.

It may seem waste of time to have troubled ourselves
at all with Mr. Bagster and his prospectus: but, excepting the special absurdity of the 'mutual benefit' principle,
which he proudly claims for his own, the document in
other respects is only an average sample of its kind.   It
makes quotation of the most successful banks, but
refrains from all mention of the less fortunate.   It parades
the dividends and premiums of to-day, but gives no
place to the dividends, or no dividends, the losses or
failures, of the past.   It leads the unwary to the belief
that an average return of 15 per cent. per annum is the
ordinary result of banking, and within the reach of
everybody: and, unhappily, there is nothing which a
promoter can allege on the subject of banking too gross
for some people to swallow.

Instead of following this Will-o'-the-wisp,—this 15 per
cent. of the prospectus, the prudent may find it a safer
policy to invest their money in the shares of old
established banks, even if the investment should yield
them only a bare 5 per cent.

The old banks have borne the searching tests of time,
and change, and panic, and stand forth purified and
strengthened by the ordeal.   But what is of still more
consequence—they understand their business: whereas,
a new bank has practically its business to learn, and the
inevitable 'footing' to pay.   Its earlier years will be a
long struggle with all the ills of infant banking.   It
must do business which other banks do not care to
retain, or it must offer to transact good business on more
tempting terms, and thus work at a margin of profit
slightly removed from nothing.   If its constitution be
hardy, it may work its way to a position of some kind
after many years; but its dividends, meanwhile, will be

of the smallest, and its shares will find their natural level, at a point perceptibly below par, rather than above it.

On the whole, the would-be investor in bank shares had best take counsel with himself, whether 5 per cent. in hand may not be preferable even to 15 per cent. in the bush.

Our discussion, thus far, of the daily work of a Country Bank, although for the most part of general application to the business of banking, has been directed more to the business of a Branch than to the administration of a Head Office,—a question to which I now propose to turn, in the hope and expectation that you may some day rise to the position of Manager-in-chief.

LETTER XXVIII.

THE OFFICE OF CHIEF MANAGER.

Preserve the right of thy place, but stir not questions of jurisdiction, and rather assume thy right in silence and de facto *than voice it with claims and challenges. Preserve likewise the rights of inferior places, and think it more honour to direct in chief than to be busy in all.* BACON.

WHEN you succeed to the supreme management of the Bank, you will enter upon duties of a higher grade, and responsibilities of wider range than you had to undertake at Oxborough. The working of a Branch will seem to you but a small matter, when compared with the management of the Central office and its thirty dependencies. Whilst Manager at Oxborough, you were one of a hundred and fifty subordinates, of all ranks; at the Central office, you will be head over all. The provincial Managers, who were your equals yesterday, will have become your official inferiors to-day.

As the Manager of a Branch, you looked to your Manager-in-chief for guidance in all large or exceptional matters: you will now have to trust for that guidance to your own head alone, and your thirty representatives at the Branches will have to look to the same source for light and leading in all difficulties.

You will have no code of instructions to guide you as Manager-in-chief: on the contrary, you will now have to edit that compilation, and enrich it with fresh matter from time to time, as experience shall suggest or necessity require. It will be your part now to instruct— not to receive instruction: to foresee and devise, and not to look to others for foresight or resource.

198

It would be unreasonable to expect you to feel no elation on the occasion of your ascent to the official throne of the Bank : but it will be well to carry your fresh honours with meekness, were it merely for this, —that the susceptibilities of those whom you have distanced in the race for advancement will, for a time, be tender of touch. You find yourself placed, at a bound, on a pinnacle of promotion, the look down from which may pardonably be attended at first with a certain giddiness and confusion of ideas : but do not let a sense of what you owe to your new position betray you into premature activity. If you would gather up the reins of government, with the skill and deliberation of one who knows what he has before him to do and means to do it, let your attitude for a time be one rather of observation and reflection than of action. Your new and varied duties, if pondered with calmness and care, will gradually assume their relative proportions and perspective, and the order and method of your manage-ment will speedily lie straight and clear before you.

One of the most onerous of your fresh duties will be your daily intercourse with your Managers at the Branches. This must be by letter, because your oppor-tunities of personal intercourse with them will necessarily be few. But you cannot conduct this correspondence with your own hand, because your other duties will leave you with little time for letter-writing. That, for the most part, must be done by the Secretary of the Bank, under your instructions. These will necessarily be brief—conveyed in a sort of mental shorthand—and it will be his work to put them into shape.

It may be, that the Secretary of the District Union Bank is one of those who can enter into another man's thoughts, and express his views as perfectly as if the thinker himself gave form and utterance to them ; but this is a gift not possessed by every one : indeed it is more rare than common. You have to reflect, in any case, that your Secretary, whatever his qualifications as a scribe may be, will have trying questions to solve, unwise

proposals to set aside, and unreasonable requests **to**
decline from time to time, at your behest.   He may, **as**
I have just said, be your faithful echo in all this ; but he
may not be.   He may be of an irritable temperament,
and take the bother and worry of reply as personal to
himself, and clothe his replies accordingly in biting
sarcasm or withering rebuke.   You will no doubt see
that this does not happen.   A martinet, as secretary **of a**
bank, can make office life a burden to its provincial staff.
Moreover, he is your other self and mouthpiece, for good
or evil in this matter.   His views are your views, in whatsoever garb of language they may be clothed.   His very
sarcasms, however truculent, go to the Branches 'in accordance with instructions' from either the Board or yourself.

And the men addressed, it has to be observed,
although your subjects now, were your equals only the
other day, and are not the less entitled to official respect
or friendly regard, because you now reign over them.
The best of Branch Managers, no doubt, has his failings :
and it is certain that the worst of them has his feelings.
Where disapproval, therefore, or even censure, has to be
conveyed, it need not be in terms calculated to affront
or wound.   A mild remonstrance will have equal weight,
and with this advantage,—it will not dishearten the
recipient, nor incense him every now and then with a
helpless rage.

A nagging and sarcastic spirit at the centre of authority, moreover, is apt to find imitators at the Branches.
The Manager who is persistently worried by the Head
Office, may be drawn at times to vent his spleen on his
immediate subordinates, who will duly pass it on to the
juniors : and thus an occasional free fight of tongues
may result, to the amazement of customers and scandal
of the Branch.

In any event, let it not be in the power of any provincial Manager to quote the example of Head Office as
an excuse for a needless severity of method with his
own little staff   Put forth your strength rather with the
snaffle than with the double-bit of authority.   Let your

intercourse with your Branches be inspired by the genial old adage—'Speak fair words and you will always have kind echoes,'—and let the management of the Bank throughout, from its Central office to its remotest Branch, be in unison therewith.

The first subject which will engage your attention, when you fairly settle down to work, will naturally be the financial position of the Bank. You will desire to know the trim of the vessel, so to speak, in command of which you are about to enter upon a voyage of momentous interest, alike to your shareholders and yourself.

Your first reference will be to the balance-sheet of the Bank, which will afford you a bird's-eye view of the situation. It will shew you, on the one hand, the total amount of money owing by the Bank to the public and its shareholders, and, on the other, how this total is laid out.

But a balance-sheet deals with aggregates only. It will set forth the totals advanced on overdrawn accounts, on bills discounted, and in other ways; but not the multifarious items of which these totals are composed.

Every bill in your bill case; every overdrawn account in your ledgers; every security you hold; whether these relate to your business at the Head Office, or one or other of your thirty Branches; must each in turn be to you a matter of patient scrutiny and careful valuation, before you can grasp the actual position of the Bank, or know the measure of its soundness throughout.

And in entering upon this immense audit and appraisement, I conclude that, in respect of overdrafts, bills and securities at the Branches, you will not rest content with less than an enquiry in every case, on the spot. You will thus reap the advantage of seeing, with your own eyes, the working of your multitudinous accounts, as shewn in the Branch ledgers; a process as we have seen, which throws an always useful, and sometimes vivid light on the way things are tending with the parties to the accounts.

Your round of the Branches will have the further advantage of bringing you into personal intercourse with the whole of your provincial staff; a matter which may be of material service in your future relations with each other. An officer whom you have never seen, and of whom you have no knowledge, except by report, will be little more to you than a lay figure, until you have had speech with him and taken stock of his business method and ability.

When you have mastered the position of every account, the worth of every bill, and the value of every security held by the Bank, you will then know whether the course of your management ought to be towards restriction or expansion: or whether, finding your resources, as a whole, laid out with safety and financial judgment, you will enjoy the satisfaction of leaving well alone.

LETTER XXIX.

BANKING FINANCE.

See'st thou good dayes? Prepare for evil times : no summer but hath his winter. He never reaped comfort in adversity that sowed it not in prosperity. QUARLES.

LET us start with the assumption that you find the District Union Bank sound to the core, and that the aggregates of its balance-sheet represent the actual sums and present values of the multifarious items of which they are composed.

But we shall understand each other better, perhaps, if we proceed at once to fabricate a balance-sheet, which shall embrace the principal heads of account common to English country banking; and thus present something tangible to the mind's eye, although the tangibility be but the fictitious liabilities and the fabulous assets of an imaginary bank.

Let us assume, then, that on your accession to the management in chief of the District Union Bank, its Liabilities and Assets are as understated, and that the apportionment of the assets rests on the following basis :—

The Reserve is taken at ONE-THIRD the Liabilities to the public :

The Advances are taken at the amount of Capital and Rest, plus ONE-FIFTH of the liabilities to the public.

203

The remaining resources of the Bank are absorbed **in** Bills of Exchange.

LIABILITIES.

On Deposit Receipts	. £1,350,000	
On Current Accounts	. 1,050,000	
		2,400,000
Notes in circulation	. . .	50,000
Drafts after date	. . . .	20,000
Acceptances by Bank	. . .	30,000
Bills for collection and other items	.	50,000

Total liabilities to the Public £2,550,000		
Paid-up Capital	. . . £300,000	
Rest, or Surplus Fund	. . 150,000	
		450,000
		£3,000,000

ASSETS.

Reserve :

Cash in hand	. . . .	£200,000
Money at call and short notice	.	350,000
Consols	. . .	300,000
		850,000
Advances, overdrafts, etc.	. . .	960,000
Bills of Exchange	. . . .	1,190,000
		£3,000,000

These figures are purely arbitrary : but they will serve, as well as others, as a basis for discussion.

And first, as regards the liability side of your position. You are indebted then, to depositors and others, some two and a half millions sterling.

Now, although it is certainly within the range of possibility that you might be called upon, at any time, to redeem the whole of this formidable liability within the compass of a few weeks, the chances are nevertheless as millions to one, against such a contingency ever coming to pass.

You will find that, in ordinary times, your deposits, as a whole, maintain a moderately uniform level. The deviations on either side of the main line of average will be slight. A decrease at one point will be met by an increase at another; the closure of some accounts by the opening of fresh ones, and so forth: the general result being that, apart from these slight movements—these ripples on the surface, so to speak—the great volume of your deposits is never stirred to its depths. The minor fluctuations, of which we now speak, are sufficiently provided for by your cash in hand: in fact this is the primary use of your till-money.

But there are times when your deposits may be exposed to exceptional attack: and you must be prepared at all times to meet such emergencies. We have seen that banks, however sound and powerful, are still as much exposed to senseless and mischievous runs, as they were in the dark ages of banking, a hundred years ago. It may be, that the District Union Bank will never be so assailed: but you cannot build upon this pleasing forecast as a certainty, and therefore make no provision against it. It may be 'odds beyond arithmetic' against your cash safe ever being attempted; but that would hardly justify your leaving its doors wide open, day and night.

Neither must you assume that you will always be able to note the signs of a coming pressure, in time to make due provision for its onset, by a contraction of your discounts and a recall of loans and overdrafts. There may be no sign given. A run does not usually advertize its advent a month or so beforehand, and some of our worst panics have come upon us without much previous

warning.   You cannot pull your resources together in
a few days, or a few weeks, if they are widely spread,
and difficult of realization.   The normal position of a
banker is like that of a general in the field, with an
enemy in front of him, against whose assault he must
be armed at all points, if he would not find himself
assailed some day, and suffer loss and discomfiture.

THE RESERVE.   To guard against all probable demands, therefore, I have put your immediately available resources—your financial reserve—at one-third the
amount of your liabilities to the public.

This provision will appear to some to be excessive.
It is certainly in excess of the reserve usually held by
some country banks; whilst it is less than that maintained by others.   The range of usage in this matter is
very great, and is governed, in some measure, by the
character of the deposits held.

In agricultural districts their feature is permanence.
In centres of industrial activity, their feature is instability.   A ratio of reserve, therefore, which might be
more than ample in one case, might be dangerously
inadequate in another.   Country banks, like yourselves, holding from one to three millions of deposits,
hold average reserves of 24 per cent.   Others, holding
from three to five millions, have reserves averaging 36
per cent.*

The deposits in your Bank partake of both classes—
some town, some country—and in placing your reserve
at 33 per cent., we have swerved slightly from the exact
line of average; but, such as it is, the deviation is on the
side of safety.

Moreover, in fixing the amount of your reserve, you
have to take into account, not only that your deposits
are subject, at uncertain times, to serious depletion:
but that the demand upon you for discounts and ad-

* *Economist,* 19th May, 1883.

vances is also subject to constant variation. Your reserve, therefore, should always be sufficient to meet every description of demand upon it; if you would work your finances without friction from one year's end to another, in times of ease, as well as in times of trouble and anxiety.

A further argument in favour of working at all times on an ample reserve, lies in the fact that, in the long run, it even 'pays' better, than by working on a small one.

A RESERVE OF 20 PER CENT. In illustration of this, let us say that, instead of a reserve amounting to one-third, you decide to finance the Bank on a reserve of one-fifth, or 20 per cent. of the amount of its liabilities to the public. In that case, your reserve will stand at £500,000 instead of £850,000, and you will thus release £350,000 for other employment.

You would employ the money, thus released, in the discount of mercantile and commercial bills of a high class—bills which would be negociable at any time in case of need.

In this way you may derive a possible gain of one per cent. in excess of what the money would yield, if left at short notice with your bill-brokers. That would represent an addition to your profits of £3500 a year. But to earn this profit, you have to discount bills to the amount of a million and a half every year, in addition to the bills you already hold, and thus proportionately enlarge your business risks.

You can barely hope to discount this formidable amount, even of the highest class of mercantile and commercial paper, without meeting with an occasional loss—a loss which may make a serious inroad at any time on your £3500, or sweep it away altogether. You will have to select your bills with super-human ability if this mischance shall ever befall you.

For the sake of argument, however, let it be conceded

that you do realize this extra profit of £3500 a year without loss or abatement ; the question still remains,— Will it be a judicious gain? Will there be no collateral drawbacks—no outbalancing disadvantage? Let us see.

I assume that the reserve of 20 per cent., of which we now speak, will be composed of the items following :

Cash in hand	£200,000
Money at call	150,000
Consols	150,000
	£500,000

Now, without subjecting your finances to the terrible strain of a 'run,' it will suffice for the argument, to imagine a drain upon your deposits at a time of monetary pressure—say to the extent of 10 per cent., or £250,000 in all. You will remember that in December, 1878, the drain upon certain banks averaged 16 per cent. of their deposits, and in the case of one of them reached 26 per cent.

To meet the supposed demand, you have only your money at call and Consols to fall back upon, because your cash in hand represents simply the till-money required to carry your business on from day to day, and cannot be diminished. After exhausting your money at call, then, you would still have to provide £100,000 to meet the drain.

To do this, you might borrow the amount on your Consols; or you could sell them; or you might re-discount a portion of your bills. But whichever course you take, it will be open to the objection that it will be sure to get wind. If it should leak out that you are borrowing on Consols, the report will be that you are being 'carried through.' If you sell them, the inference will be that you are hard pushed. If you resort to the bill-market, and thus make your first appearance there as a re-discounting bank, the fact will hardly fail to pass without comment more or less damaging.

Rumours such as these, at a time when the very air is charged with discredit, conveyed in letters 'strictly confidential,' from friends in the City to correspondents in the provinces, are swift to spread, and might enlarge a natural drain upon your deposits to serious proportions, or even convert it into a ' run.'

You remind me that there are your overdrawn accounts to fall back upon, and also that you might reduce the volume of your discounts. That is true : but either of these processes takes time, and that may not be at your command. Even the most affable. amongst your depositors would be sorely amazed, if you were to ask them to call again in a month or six weeks, by which time you expect to have got in some of the money which you have lent to their friends and neighbours. There is, in fact, only one way of meeting the difficulty, and no way of evading it,—the means to meet a sharp drain upon your deposits must always be in your coffers, or at your immediate control— before-hand.

There will be no time for calling in advances, or awaiting the falling due of bills. The peremptory people who line the outside of your counter, awaiting the payment of their deposits, will each have his pound of flesh, there and then, even if you sink under the operation.

Let us assume, however, that by sales of Consols, the re-discount of bills, or otherwise, you have met the drain, and that you have subsequently restored your reserve to its normal amount—namely, one-fifth your liabilities — by a rigorous curtailment of your discounts and advances to the extent required.

But with what cost to others will this have been accomplished? What amount of anxiety, inconvenience, and loss, will the withdrawal of your usual facilities, to the extent of a quarter of a million, have inflicted upon numbers of your constituents? To expect that

14

they will pass the infliction by, and humbly kiss the rod, would be to take a too complacent view of the matter. The people whose discounts you have restricted, or whose overdrafts you have called up, will not hold themselves bound to you a day longer than they can make arrangements with other banks for a transfer of their accounts. Neither will they be silent on the subject of your treatment of them, nor tongue-tied as to its cause. They will not scruple to publish abroad that you sacrificed them to save yourselves.

And such an imputation may prejudice your business in another direction—it may arrest and turn aside the backward flow of your deposits. Those who have withdrawn their money from your Bank, as a matter of precaution, will be apt to take it in the end to the bank which has shewn most strength during the crisis.

But whatever steps it may be necessary to take, you must not hesitate for a moment at any sacrifice needful for the safety of the Bank—not the sacrifice of your Consols at any price, nor the loss of half your business, if need be ; because no effort must be spared, within reach of human accomplishment, whatever the cost may be, to avoid the catastrophe of a stoppage.

The working of a bank, then, on an inadequate reserve, might bring it, under conceivable circumstances, within the range of consequences, weighed against which, the profit arising from such a course of working would be as dust in the balance.

The principle is liable to the further objection that it will deprive your arrangements with your customers of that quality of fixity which they ought to have ; and on which your constituents, with fair shew of reason, have a right to repose. You cannot work a bank with justice to them, or advantage to yourself, on the hand-to-mouth principle. Your reserve ought always to be sufficiently ample to meet, not only all ordinary, but all exceptional demands upon it, without disturbing existing arrangements.

You must give yourself elbow-room in the government of your finances. To be all liberality at one time, and to be putting the screw on all round at another, is a system of management which may deprive you of some of your best accounts, but is not calculated to attract fresh ones.

When a man in business finds himself in search of a banker, he will naturally give the preference to the strongest bank; because, if he is a borrower, it is of consequence to him that his banker shall always be able, panic or no panic, to afford him his usual monetary facilities. On the other hand, if he is a lender, the bank with the strongest balance-sheet will be the most likely to commend itself to his choice.

In evidence of this, I have before me the returns for ten years of four English joint stock country banks, each having nearly the same amount of Capital and Rest.

It has been the usage of two of these to work on an average reserve of 15 per cent.; and their deposits shew an increase, for the ten years, of 45 per cent. on their previous amount. The other two have worked on an average reserve of 30 per cent., and their deposits shew an increase of 80 per cent. on their previous amount.

Now if these last named Banks had worked on a basis of 15 per cent., that would have released to them £600,000 of their reserves for more profitable employment; which, on the basis of our former estimate, would have brought them in an extra profit of £6000 a year. But in that case, the increase in their deposits, other things being equal, would have been less than it actually was by £1,200,000. In gaining £6000 a year, therefore, by working on a small reserve, they would have failed to acquire fresh business bringing them in £12,000 a year.

Other influences, no doubt, besides the relative strength of balance-sheets and reserves, may have had the effect of attracting depositors more or less to one bank or the other; but making all allowance for this, it is at least a reasonable proposition, that the immediate gain which may arise from working on a small reserve, may in the long run be largely outbalanced, in mere pounds, shillings, and pence, by working upon a large one.

There is one other point from which to regard the question of your reserve. We have seen that the nominal result of your working on the smaller one would be an apparent increase to your profits of £3500 a year. Under the most favourable circumstances, and making no abatement for loss of any kind, this would enable you to increase your dividend from 15 to 16 per cent., and no more.

But one per cent. additional dividend per annum, at the cost of normal financial weakness, intermittent anxieties, and constant working at high pressure, would surely be a dearly bought advantage, even if it had no other drawbacks ?

Let no suggestion, then, from shareholders too eager for dividend, tempt you to snatch a precarious piofit and a fleeting popularity, by working on an inadequate reserve. The safety and steady progress of the Bank stand far in front of all other considerations, and must never be put in jeopardy, whatever the effect on your dividend may be. Better fifteen per cent. and safety, than twenty per cent. and danger.

The present market value of your share capital is £900,000. What if a movement upon your deposits should overtake you with an insufficient reserve, amidst all the unreason and terror of a panic, and you have to stop payment? The one per cent. which you may have added to dividend by working on a small reserve, will be a conscience-smiting set-off to a shrinkage in the price of your shares from nine hundred thousand pounds to nothing, in a day. Even if, after paying off your deposits and other liabilities, you had still your Capital and Rest intact, and were able, out of these, eventually to return £15 per share to your proprietors; the loss to them would still be a calamitous one. Prior to the stoppage, the market price of the shares was £30. There would consequently be a loss of £15 per share, or £450,000 in all. In other words, the goodwill of your business, which this sum would represent, will have vanished into air. To have put in peril a business bringing in £50,000 a year, for the paltry sake of an additional £3500, would be a startling illustration of what it is in the finance of banking to be penny wise and pound foolish.

A RESERVE OF ONE-THIRD. Let us now consider the effects of the withdrawal of £250,000 of your deposits, should you decide to work the Bank on the basis of a reserve of one-third, as set forth in our balance-sheet, viz. :

Cash in hand . . .	£200,000
Cash at call, etc. . . .	350,000
Consols	300,000

In all £850,000

You would of course meet the withdrawals ·as they arose, out of your moneys at call and short notice ; because these moneys have been thus set apart expressly to provide against unusual demands.

You would take this course, for the further reason that it would enable you to meet the drain, without having to press any of your customers for a reduction of their advances, or a limitation of their discounts, at a time when such pressure might be a serious loss and inconvenience to them.

By this abstention you will secure not only their good will, but their good word, which may not be without its value even in the near future.

The Bank whose customers can proclaim, that their usual facilities were extended to them without grudge or abatement, throughout the money pressure, will clearly have a better chance of enlarging its constituency, than the Bank which has earned for itself the reputation of having sacrificed a score or two of its clients to save

itself   The fact that you have met the demands upon
you at all points with ease and equanimity, and that you
have not recalled a single overdraft, or refused the discount of a single good bill, will have the further effect
of bringing back to you the deposits which have been
withdrawn from you under the influence of fear; and
may possibly attract to your exchequer not a few of
those which have been taken from your weaker neighbours, if you have any.

After the cessation of the drain, your liabilities, as
reduced thereby, will stand thus:

To depositors, etc. . .	£2,300,000
Capital and Rest . .	450,000
	£2,750,000

whilst your assets will stand as shewn in the first column
of the statement following.

But if we are to apportion your assets on the basis
adopted in the construction of your balance-sheet, they
will have to be gradually brought to the figures of the
second column.

Reserve	£	£
Cash in hand . .	200,000	200,000
Cash at call . .	100,000	266,000
Consols . .	300,000	300,000
	600,000	766,000
Advances . .	960,000	910,000
Bills of Exchange .	1,190,000	1,074,000
	2,750,000	2,750,000

Your advances at present, it will be seen, are £50,000,
and your bills £116,000 in excess of limit, and must be
reduced accordingly, in order to restore your reserve to
its normal amount, of which it is exactly the sum of these
two items short, namely, £166,000.

But it may not be necessary to take steps to enforce this readjustment. The back-flow of your deposits, enlarged possibly by affluents from other sources, may of itself gradually restore your finances to their former equipoise, without your having to disturb a single profit-able account, or the discount limit of any good client.

If this shall prove too sanguine a view, your large reserve will at least have given you this point of vantage —it will have given you time: so that if you find that reductions have, after all, to be made in overdrafts and discounts, you will not have been driven to applying the knife summarily to some of your best accounts. You will be able to await the result of that operation on certain of your discounts and advances, which you may not be disinclined to curtail in any case.

In what amounts the resources of an English Country Bank, like the District Union, with its thirty Branches, ought to be apportioned to reserve, overdrafts, and discounts, is necessarily a matter of opinion, which will be governed to some extent by surrounding circumstances in each case.

But whatever limit you do assign to these great heads of account, you must be prepared for a daily tendency in your actual figures to deviate from them. Your *pro formâ* balance-sheet—that is, the statement of how your resources ought to stand,—has, therefore, to be reconstructed every time your books are balanced, if you would have a continual and exact knowledge of the deviations from standard of the appointed totals of your resources. But it is not necessary, neither would it be expedient, to proceed at once to rectify every divergence as it arises betwixt your actual and *pro formâ* figures; because in the ordinary course of things such deviations will frequently rectify themselves. An excess of discounts one week, may be balanced by a decrease in the next. An overplus in your cash one day may be more than absorbed the following day. Heavy checking on some accounts may be coincident with heavy lodgments on others. So long, therefore, as your figures exhibit

only a limited range of departure from standard, you will
properly abstain from interference, and allow them to
right themselves if they will.   But if you find the total
of your overdrawn accounts, for instance, shewing a
steady increase week by week, with an obvious tendency
to stand permanently in excess of the limit which you
have assigned to them, you will have to apply the curb
firmly: because the celerity with which your resources
will flow in this direction, if unchecked, offers a remarkable contrast to the tardiness with which they will flow
back again when you want them.

That is a mole-eyed method of banking, which looks
merely to the safety and profit of proposed accounts,
and accepts them accordingly, without regard to their
incidence on the financial position of the Bank.   A
dividend thus inflated is not the be all, although it might
well become the end all, of a bank.   However tempting
in point of gain offered transactions may be, a manager
has to refuse them, no matter with what degree of
reluctance, if their adoption would have the effect of
seriously disturbing the regulated balance of his finances.

COMPOSITION OF THE RESERVE.   We have thus far
discussed the value and incidence of your reserve as a
whole.   We have still to consider the question of its
component parts.

As regards the cash in hand, which is put at £200,000,
it represents 8 per cent. of your deposits.   Some will
deem the amount too small, but no one, I think, will
look upon it as excessive.   It is intended to cover, and
will sufficiently cover, under ordinary circumstances, the
difference between your receipts and payments of cash
on any one day.

The amount of your cash in hand, moreover, will be
governed in some measure by the next item—cash at
call and short notice, £350,000; because moneys thus
placed can be put into your till practically by return
of post.   Regarded in this light, your cash virtually in

hand amounts to £550,000, or about 23 per cent. of your deposits.

The cash in hand and at call held by 101 joint stock banks at 31 Dec. 1882, amounted to 59 millions, as against 257 millions of deposits.* The deposits, therefore, exceeded the cash in hand and at call in the ratio of 4.35 to 1. Your position is almost identical with this: your deposits exceed your cash in hand and at call by 4.36 to 1.

Your Consols are put at £300,000, and they yield you interest at a trifle over 3 per cent.; but your moneys in the hands of the bill-brokers will not yield you such a return. On the average of the last ten years, as we have seen, the yield would have been £2 2s. 8d. per cent. Why not, therefore, you suggest, put more of your reserve in Consols and less of it at call? Why not half a million in Consols, and £150,000 with the brokers; and thus net an additional income of £1750 a year?

But by thus reducing your money with the brokers to £150,000, you leave a margin between you and your Three per cents. so limited, that fluctuations in the ordinary movements of your business may oblige you to resort to your Consols more frequently than would be expedient. Every now and then you may have to buy or sell; and as a rule you will have to buy when money is cheap, and sell when it is dear. You will thus, for the most part, have to buy in the dearest, and sell in the cheapest market. You might of course avoid selling, by borrowing on your Consols: but frequent borrowing, or selling, or buying had best be avoided. Do not let the adjustment of your finances become subject to the fidgets. Give yourself at all times a sufficient margin within which to work. This will pay you better in the long run, than by working things continually within a hair's breadth of necessity and within a stone's cast of danger.

But why Consols, you ask, and always Consols? Why

---

* *Economist,* 19th May, 1883.

not invest a portion of the reserve in other first-class securities yielding a better return of interest?

The reason is this—Consols stand unrivalled and alone in the supreme quality of convertibility. They are the one security which you can, with absolute certainty, turn into cash at any hour of any business day in the worst throes of panic. You cannot rest assured of this in respect of any other description of securities —not even of the British Government itself Your Consols are virtually so many Bank of England Notes in a latent form, but with this advantage,—that they yield you three per cent. whilst practically forming a portion of your till-money.

RE-DISCOUNTING. The re-discount, or sale of a portion of its bills, is often an important feature in the financing of an English country bank.

If you sold £500,000 of your bills, you could discount an equal amount in fresh ones with the proceeds, and, as a rule, make a profit on the transaction; but not always. It would be a reasonable estimate to put the profit on such transactions at one per cent. per annum, or £5000 a year. But against this you have to set the possible loss on the extra £2,000,000 in bills, which you will have to discount every year in order to realize this profit.

Even that is a minor objection. Your liabilities to the public already exceed your paid-up Capital and Rest in the proportion of nearly six to one; and it would not be desirable to add, by your own act, half a million to these liabilities, and thus raise the disproportion to a higher figure.

The District Union Bank, as the holder of so large an amount of deposits, ought never to be seen in the re-discount market. It ought to work within its own resources. Not to do so, would be to inflate its proper business beyond its natural limits, and to increase any strain upon its credit in adverse times.

But the objections which apply to banks having ample

resources within themselves, do not apply to banks placed in districts of great industrial activity, where deposit money is scarce and the demand for loan capital is great. There is nothing opposed to sound banking principle in banks, thus placed, supplementing their resources, by re-discounting portions of their bills, and thus drawing supplies from the London market. A bank, by this process, merely transfers that portion of its discount business to London, which is in excess of its local means to meet it.

This I say is a legitimate branch of the business of such banks, provided the banks do not allow it to tempt them to maintain a too limited reserve to meet their other liabilities. If it be a wise and necessary course for a bank which never re-discounts a bill, to maintain at all times an ample reserve to meet any possible demand upon its deposits, it cannot surely be less incumbent on a re-discounting bank to do so? If the District Union Bank holds a reserve of one-third the amount of its deposits, in its present position; it would surely not hold less than a third, if it should add one-fifth to its other liabilities in the form of bills re-discounted? The deposits of a re-discounting bank are not less likely to be drawn upon in times of pressure, than those of other banks : the same relative adequacy of reserve ought, therefore, to be held against them.

It will go against the grain, no doubt, when a Manager finds himself obliged at times to replenish his reserve by re-discounting bills, at a percentage considerably beyond what the proceeds will yield him at call; but he must accustom himself to face this form of depletion with Spartan endurance, and to meet any suggestion to the contrary, come from what quarter it may, with resolute resistance. The re-discounting bank which should disregard the principle of maintaining at all times a sufficient reserve, and rely exclusively on re-discounts to replenish its till when necessary, would become virtually beholden to the good-will and ability of its London agents or bill-brokers, to carry it through the first monetary crisis.

The Bank which should rest its financing on so narrow a plank as this, would manifestly place itself within measurable range of disaster: for it is no disparagement to London banks or London bill-brokers, to imagine a time, in the monetary vicissitudes of the future, in which they might be unable to afford it the assistance required. There has been a time, within living memory, when you could not discount even an Exchequer Bill of the English Government in all Lombard Street.*

The danger of the situation to such a bank will be seriously enhanced, if its London agents and brokers already hold as much as they care to hold of its indorsements, in the existing condition of the money market. And another danger may lie in this—the choicest bills of the bank may be already under re-discount. Its portfolio may have been denuded of all, except bills of a quality which would only pass muster in ordinary times. When most in need of bills of supreme quality, it may have none of them to carry it through the Black Friday of the future, should that evil day ever come again.

Let us hope that it never may; but that the Bank which has placed itself in a position so full of peril may, nevertheless, be pulled through somehow, and the very worst avoided. In this event, the anguish of mind which its Directors and Manager will have passed through, during the terrible march of the crisis, will have revealed to them, with an emphasis to be remembered, the sickening possibilities which may attend the working of any bank on an inadequate Reserve.

* The late Mr. Masterman made this statement in the House of Commons, in October, 1847; and the Act of 1844, to the best of my recollection, was suspended the following day.

LETTER XXX.

ADVANCES.

It is certain that the greatest part of trade is driven by young merchants upon borrowing at interest; so as if the usurer either call in or keep back his money, there will ensue presently a great stand of trade. BACON.

UNDER the heading of Advances, in your balance-sheet, are included overdrawn accounts, temporary and special advantages, and, to avoid detail, various minor heads of account; but for all purposes of argument, it will suffice to treat the whole as consisting of overdrafts and advances.

The limit we assigned to these was £960,000, and was thus arrived at:—

Paid up Capital and Rest .	£450,000
20 per cent. of Deposits, etc. .	510,000
	£960,000

The figures are purely arbitrary, as were those on which we based the other apportionments of your assets. Whether they represent the exact quota of your resources which may with prudence be thus employed, is a point on which opinions will differ,—some will think the proportion too restricted; others will regard it as over-much.

The usage of London banks in this matter necessarily differs from that of the provinces, because metropolitan deposits are subject to greater fluctuations than those of country banks : a London bank must, therefore, retain a larger relative proportion of its resources in living forms of asset. The deposits in country banks consist, for the greater part, of the savings of quiet country people ; who do not trouble their heads, as we have seen, about the state of the foreign exchanges, the reserve of bullion, or the ups and downs of the money and share markets. They are not of a speculative turn. In the management of their banking affairs they are rather restful than fidgety ; and will at times leave their deposits for years undisturbed, except for the accretion of fresh savings or accrued interest. They know that the money is at their command, principal and interest, in full, at any time when wanted ; they are therefore content to let it rest at a moderate rate of interest, until a good mortgage offers itself, or a tempting bit of property comes on the market.

No doubt there are varieties of provincial depositors to which this pastoral sketch will not apply. There are portions of country deposits, especially in the larger towns and cities, which are as restless and fugitive as those of the metropolis :—nevertheless, the dominant feature of provincial deposits is a limited range of fluctuation and consequent steadiness of total.

It is this stability in the general mass of their deposits, which enables country banks to employ a considerable percentage of them in overdrawn accounts and advances ; but this percentage will be governed, to some extent, by the nature of the overdrafts. Many of these, no doubt, will be as fixed in character as your Bank buildings or your office fittings, and therefore equally unavailable for the payment of deposits. At the same time, these permanent overdrafts are your most lucrative form of account ; and they will always be the last which you will seek to disturb, so long as they continue within their appointed limit, in the marshalling of your assets.

On the other hand, your temporary advances on first-class railway stock, or on produce warrants, or other marketable securities, are only second in a financial point of view, to bills of exchange themselves. You cannot, it is true, re-discount such advances and turn them into money at any moment; but they will turn themselves into money, when due, equally with paper of the first quality. They will afford you the principal means wherewith to maintain the equilibrium of your finances, with least friction; because, being impersonal advances,—loans based more upon the value of the security than on the responsibility of the borrowers, and made at the lowest rate of interest to which the market can be pressed down,. —you have no hesitation in regulating the amount of such loans in absolute accordance with the requirements of your own business. In these and other forms of temporary advance, you have a quasi Reserve, of which you can avail yourself at any time, in whole or in part, without scruple and without offence. When the demands upon you for more lucrative forms of advance increase in volume, you allow your railway and other forms of temporary loans to run off in a corresponding ratio: when these demands slacken, the outflow of your resources towards such temporary employment will re-commence. The principle will be well-nigh self-acting, like the ball-cock in a cistern.

BANK CREDITS. Certain of your customers import produce from foreign parts, for which, in some countries, they have to pay before shipment. The seller abroad will not part with his commodity before he has value received, in money or its equivalent. This is provided by the importer sending the seller your letter of credit, which authorizes him to draw upon your Bank up to a certain indicated amount. Another form of credit gives authority to firms abroad to draw upon the Bank 'against documents '—that is, for the invoice amount of goods, produce, or commodities, at specified limits of price, which are not to be exceeded.

The risks run in the issue of credits chiefly depend upon the arrangements which you make with the parties to whom you issue them. You are bound to accept the drafts drawn under these documents when they are presented for acceptance, if the drafts are in order,—whatever may have happened to your customers in the meantime. From the date, therefore, on which you issue a credit to a customer, he becomes indebted to you for whatever sums may be drawn upon you under it.

If the Credit is for a specific amount, you must regard that amount as so much advanced to the customer on overdraft, and deal with it accordingly. The fact that you may not be called upon to pay the money for months—possibly not at all—does not alter the fact, that you have undertaken a responsibility which you may have to face, and against which you have to protect yourself the moment it begins to run.

If the Credit is for an indefinite amount; that is to say, if the bills drawn under it are limited to the value of certain produce or commodities at indicated prices, you will no doubt see that your customer provides you with a margin, in cash or convertible securities, which will be amply sufficient to cover all contingencies.

There are persons of good judgment, who look upon this description of transaction, as being the busines rather of a mercantile house than a country bank. It involves certain obvious risks; it enlarges the volume of your liabilities; it requires special mercantile knowledge to conduct it with safety; and even with the best of knowledge, you will hardly escape collision on disputed points and an occasional law-suit. Moreover, the rate of commission has now become attenuated to a point that renders the business barely worth the doing; except with customers who have other claims upon you, and to whom you cannot refuse this form of accommodation when they require it.

To revert briefly to your advances as a whole: the question remains—Will it be prudent to lock up 20 per cent. of your deposits, in addition to your paid-up Capital and Rest, in this form of banking asset,—the remaining 80 per cent. of your deposits being represented by cash, Consols, and bills of exchange?

It is a question of usage and expediency. We have already discussed the advantages which accrue to a bank from a strong balance-sheet. We have seen, on the other hand, that profits derived from an over-investment of its deposits are often delusive, and more than lost, in the long run, by collateral disadvantage and danger. Against profits thus earned, you have to place the profits that ' might have been '—profits arising from that increase of business which a strong balance-sheet is calculated, as we have seen, to attract, and a weak one to repel.

And you have also to keep in view that the sum of your commitments in the direction of authorized overdrafts is not merely what your debtors owe you at the moment, but what they might owe you, if they should avail themselves of their limits of overdraft to the full. It is improbable that all your over-drawn accounts will at any time stand at the extreme range of their limits; but it is more than probable that your accounts will make a nearer general approach to that position in a time of pressure, than in a time of ease.

But whatsoever limit you decide to adopt as the maximum of your overdrawn accounts, it will be well to keep in mind that on one side of it lies safety, and on the other the path to danger. There is no channel into which your funds will flow with greater alacrity, if they are not watched with care and checked by the strong hand. The overdrafts of a bank bear some such rela-

15

tion to its stability, as dead-weight in cargo bears to the sea-worthiness of a ship. Your overdrafts constitute your financial dead-weight : admit too much on board, and thus get below your load-line, and you will find the Bank labouring heavily the first time you have to face a head sea of discredit.

LETTER XXXI.

ADVANCES TO SHAREHOLDERS.

A great part of the proprietors when they paid in their first instalments, opened a cash account with the Bank, and the Directors . . . . allowed many of them to borrow upon this cash account, when they paid in upon all their subsequent instalments. Such payments therefore only put into one coffer what had a moment before been taken out of another.

WEALTH OF NATIONS.

You have a primary lien on the shares of your Bank by your Deed of Settlement. In case of need, you can hold them as against all other creditors, until your advance upon them, principal, interest and costs, is paid in full. Your £10 shares sell with steadiness in the open market at £30 each, and you take them at that price as cover for advances.

But even in the case of London and North Western Stock you require a margin when you make an advance against it. If so, why omit a similar precaution when you make advances on the security of your own shares? Moreover, the price of its shares, however sound a bank may be, is subject to swift and serious depression in periods of distrust or panic. The shares of many of the soundest banks in the Kingdom went down in a few weeks, in the scare of 1878, some 30 to 40 per cent. An equivalent drop in the price of your shares, would bring them to £20, and leave your margin 33 per cent. on the wrong side;—for every £3000 advanced against the shares, your security would have shrunk to £2000.

It is no answer to this objection, to plead that no such drop in your shares did or ever will take place. We

227

are not as yet in sight of the millennium of finance, nor
the perpetual repose of bank deposits; and the course
of panic is capricious.

The storm passed high over the heads of the smaller
joint stock banks in 1878; but it does not follow that the
next disturbance in our monetary atmosphere will take
the same direction.

Moreover, the true value of its own shares to a bank,
is not their current price in the market, but their intrinsic value—that is, the amount which your paid-up
capital and rest would yield per share, if rateably divided
amongst your proprietors.

There are 30,000 of your shares, and your capital
and rest amount to £450,000. The intrinsic value
of each of your shares is therefore £15; or about
half the value at which you take them as a security for
advances.

Now, if a bank shall make it a part of its business to
allow advances on its own shares at market price,
looking to them as its sole and sufficient security, and
without regard to the means of the borrower, it must
happen in time, that a portion of its capital will be held
by people of little or no means.

What this portion may attain to, will depend upon
circumstances. It may never exceed a small percentage,
or it may reach a large one. But let us take a moderate
figure, and say that 5 per cent. of its capital, or 1500 of
its shares, shall come to be held, in process of time, by
persons who are indebted to the Bank to the full market
value of their holdings,—£30 a share, and have no other
means or property to fall back upon.

Let us, then, imagine that by reason of frequent
losses, an unprofitable and decaying business, or any
other cause, you decide to wind up. In that event one
half of the £45,000 which you may have advanced
without other security to the impecunious amongst your
proprietary, would become a loss.

It may be about an even chance, as you protest, that
the skies shall fall, as that anything can ever lead to the

winding up of the District Union Bank; and the contingency is sufficiently remote, with such a balance-sheet as yours, to render it an unimportant factor in your calculations. But the contingency is one, nevertheless, which cannot be altogether ignored, in any view of the matter which shall claim to be exact, and to embrace all eventualities.

It has further to be observed, that the man who owes his bank the full market value of his shares in it is, strictly speaking, only a shareholder in name. The Bank has virtually provided him with the means wherewith to purchase the shares, and they are pledged to it to their full market price. The shares, it is true, stand in his name, and he is entitled in right of them to attend all meetings of shareholders and to carry himself thereat, in all respects, as if he were an independent shareholder and did not owe the Bank a shilling.

But, apart from the obvious objections to shareholders of this type, there are others of equal gravity. No one ought to become a shareholder in a bank, unless he is in a position, not only to pay for his shares with his own money, but also to meet, from the same source, whatever calls may at any time be made upon them.

Your Directors have the power to make this an indispensable condition of proprietorship: they are empowered by your Deed of Settlement to reject, as a shareholder, anyone of whom they do not approve.

The proprietary of a bank, were they thousands in number, are merely a huge business firm, and ought to have the same liberty of choice which any private firm has, in the selection of fresh partners. This privilege of choice they delegate to their Directors; and if it is not exercised, portions of the stock may gradually drift into the hands of persons of insufficient substance—with the results which we have just indicated.

There is a yet further objection to advances on the security of your own shares, which is this;—If you lend back your paid-up capital or any portion of it to yourselves—for that is the practical operation of such advances—your capital becomes diminished for the time being by the total amount thus lent, and your financial strength will be weakened in like degree.

It does not follow that those of your shareholders, who require to borrow money, must therefore be driven from your doors to seek for it elsewhere. It only follows that they ought to cover the money borrowed, by security other than their bank shares; or that they should be safe beyond all question for the loans without security at all.

But even shareholders of means, or supposed means, do fail occasionally, and their shares become forfeit to the Bank. When this happens, the shares ought to be sold with the least possible delay ; because, so long as they remain unsold, they are simply a cancelment of that portion of your capital which they represent. The Bank, for the moment, has absorbed a portion of its own substance.

LETTER XXXII.

LARGE ACCOUNTS.

When you are indebted any great sum, your creditor observes you with no less regard than if he were bound to you for some huge benefit, and will quake to give you the least cause of offence, lest he lose his money. BEN JONSON.

IN your preliminary enquiry into the position of your overdrawn accounts, you will no doubt take special note of those, if any, which are largely in excess of the average of your individual advances. I say, if any, because it is to be desired that your Bank may have no such untoward burdens to carry, as a few huge accounts, absorbing a large portion of its capital, and uncovered, or imperfectly covered, by security. Every bank failure which has happened during the last forty years, has been brought about by reason of facilities of scandalous extent granted to three or four favoured accounts.

I have before me some particulars, taken from the detailed balance-sheet of a bank, with a paid-up capital of a million and a magnificent connection, which failed in 1857. Three-fourths of its business were as sound as a banking business could be; but the other fourth was represented by a few accounts, which absorbed amongst them a million and a half of money, in advances and discounts which were well-nigh worthless. A powerful bank was thus brought to the ground, and a business worth £70,000 a year scattered to the winds.

The balance-sheet of another bank, which failed in 1866, reveals the same story: a large paid-up capital and a valuable connection; more than half its business of first-rate excellence; the remainder as bad as it was in the power of foolish men to make it.　Its large capital, and half as much again, were swallowed up in a few monstrous accounts, with the usual result—a final break down and utter wreck of an institution, which, under sane management, had before it a long career of usefulness and success.

The figures now quoted, however, although sufficiently startling, were terribly surpassed by those of Overend, Gurney & Co.

The Black Friday of 1866 was signalized by a failure which, for a time, stood alone in its bad eminence amongst the calamities of banking.　The lowest deep in banking disaster, it was felt, had been reached at last.　It was held to be beyond belief, that a noble business could ever again be wrecked by such high-handed incompetency, and millions of money cast away with such disastrous prodigality.　But the bursting up of the City of Glasgow Bank dissipated these complacencies as with a thunderclap.　The losses of Overend, Gurney & Co. were enormous, but they stood eclipsed in the awful shadow of the other failure.　Shameful as were some of the figures of the great discount house, they failed to reach the altitude of five millions of loss on four accounts.

If it be asked how such evils arise and are developed, the answer is not far to seek—they arise from transactions entered upon, either in sheer ignorance or in reckless violation of the fundamental principles of banking ; and once entered upon, they develop themselves with fatal swiftness of growth.

If the Directors and Managers who are accountable for these things, had controlled their advances on the commonplace principles followed by you at Oxborough, such overwhelming loss to shareholders, and shame and scandal to British banking, would never have arisen.

When you assume the management in chief, therefore, of the District Union Bank, the homely ways of banking which you have followed in Oxborough with success, will be found of equal soundness if practised at head-quarters, although you may have to apply them on a larger scale. But let the largeness of the scale be always within the limits of moderation, and let your face be resolutely set against 'big accounts,' no matter how large the apparent profit on them may be, unless you are covered in every case by sufficient and immediately convertible security.

No doubt there are firms in England, to whom it would be as safe to advance without security £100,000, as it would be to advance £1000 to others. Nevertheless, for the District Union, or any other Bank, to advance a third of its capital on any one account, without immediately convertible security, would under any circumstances be an act of financial temerity, which might place its management some day on the same platform with those developments of banking, the outcome of which the nation has more than once beheld with shame and resentment.

Even if covered by convertible securities, the amount would be dangerously large. If the borrower should stop payment in a time of monetary pressure, when failures most abound, and when the public appetite for evil report is at its highest capacity of digestion, the result might be seriously detrimental to the credit of your Bank. Even if after many days you get your money back again, a doubt will have been engendered as to the prudence of your management, which may not be without its effect on the future of your business. The putting of too many eggs in one basket, has a homely significance even in the ordering of a banking business.

With such a capital as yours, it would be more expedient to lay £100,000 out in a hundred advances of £1000 each, than in a block to one huge borrower. For one reason, the risk would be less. It is better to have a hundred men liable for a given sum, than only one man. Even if you select your smaller borrowers so badly, that a score of them shall collapse during the course of the first commercial crisis; these petty failures, compared with the smashing up of your big customer, would be as the rattle of musketry to the explosion of a shell.

And there is another argument in favour of the smaller class of accounts. They pay better. The turn-over on such accounts is relatively greater than on large ones. The capital of the shopkeeper is turned over more frequently than that of the merchant. A business which involves large transactions, at long dates, in distant lands, is easily distanced in the matter of turn-over, by one conducted on the principle of the 'nimble penny.'

And there is yet another consideration. You are less liable .to be drawn in, when the account is of moderate amount. When a client, whose overdraft is already up to its limit, comes to you on the third of the month, and threatens that unless you assist him with a further advance without security to meet his acceptances for the morrow, he must suspend his payments; I conclude that you will refuse to be thus 'cornered.' You will prefer to stand where you are. You will decline to furnish him with a fresh grant of the Bank's money, in order that he may pay certain creditors in full, and leave the Bank by so much further in the lurch.

But when the great Anglo-Indian house of Synkheim Brothers, with a capital of a million, 'as everybody knows,' and on the strength of which they are already in debt to their bankers a tenth part of that amount: I say, when these gentlemen come to their bankers, with a list of their acceptances for the month, amounting, let us say, to some fifty thousand pounds, the case is different. It ought not to be, but unhappily it is so. The Brothers Synkheim represent to the Bank Manager that their shipments of Manchester and other goods to the East have been unusually large, and the markets for their sale unusually adverse; and that, in consequence, their remittances by the present mail will not suffice, without a further temporary advance from the Bank, to provide for their acceptances now becoming due.

The Manager, awed by the presence of the members of a firm worth a million of money, summons courage, nevertheless, to murmur something about security. This the firm would cheerfully give; but, as it happens, the whole of their resources at the present moment are unfortunately at the other side of the globe.

We all know what has too often happened; the extra advance will be conceded, and the power of the Bank to resist further involvement by so much impaired.

A bank can make its mind up, without serious effort, to face the loss of a thousand or two; but no bank can regard, without dismay, the possible stoppage of a house owing it £100,000. It would be infinitely better for all concerned, as a rule, to let the house go down at once— even if it should carry the Bank with it, rather than put to risk another pound.

But this has not been the usage always. On the contrary, we find that in too many cases, a few large accounts are allowed to grow to abnormal figures, until a point is reached when the borrowers become masters of the Bank, and they and it drive blindly on to mutual perdition.

You put the question—Are such culpable perversions of banking principle possible in the future? Will credit ever again be shattered, or the public conscience outraged, by a second Overend & Co., or another City of Glasgow Bank? I think the question may confidently be answered in the negative.

For one reason, nearly every joint stock bank in the three Kingdoms is now bound to publish a balance-sheet, at least once a year; and that balance-sheet has to be signed and certified by three of its Directors and its Manager as true, under penalties which few gentlemen will care to face, if it prove to be false. If they have put their signatures to a deliberate mis-statement, the shame and the punishment will now be sure and swift.

But, in addition to the testimony of the Directors and Managers, there will henceforth be required a declaration on the face of every balance-sheet, signed by independent auditors, that it affords a true and accurate statement of the affairs of the Bank for the time being. I hold this certificate to be of more importance even than that of the Directors themselves, without thought of disparagement to them.

In the first place, in nearly every case, it will be the declaration of men whose training for life has been the analysis of accounts and the science of book-keeping. In the methods of research which are necessary to a responsible audit, they are experts, whom no sleight of hand in double-entry or fraudulent arithmetic will serve to hoodwink for a moment.

In the second place, the testimony of a public auditor is disinterested. He has no object to serve in deceiving the public, or the shareholders, as to the actual position of the Bank. His interest is to tell the truth, come what may.

Lastly, the auditor is not appointed by the Directors. He is chosen annually by the shareholders, and his remuneration is fixed by them. He is not therefore a servant of the Board; it can neither influence nor dismiss him. He is virtually the detective of the shareholders,—chosen by them to keep an eye upon the Directors: not necessarily an eye of doubt, or suspicion; but to test and verify their annual statement of facts, and make assurance of their figures doubly sure.

A fraudulent balance-sheet, under the altered condition of things, appears to me, therefore, to be no longer a possible thing. It is impossible that the books of any bank can ever again be materially falsified by the most astute or the most nefarious of officials, without immediate detection.

Therefore, there can be no more falsified bank balance-sheets. Losses in banking will no doubt arise at times in the future, if banking principle be disregarded; but they will be subject to early detection and prompt exposure. There will be no more ruinous bolstering up of large and dangerous accounts. The auditors will see to this, if the Directors do not: so that a second edition of the City of Glasgow Bank, even on a reduced scale, is henceforth beyond the range of probability.

LETTER XXXIII.

BILLS OF EXCHANGE.

Amongst many roses some thistles grow, some bad weeds and enormities, which much disturb the peace of this body politick, eclipse the honour and glory of it, fit to be rooted out and with all speed to be reformed. ANATOMY OF MELANCHOLY.

THE bill of exchange is the highest form of banking security. It even excels Consols, as such, in one respect—its principal sum is not subject to depreciation; it will be paid in full when it reaches maturity; whereas an equal sum invested in Consols would yield on realization simply the price of the day. The price may have advanced, it is true, but it is equally possible that it may have receded. A bill, moreover, is unsurpassed in facility of transfer. The mere signature of the indorser transfers all property in the instrument to you as effectually as if the transfer were embodied in a conveyance of the regulation length on lawyers' vellum.

If the first bill of exchange had been framed by a leading conveyancer, reduced to shape in a committee of the whole House, and had suffered periodical amendment at the hands of the Legislature ever since, it becomes a curious speculation what complexity of form and measure of length this simplest of documents would have attained by this time. Fortunately for the commercial interests of the human race, it has escaped this ordeal, and remains to us an instrument altogether matchless in brevity of form, facility of transfer and simplicity of title. There is no difficulty in settling the title to a bill of exchange. You have but to assure yourself that the indorser is none other than himself and the point is settled. And you can with equal promptness and ease render the document inalienable, except by your own act and deed, by the simple process of specially indorsing it to the Bank, whereby you render it useless plunder to a thief

At a previous stage of this correspondence, we sought to analyse the class of bills which you would chiefly meet with, in a quiet country town like Oxborough.

We have now to glance at the varieties of paper with which you may have to deal, in the populous and busy commercial town where your Bank has its head-quarters, when you come to rule as its Manager in chief.

In the first order of merit, come bills bearing the names of banks or banking houses, as drawers, acceptors, or indorsers, together with other names of high standing. These bills stand A 1 in the estimation of the discount market, and the fanciful speak of them as gilt-edged. Then we have 'remittance paper'—bills drawn by houses abroad on banks, or correspondents in England. Then comes 'inland drawn' paper—bills drawn by the shippers of goods on the agents in England of the houses abroad, to whom the goods are shipped. Anon we come upon brokers' paper—bills drawn by importers against commodities placed in brokers' hands for sale. Then we reach the immense class of bills arising out of our manifold trades and industries, which pass under the term of 'trade paper:' and finally, we have a nondescript class, of limited amount, consisting of promissory notes or loan-bills; such as those of Bowdler on Starkey, and the like.

It may chance, however, unless due caution has been exercised by your predecessor in office, that bills are to be found in your portfolio which do not come strictly within any of these definitions. We have seen that even in quiet humdrum Oxborough, bills may be fabricated and set afloat against values purely fictitious.

But bills may be drawn against values only too ponderous. Bills, for example, are sometimes drawn against ships or steamers in the course of construction. Where the acceptor is a man of sufficient means himself, or where he has an 'ownery' for the vessels, from whom he is able to collect the money needful to meet the bills as they mature, there is little to be said: but if his ownery is not in hand,—if it consists of persons who owe their existence for the most part to a hopeful imagination,—he will not be able to meet his acceptances at maturity; and if the builder cannot take them up, the bills will have to be renewed and additional ones drawn, to provide the wherewithal to complete the vessel and send her to sea.

What may next happen is problematical.; she may prove a lucky ship, or she may prove to be the reverse: but in either event, the native element of vessels thus launched and sent to sea, is manifestly paper. They float as much on bills as on the ocean wave; and the outcome to the discounters of such paper—as witness the experiences of Overend, Gurney & Co.—is ordinarily more disastrous than exhilarating.

It is not the province of banking to discount bills, the proceeds of which are to provide the acceptors with fixed capital. A man may properly be drawn upon against goods, produce, or commodities which he is turning over in his business from day to day; but not against his buildings or machinery. These are not floating capital. He cannot meet his acceptances with factories or fixtures, buildings or machinery. These represent his fixed capital, and are provided by himself out of his own means, or they ought to be. In any case, they are no basis to run bills of exchange upon; neither are vessels in course of construction, or navigating the high seas.

A ship-owner, or ship's husband, may properly be drawn upon for sails, or cordage, or stores supplied to his ships, because there is a tangible fund in his incoming freights to meet such marine engagements: but when he accepts against the hull of a ship, he passes the recognized limits of negociable value, and his paper becomes ultra-marine in the estimation of the bill market.

Your largest holding of paper will, no doubt, consist of trade bills, the features of which we discussed at length in a former letter, and of which we took for an average sample the draft of Cartridge on Booker & Co.

Next in probable amount will come your holding of 'brokers' bills,'—a description of paper unknown to Oxborough—drawn by the owner of produce upon the broker in whose hands he has placed it for sale. The bill is usually accompanied by the written undertaking of the broker to apply the proceeds of the merchandise in payment of the bill. When this undertaking is supplemented by a warehouse warrant, shewing that the merchandise has been transferred into the name of the Bank, no safer transaction could well be offered you.

But the legal transfer of the property into the name of the Bank is indispensable, if absolute security is to be insured. If this is not done, neither the owner nor the Bank has control over the produce or commodity advanced upon. In that respect they have to trust entirely to the honour of the broker. It is rarely that this trust is abused, but it has been in certain flagrant instances; and this species of malversation will always be a possibility, where the letter of hypothecation is not backed by a warehouse-warrant in name of the Bank.

It is difficult to understand why this should not be done in every case, on principle; unless we are to concede that the borrower of money has a greater claim to be the holder of the commodity borrowed upon, than the Bank which lends the money; a contention which is clearly untenable, not to say ridiculous. By all laws of reason and business usage, the lender of money is held to be the natural holder of the property advanced upon.

You question whether leading brokers will take this view of the matter. If so, all that need be said is, so much the worse for the leading brokers; because they will thus divert such business into the hands of less substantial people, who will not be deterred by sentimental

16

scruples from giving business validity to business transactions.

With respect to bills drawn, indorsed, or accepted by banks, at home or abroad, of undoubted means and stability, and bearing other 'names of high standing, there will be no difficulty of selection. They will turn into bank notes of their own accord, as they fall due, and you will be without a care or anxiety in respect of them.

Bills drawn by houses abroad on their correspondents in England against actual shipments of merchandise to this country, and known to banks and bill-brokers as remittance paper, are frequently drawn upon banks or houses of the highest mercantile standing, and are in high repute and favour in the discount market.

As between this class of bills, and those drawn by English shippers on the agents in England of houses in India, China, or elsewhere abroad, there is this difference: in the case of remittance paper, the bills are drawn against value on its way to this country; in the other, the bills are drawn against value which is leaving this country for distant parts of the globe. A bill drawn against value which will be in hand before the bill falls due, obviously rests on a different basis from a bill drawn against commodities which, at the maturity of the bill, are being realized in the distant markets of the East or West.

KITE-FLYING. We have thus far dealt with bills drawn against 'value' actually given by the drawers and received by the acceptors of the bills; although we have not found the value of approved quality in every case. Nevertheless, we have found a value of some kind, underlying and forming the basis of each transaction. Every genuine bill of exchange is in fact the presentment and voucher of a mercantile or trading transaction, which has actually passed between the parties to the instrument. But we have yet to speak of certain bills of more nebulous quality—bills drawn and accepted against values received which have no existence —bills which have their origin and exclusive base in the predatory instincts of their makers. You have met, as we have seen, with an obvious 'kite' or two at Oxborough; but the character of this class of bill is not always so apparent: there are diversities of kites, as of other things.

When Mr. Julius Webber tenders for discount his draft on Wefton & Co., and you already hold certain drafts of theirs upon him, both being customers of your Bank, and both in the same line of business, you will not only look askance at the proffered transaction, but will naturally desire to know the basis on which the bills already afloat are supposed to rest. You will be vehemently assured, no doubt, that actual value has passed in every case. When Wefton & Co. run short of a certain class of goods, the friendly Webber lets them have some of his, and draws against them; similarly, when his stock requires 'assortment' they, with equal courtesy, furnish the needful and draw upon him therefor with equal promptitude. Nothing, they will assure you, could be more regular than their drawings upon each other.

In a certain sense—possibly not; but when two firms in the same trade take to exchanging goods with each other, and to drawing bills against the total of each exchange, instead of for the difference only, it is manifest that such bills have no more real foundation to rest upon, than if the same bale of goods were shuttlecocked backwards and forwards between the parties, whensoever either of them was moved with the desire to draw.

Let us suppose that Webber has bills running on Wefton & Co. for, say, £1500, for which he has sold and delivered them goods of equal value; and that Wefton & Co. have drafts running upon him for a similar amount, and for which they have supplied him with

actual value in goods. It is clear that by these operations they have raised £3000, without thereby adding a
shilling of value to their respective stocks in trade. It
is further manifest that by this financial hocus-pocus,
bills might be set afloat to an amount, not merely equal
to, but largely in excess of their combined stocks
in trade,—if banks could be found incautious enough
to discount paper of this light and airy description.

And there are other methods of kite-flying, equally
plausible, more difficult of detection, and only a shade
less censurable.

A. has imported a cargo of produce,—value, say, £5000,
which he sells to B., who buys it on speculation, and
re-sells it also on speculation to C., who disposes of it to
D., a wholesale dealer; who finally parts with it to the
trade, and draws upon the smaller buyers against sales.
Now, if bills are drawn at every stage of the process, as
they may easily be, a single cargo might thus be used
as a base to set afloat bills to three or four times its
value. The proceeds of each bill ought, in strictness,
to be applied, as soon as the bill is drawn, to take
up and cancel the previous one; but this is not the
usage. As a rule, A., B., C., and D., will prefer to have
£5000 each to play with for a few months, and their
respective bankers meanwhile will be the holders of
£20,000 in bills, three-fourths of which amount have
gone for the time being into other forms of commercial
speculation.

There is yet another description of paper against
which you have to be on your guard. The drawer and
acceptor of the bills may both be respectable English
firms; and there may be nothing on the face of the bills
to suggest irregularity. The drawer is an importer of
the produce or commodity which it is the special
business of the acceptors, his brokers, to deal in and
dispose of, and everything seems fair and above-board;
until some day, to your amazement, both firms give way

together.   You then discover that the bills were drawn, not against produce or commodities in the hands of the acceptors, but to provide the drawer with means to make advances to growers abroad, in anticipation of expected crops.

You further find, that the parties have been carrying this speculative game on for years, and that the frequent result of such trading has followed, and brought both concerns to grief.   You have been an unconscious instrument in effecting your own heavy loss, and abetting them in their own undoing.   You have been treating as genuine commercial paper a series of flagitious kites.

Your excuse is, that the bills had every appearance of validity.   There was respectability at both ends, and probability in the ostensible transactions; but unhappily there was a want of candour.   The bills, in every case, purported to be drawn as against so much value in hand and not against so much value in expectation. Had they been so drawn, it is needless to observe that they would never have seen the inside of your bill-case.

The polite moralist may draw a distinction betwixt the fabrication of bills of this description and the vulgar game of thimble-rig; but the banker who finds himself hocussed by such paper is apt, in his rage, to think that in dealing with a professed trickster, he would at least have the advantage of being on his guard.

You ask how you are to detect such paper when offered?   By the simple process of requiring, as in the case of other brokers' paper, that the acceptors shall hypothecate and transfer to the Bank the commodity against which the bills are drawn.   By a resolute enforcement of this necessary condition, you will avoid being the holders, henceforth, of bills drawn against values in the air.

But if we would know one of the causes of recurring panic and widespread banking loss, we have to look at methods of kite-flying, practised at higher levels and on areas of wider range, than are accessible to the Webbers and Weftons, or the Bargoods and Laxeys of trade; whose offences, compared with those of the larger practitioners of the craft, dwindle to petty larceny.

More than once during the current half century, bills have been drawn by certain large houses of the period on each other, against merchandise purporting to be on its way either to England or to English houses abroad, to the extent of millions—merchandise which had no existence beyond its fraudulent inscription on the face of fictitious bills.

The credit given to these houses was not made to rest on the homely principles on which banking at Oxborough is conducted. The credit given was not based upon an intimate knowledge of the parties themselves, their habits of life, their business capacities, their liabilities and their resources; but was accorded with lavish hand, in ignorance of these essential facts and regardless of the conclusions to which they might lead.

Neither would there seem to be much ground for hope that matters will be different in the future, so long as the engagements which any mercantile house may come under, in excess of its capital, are subject to no law of control, beyond what the house may see fit to impose upon itself. Limits are assigned to other things. We breathe and move in a labyrinth of legal and moral restraint; but there is no limit, in law or equity, to the most baleful expansion of commercial credit. In the progress of each decade, it grows and spreads unseen, until its presence, like the fire-damp, becomes known only by explosion.

If the paper of each house were to centre in any one bank, or discount house, some limit might be put to this fertile source of banking misfortune; but this is impracticable. Such paper is scattered throughout the country: here a little, there a little: each banker knowing how much he himself holds, but knowing nothing of the aggregate paper afloat of each house.

In this ignorance, he hugs himself with the belief that his few thousands on a house worth its plum, are as safe as the bank notes in his till—a form of delusion from which, every ten years or so, he has a rude awakening.

I protested five and thirty years ago, that the then recent losses on this pernicious brood of ' kites,' were sufficient to strike bankers dumb—but they would appear to have had the more serious effect of striking certain of our number blind. We have lived to witness developments of the bill system of 1847, and of other so-called forms of banking, on a scale of magnitude, in comparison with which the figures of that time shrink into abject insignificance. The practitioners of that early period were as pigmies, compared with the leviathan operators of a later time.

One cause, which has rendered the manufacture and negociation of such bills practicable, still exists. The intense competition for so-called high-class paper among London and other banks and discount houses, is still such as to enable any astute and speculative firm to have discount facilities in half-a-dozen different quarters at the same time.

Now, one old-fashioned rule of country banking was, and still is, to require that a man shall have only one banker, and to close his account if it is discovered that he has two ; and you will do well to adhere in all cases to this prudential rule in respect of your own customers. How can you know, with any approach to exact figures, what a man is doing, or how his affairs stand, if he is transacting a portion of his business elsewhere ? The very fact of his doing so excites a suspicion that he has some reason for withholding certain of his operations from your observation. When you lend him money, and discount his bills, you have a right to know the whole of his banking transactions ; otherwise you may awake some day to the knowledge, that he has been availing himself of facilities elsewhere, by means of which he has succeeded in deluding you as to his real position.

And you will find that some of the discount establishments in London afford such facilities to parties whom they know to be customers of country banks. Even with money of your Bank lying with them at call, they hold themselves at liberty to compete against you, with your own customers, for discounts, at your very doors. It is not a neighbourly policy, nor altogether a wise one; it is a question whether it even 'pays.' The broker who should practise this sort of competition would have no ground for complaint, if he found the money placed with him at call or short notice by the bank competed against, taking to itself wings to seek a more friendly shelter.

Would it not be a better way, even as a question of profit and loss, for a London bill broker gradually to limit the discount business coming to him from the provinces, to the bills of Country banks seeking re-discount? The same volume of country paper would still have to seek London for discount; but then, all such paper would reach the brokers through the medium of bankers on the spot. The broker would thus have the assurance that the bills had been selected by those who had un-rivalled means of judging of their regularity and safety; and this assurance would be strengthened by the indorsements of the banks. A broker's chances of loss on country paper would thus be reduced to vanishing point. If such a policy were gradually adopted—if London dis-counters of bills were gradually to close the door against all country business, except that coming to them from Country banks, or from provincial houses having no local bankers, the 'fast' firms of the future would find themselves pulled up by their bankers, long before their liabilities could reach the monstrous figures of the recent past.

By dealing direct with provincial customers, the dis-count broker no doubt obtains a rate of discount slightly in excess of what he would obtain, if the bills came to him through a Country bank and under its indorsement. But if against the small fraction of profit thus realized during, say, the last ten years, were placed the losses on such transactions; who can doubt on which side the balance of advantage would incline?

You ask how a Country banker, under the existing order of things, can best guard himself against danger in furnishing his bill-case with its necessary quota of first-class paper? You say that if enquiry had been made as to the position of any one of the large houses which have failed during the last quarter of a century, the answer, up to the very eve of their failure, would in all probability have been that their credit was beyond question. That is true, and because it is true, I would submit that a country bank had best secure its first-class paper through a first-rate discount house, and under its guarantee. This would render the operation safe beyond the reach of doubt, and would be doing by the bill brokers as you would have them do by you; you would thus avoid meddling with their business, as you would have them abstain from interference with yours.

Let us suppose that you choose instead, to select your first-class paper on the strength of your own judgment, and thereby gain a quarter per cent. per annum on each transaction. On a bill for £5000, having three months to run, your gain will be £3 2s. 6d., and no more. This will be the extent of your gain, by working without the light of a broker's experience, or the substantial backing of his guarantee.

Let it be the result of a discount business thus personally conducted, that the bill becomes a loss—a contingency which would not be without precedent—and the gain of £3 2s. 6d. for the sake of which you have risked so much, will seem pitiful indeed. Beware of these petty allurements of gain, which are as calculated

to swallow dividends up, every now and then, as to
enlarge them. ' I was caught by a morsel,' was the
mournful reflection of the fish in the adage.

When you have completed the investigation of your
bill-ease and made a synopsis of its contents, and would
know the financial value of the whole,—deduct from the
total, the amount of your promissory notes and loan
bills, and all paper of dubious quality, if you hold any,
and the difference will be the result required. In other
words, the amount remaining in your bill-case, after this
deduction is made, will represent the net amount of
negociable paper which you hold—that is to say, the
total of your bills available for re-discount in case of
need.

What proportion of unmarketable paper it may be
prudent for you to hold at any time, must be determined
by the same laws which guide you in fixing the limits of
your other forms of asset.

In constructing your balance-sheet, we assumed that
the whole of the £1,190,000 in bills of exchange
were of negociable quality. These, added to your
cash and Consols, represent a total of readily available resources, equal to 80 per cent. of your deposits—
a position of undeniable strength. But, if certain
of your bills are not negociable, this percentage will
have to be reduced : if you hold unmarketable paper
to the extent of say £300,000, the percentage would
drop from 80 to 68—and your financial barometer
would indicate a fall of 12 degrees. The amount you
hold of promissory notes or loan bills may, therefore,
be an important item, in estimating from time to time
the general strength of your position.

The degree of that strength, it may be well to note,
is always to be measured by the proportion which
your fusible assets bear to your liabilities to the
public. Your cash in hand and at call may be regarded
as assets in actual fusion : your Consols and negociable

bills as fusible into cash in a high degree: your promissory notes and loan bills as in-fusible, within any
exact time; and the bulk of your overdrafts as opposing
an obstinate resistance to fusion, whatever heat of application may be brought to bear upon them.

LETTER XXXIV.

RESERVE LIABILITY.

Set it down to thyself, as well to create good precedents, as to follow them. Reduce things to the first institution, and observe wherein and how they have degenerate : but yet ask counsel of both times : Of the ancient time what is best ; Of the latter time what is fittest. BACON.

THE failure of the City of Glasgow Bank may be said to have brought unlimited liability in banking to a violent end. As the circle of ruin occasioned by the catastrophe widened in its sweep, from day to day, the consternation among shareholders in unlimited banks became intensified. Men began to ask themselves, whether it was not an act of insanity, to continue owners of a description of property, the holding of which had brought even wealthy men to the ground, and hundreds of the well-to-do to privation or beggary, with as little warning as an earthquake gives.

The terror, as we know, was exaggerated. It was proveable that there could never again be such a lengthened course of falsification, never such a piling up and secret hoarding of accumulated disaster. Nevertheless, the fear remained. 'That which has been is that which may be.' To the minds of many, there appeared to be no choice between getting rid of their bank shares at once, or finding themselves sucked down in some other banking maëlstrom.

The banks were thus threatened with the loss of the most cherished names amongst their proprietaries. Men of wealth and position would gradually sell out;

252

and persons with little substance and less standing would gradually take their places.

One would make a struggle to meet a definite liability, and might rely on friends for assistance : but a limitless debt appals the imagination, and breaks the heart of effort. The victim will not even look it in the face, but goes miserably under at once.

Unlimited liability, it was held, might thus become in time the mere shadow of itself—a husk without its kernel. The unlimited liability of a body of shareholders of limited substance, would cease to reckon for much, in the event of a breakdown and adverse liquidation.

The question, therefore, became urgent,—was it possible to assign some limit to the liability of shareholders, and yet make ample provision for the security of depositors ? If this were feasible, the banks would be able, not only to retain their proprietaries intact, but men of property and influence would become holders of bank shares, who had never held such shares before. The solution of the difficulty was found in the principle of 'reserve liability,' and was embodied in the Act of 1879.

The Act empowered every bank, with the consent of its shareholders, to increase, if it should see fit, the nominal amount of each of its shares, and thus enlarge to any extent, the total of its subscribed capital—a process which was impracticable as the law then stood.

The Act further empowered every bank which should register under it, whether with its capital thus enlarged, or as its capital actually stood, to place the whole, or any portion of its uncalled amount, in the form of reserve liability.

The Act, therefore, enabled every bank which adopted its provisions, to set aside and hypothecate a certain portion of its registered capital, as an inalienable fund for the protection of its depositors, in addition to the protection already afforded them by its paid-up capital and rest.

A bank could thus create for depositors a security which claimed to rank in substance and availability with unlimited liability itself—diluted, as that form of liability might become, by the defection of the strong and the infusion of the weak.

It became a reasonable proposition, that a liability for a given amount, which was limited but available, might be of larger yield than the liability of a deteriorated proprietary, which was unlimited, but comparatively barren. It was held that a million, which was certain of collection, might prove a more absolute security, than unlimited millions of sterile liability.

But the Act, whilst it thus effectually protects the depositor, still further safe-guards his interest in other ways. Every bank, as we have before stated, which registers under the Act, has to publish a balance-sheet, which shall set forth its exact financial position at least once a year.

It has further to submit the whole of its books and accounts, its money and securities, to the investigation of public auditors, in order that they may certify, or decline to certify, as the case may be, to the correctness of the balance-sheet.

Every bank has, in addition, to append to its title the word ' limited.' In the case of banks with large capitals paid up and large reserve funds, this precautionary term was regarded by many as needless, and, to a certain extent, misleading. The law required it to be applied alike to the London and Westminster Bank, with its £13,000,000 of capital and rest, and the Bank of Swindelhurst, which may have started business with a capital limited to a £10 note, there being no law to the contrary. The mere title of a bank, it was urged, conveys of itself no distinctive idea to the mind of a certain type of depositor. A bank it is a bank to him, as the primrose was to Peter Bell, and it is nothing more. But as

it was open to every bank, by way of rider to the
obnoxious term, to have imprinted on its documents,
if it should see fit, the amount of its capital and rest;
this special objection to the limiting word was without
bottom.

All fears, indeed, as to its effect on the minds of
depositors have proved groundless, and have long since
vanished. To find the word 'limited' as an appendage
to the title of a bank is no detriment nowadays; it
is rather held to be a distinction. It is known and
recognized as an assurance that the Bank's affairs are
thoroughly gone into, and truly set forth, at least once in
every year.

No measure, perhaps, has ever worked a revolution
so momentous or so swift, in the financial basis of
our banking system, or had a more critical time in
Parliament. The session of 1879 was within three days
of its close before the Bill had reached even the stage
of second reading, and 'reserve liability,' as expounded
in the Bill, was still a financial conundrum to the House.
Fortunately, a definition of the principle was thought
of at the eleventh hour, and embodied in a clause,
which expressed in a few lines, what occupied as
many pages in the print of the Bill. The amending
clause was frankly adopted by Sir Stafford Northcote,
who had charge of the measure on behalf of the
Government; and, with cordial help from both sides of
the House, the Bill was rushed through the Commons,
in time to pass with equal swiftness through the Lords,
and receive the Royal assent, literally at the twelfth
hour.

The Bill could no doubt have been improved in
certain points of detail, had time permitted: but the
almost universal adoption of the Act, as it stands, may
be taken as evidence that its defects are slight compared
with its advantages. The great principle of reserve
liability, which it embodies, has been accepted on all
hands, by depositors and shareholders alike, as a whole-

some substitute and reasonable equivalent for unlimited liability.

In evidence of this, I have before me the returns of forty of the Banks which have registered under the Act, and which shew an increase of nearly £30,000,000, or some 15 per cent. in their deposits, since the date of registration.

At the date of the passing of the Act, there were in the three Kingdoms eighty-two unlimited banks, and of these seventy-five have since registered under the Act, leaving only seven Banks now unregistered. But the banks which have availed themselves of the Act, have done so in a wise and liberal spirit. In seeking to put a limit to their liability, they have so broadened the basis on which their credit stood, as to leave their liability still practically unlimited. Their subscribed capitals and profits in rest, which in 1879 stood at 82 millions, now stand at 166 millions; so that, in availing themselves of the Act, they created fresh Capital to the extent of more than 80 millions, as further security to their depositors.*

---

* The following summary, which has been chiefly compiled from one of those interesting and valuable returns for which the banking community is so frequently indebted to the ' Economist,' will give more exactly the figures of the movement.

Position of Seventy-five Banks registered under the Act of 1879.	In 1879.	31 Oct. 1884.
Capital paid up	£27,739,000	£30,367,000
Capital to call . . .	40,373,000	44,288,000
Capital in reserve liability . .	nil.	76,592,000
	£68,112,000	£151,247,000
Rests, or reserve funds . .	13,807,000	15,512,000
	£81,919,000	£166,759,000

Seven Unlimited Banks.

Paid-up capital	£1,017,000
Reserve funds	804,000
	£1,821,000

This is the equivalent which the banks have given for limited liability. Their deposits amount to 270 millions, and their resources to meet them sum up in all to 437 millions. So much for 'limited' liability under the Act of 1879.

LETTER XXXV.

CAPITAL AND SHARES.

Albeit much of that we are to speak in this present cause may seem to a number perhaps tedious, perhaps obscure, and intricate. . . . . They unto whom we shall seem tedious, are in no wise injuried by us, because it is in their own hands to spare that labour which they are not willing to endure. HOOKER.

YOUR Bank is registered under the Act of 1879, with a subscribed capital of £1,200,000, divided into 30,000 shares of £40 each, on which £10 have been paid up—the remaining £30 per share, or £900,000 in all, having been placed in 'reserve liability.'

You have called into existence this novel description of capital, and it will expressly exist for the protection of your depositors, in addition to the £450,000 of your paid-up capital and rest. It will afford them a guarantee for nearly a million sterling; a guarantee which cannot be tampered with, or diminished, because you cannot call up or use any portion of it for the purposes of your ordinary business. It can only be called up, in the words of the Act,—'in the event and for the purpose of the Bank being wound up.' It is a perpetual guarantee, which can be neither abridged by use, nor barred by the Statute of Limitations.

The security, therefore, which you offer to your depositors would appear to be sufficiently ample.

Your assets actually in hand, according to your balance-sheet, amount to . .	£3,000,000
But in addition to these you have capital in reserve liability to the amount of .	900,000
Making together	£3,900,000

But your liabilities to your depositors and others amount only to £2,550,000. So that your resources exhibit a margin of £1,350,000 in excess of your liabilities.

Your means of payment are consequently 65 per cent. in excess of your indebtedness. For every £100 which you owe to a depositor, you give him security for £165.

The term 'limited,' therefore, as applied to your Bank without qualification, is somewhat misleading. There is certainly a limitation of liability, such as it is. Your shareholders are not bound to find more than 65 per cent. beyond what you are owing to your depositors: against your debt to them of two millions and a half, you are limited to giving them security for more than three millions nine hundred thousand pounds. In other words, your margin for contingencies is £1,350,000: that is to say, you might make bad debts to that amount, and still have resources left, which would enable you to pay your depositors twenty shillings in the pound.

But the idea of the bad debts of a bank like yours ever coming within measurable distance of such a total, is preposterous. Even a Board of financial lunatics, with a maniac for Manager, could not pile up such a mountain of loss, if they had a whole decade to do it in, without detection or disturbance.

But they would not go undetected nor undisturbed for a tenth part of that time. Within the compass of the first twelve months of their maladministration, these gentlemen would find themselves, under the new order of things, put in financial durance by the auditors, to await the just wrath of their shareholders.

No doubt there will be banking losses in the future. To a certain extent they are unavoidable; but they can never attain to vast and overwhelming totals again, because hereafter they will be checked in time. There can never again be successful concealment of evil-doing stretching over periods of time. You will have to render an annual account of your stewardship, and that account must henceforth be verified by the sharpened vision of skilled accountants. Losses will henceforth have to be dealt with as they arise. The nursing of doubtful accounts to figures more and more portentous, year after year, will no longer be possible. The enormities of our banking past, can never be re-enacted; the banking misfortunes of the future will be trifles light as air, compared with the desolating experiences of the past.

We have thus far dealt with the proportion which your entire capital, called and uncalled, bears to your liabilities. This proportion is the measure of your ultimate stability as a Bank.

But this larger question involves a less—namely, your immediate stability—of which a popular, but inexact measure, is found in the relative amount of your working capital. This is taken in your balance-sheet at £450,000 —that being the united amount of your paid-up capital and rest.

In the same document, your liabilities to depositors and others are taken at £2,550,000. The ratio of liabilities to working capital, therefore, in your case, is as six to one.

But this ratio differs greatly amongst banks. In some it is only as two to one; in others, the excess is even as eight or ten to one. There is no accepted rule in the matter, and it would be difficult to frame one. The Bank with the lowest ratio of working capital may, in reality, be as safe for its engagements as the bank with the highest. It is mainly a question of assets. If they are equally sound in either case, the proportion of working capital to liabilities is of secondary importance.

Nevertheless, the public will be apt to regard the immediate stability of a bank, which is only indebted to twice the amount of its paid-up capital and rest, as more assured, than that of a bank whose indebtedness stands at ten times the amount of both. To avoid either extreme, I have placed the District Union Bank in an average position, about midway between ten and two.

If this be accepted as the normal ratio which your working capital should bear to your liabilities, the question next arises,—how to provide additions to your capital as they may be required, which shall yield the greatest advantage to your shareholders, and give most contentment to your depositors?

Your shares are registered as £40 each, with £10 paid and £30 in reserve liability; but you are doubtful whether it would not have been equally politic to have placed only £20 in the latter form, and thus left £10 further to call on each share. Let us, therefore, put your method to the test of figures. Let us assume that, in the course of time, your deposits shall become doubled in amount, and that your working capital, in consequence, has likewise been doubled, by successive calls on your existing shares, which would then stand at £20 paid, and £20 in reserve liability. Let us further assume that your Rest, sharing in the general prosperity of your business, has experienced the same ratio of increase, and now stands at twice its former amount.

Your position will then be as follows :—

Deposits	£5,000,000
Assets in hand :—	
As against Deposits . . .	£5,000,000
" Capital Paid up . .	600,000
" Rest	300,000
	£5,900,000
Add Capital in reserve liability .	600,000
Aggregate resources	£6,500,000

Showing a surplus of a million and a half, or 30 per cent. in excess of your liabilities to depositors.

Let us now put the other method to the test of figures, and assume, that you have provided the addition to your paid-up Capital and Rest by successive issues of new shares, identical in all respects with your existing ones, and that they have been distributed rateably amongst your proprietors.

The average price at which your shares have sold for many years past, appears to have been £20 premium. If you issue the new shares therefore at, say, £10 premium, you may confidently rely upon their being taken up with avidity.

This amount of premium, on 30,000 new shares, would enable you to add £300,000 to your Rest, and thus raise the total of that fund to £450,000; whilst on the shares thus emitted, there would be a profit, measured by the market price, of £10 on each,—thus affording your proprietors a share bonus of £300,000. Your position would then be as under :—

Deposits	£5,000,000
Assets in hand :—	
As against Deposits . .	5,000,000
" Paid-up Capital .	600,000
" Rest . . .	450,000
Total in hand . . .	6,050,000
Add Capital in reserve liability	1,800,000
Aggregate resources £7,850,000	

These figures give a surplus of £2,850,000, or 57 per cent. of means in excess of liabilities.

From a depositor's point of view, there can be no doubt which position of the two will most commend itself to his favour. He will rather that his margin of

safety stood at 57 per cent. than at 30 :\ he will rather
that your resources exceeded your indebtedness by
three millions sterling than by only a million and a
half.

Moreover, if you admit the principle, that the security
which you give to depositors ought to increase rateably
with the increase in your deposits, your method of provision would not meet this requirement. To make a
call upon subscribed capital already in existence, makes
no addition to its amount : it merely alters its form.
Your subscribed capital, when your deposits were only
2½ millions, stood at £ 1,200,000 ; and it would stand at
that figure, and no more, when your deposits had increased to 5 millions.

It is true, as you point out, that by your method, the
remaining liability on each of your shares would be
reduced to £ 20 ; whereas, by the method actually adopted,
the liability would continue at £ 30. What effect this
might have on the market price of your shares is hardly
worth discussion. It will probably have none ; but, put
it at what you may, it will be but a feather's weight of
set-off, against the moral disadvantage of allowing your
deposits to be doubled in amount, without adding a
pound to your subscribed capital.

In the altered conditions of English banking which
the Act of 1879 will enforce, it is impossible, humanly
speaking, that the shareholders in any bank will ever
be called upon to find a sixpence on account of their
reserved liability. Before that point can be reached, a
bank must have squandered, in a single year, the whole
of its paid-up capital and rest in bad debts, which is
beyond rational belief Even in the most recklessly
managed banks on record, it has taken periods of years
to reap such a harvest of disaster.

Reserve liability, then, virtually exposes a shareholder
to nothing, and costs him nothing. It is a liability which
he may dismiss from his thoughts, as a thing which will
never touch his pocket or trouble his rest.

But although the liability may be thus lightly regarded by shareholders, it will afford an abiding ground of assurance to the minds of depositors. Reserve liability is to them the equivalent of so much capital locked in your cash vaults, in trust for their special protection.

It may not exist in the actual form of bank notes or gold, but it is convertible into these at any time when occasion demands. No portion of it can be called up and exposed to the risks of your business: it is an inviolable fund, which you cannot tamper with, or deplete, even if you would.

Seeing then that reserve liability costs shareholders nothing, whilst it gives lasting assurance and comfort to depositors, in proportion to its amount, it would seem an act of bootless thrift not to make it ample.

In making any additions to your capital, you will proceed tentatively; you will not seek to enlarge it the moment the general level of your deposits indicates a rise. You will defer taking action till it is seen whether the increase is casual or permanent: whether it is the result of a gradual and durable rise over the whole area of your district, or an exceptional and transitory increase here and there.

This precaution is necessary, because, although an increase in your deposits ought to be followed eventually by an increase in your capital, it does not follow that the reverse of the principle holds good. Theoretically, a reduction of your deposits ought to be followed by a proportionate reduction of your capital; but in banking, theory has sometimes to give way to practice and expediency.

For a bank to reduce its capital, on any pretext, is to adventure upon a ticklish operation. If it does so, because its depositors have seen fit to withdraw certain of their moneys, a reduction of its capital is not calculated to entice the deposits back again, nor to attract fresh ones. To advertise even the District Union Bank as 'limited and reduced,' might give the impression, to the minds of the ignorant, that the Bank has got into trouble and is going to wind up. You must be well assured, therefore, that any important increase in your deposits has in it the element of permanence, before you make a relative increase in your capital; because banking capital, once paid up, is practically beyond recall.

LETTER XXXVI.

PROFIT AND LOSS.

Proportion thy expenses to what thou hast in possession, not to thy expectancies; otherwise, he that feeds on wind, must needs be griped with the cholic at last. FULLER.

IT is still a matter of wonder to many·people how banking profits are made; how, especially, while the Bank of England rate of discount, on the average of years, rules at barely 3¼ per cent., Banks can realize, and do annually disburse, dividends ranging from 10 to 20 per cent. on their paid-up capitals.

But the problem is not difficult of solution. We have merely to take your balance-sheet, and construct upon the basis of its principal figures, what shall be at least an approximate guess at the results of your operations for any given twelve months.

PROFITS OF BANKING. It will simplify the calculation, if we assume that the expenses of the Bank will be covered by the commission charged on its overdrawn and other accounts and transactions. These charges are de· signed to cover such expenses, and ought to suffice for that purpose.

Your Capital and Rest, being your own property, and not therefore subject, like your deposits, to withdrawal, may safely be laid out on a class of accounts to bring you in a steady 5 per cent.

Your deposits, on the other hand, not being your own money, but that of other people, and subject to repayment at short notice or at call, must be invested in less productive but more available forms of security. If invested in the proportions of cash in hand and at call, Consols, bills of exchange, and other items, as set forth in your balance-sheet, your deposits will bring you in from $3\frac{1}{4}$ to $3\frac{1}{2}$ per cent. on the average of years,—that is, on the supposition that your discounts and temporary advances will yield you, all round, one per cent. above Bank rate.*   It follows, that if your rate of deposit interest is from $2\frac{1}{4}$ to $2\frac{1}{2}$ per cent., your deposits, as a whole, will yield you a return of one per cent.

Proceeding upon these data, we have the following result, as the estimated sum of your profits :—

Capital and Rest	£450,000 @ 5%	£22,500
Deposits	..	2,400,000 @ 1%	24,000
			£46,500
This would enable you to pay your usual dividend of 15 per cent., or .			45,000
and leave a surplus of . . .			£1,500

To this will have to be added the profits on your circulation of notes, and on the other minor items in your balance-sheet.   Your surplus, thus supplemented, ought to provide you with a margin amply sufficient to cover bad debts.

---

* Average Bank of England rate of discount for ten years, ended 31st December, 1884—£3 3s. 11d.

Average rate for Call and Notice Money with brokers, same period, £2 2s. 8d.

£200,000 in till, yielding	Nil.
350,000 at call, at £2 2s. 8d. per cent. . .	£7,465
300,000 Consols, at £3 per cent. . . .	9,000
1,040,000 Discounts } at £4 3s. 11d. per cent. .	65,035
510,000 Advances	
£2,400,000, yielding	£81,500

= $3\frac{3}{8}$ per cent.

These figures give prominence to the fact that the
profits of a bank, beyond what are derived from the
employment of its own capital and rest, largely depend
on the amount of its deposits.   Let your deposits, for
example, be increased by half a million—your other
figures remaining the same—and you add £5000 to your
yearly profits : or reverse the operation, and the result
will be reversed.

It has to be admitted that this method of arriving at
the constructive profits of a country bank, is a rough
and ready one, and would require, in almost every case,
manifold adjustments to give it complete exactitude :
but it may serve to shew how large dividends may be
honestly earned and lawfully disbursed by country
banks, even when a low general rate of interest
prevails.

RISKS OF BANKING.   The business of a bank is swift
of movement and enormous in volume.   It combines
the widest area of risk with the lowest rate of profit.
The business of a trader is by comparison slow in movement, limited in volume, and carries a high rate of profit.
It combines the smallest area of risk with the largest
rate of gain.

Your Bank will be glad to employ any portion of its
deposits in the discount of high-class paper at a net
profit of one per cent. per annum.   On a bill at three
months' date for £5000, your profit would consequently
be £12 10s., and no more.   But a merchant or trader
would not consider even 5 per cent. an exorbitant rate
of profit, on any ordinary line of trading or mercantile
operations.   That percentage, however, on £5000, would
produce £250, or twenty times the rate of banking
profit.

Let us suppose that the bill for £5000 is drawn upon
one of those large houses which do fail at times, and
that the dividend is five shillings in the pound, which
unhappily would be a more than liberal estimate, and

that you are thus saddled with a loss of £3750. It may not strike you at the moment, but you will find by a simple process in arithmetic, that it will require three hundred times the profit of £12 10*s*. to repair the loss. In other words, you will have to discount, without loss, fresh sheaves of high-class paper to the startling total of a million and a half, in order to replace the deficiency on this ill-starred bill for £5000. A banker's choice of first-class bills had needs be infallible, when these may be the consequences of a single slip.

It has further to be noted, that the risks of a banking business are not measurable by the moneys owing to a bank on discounts, overdrafts, or advances, on any given day ; because the items which constitute these aggregates are in the course of perpetual change. As series after series of risks run off, they are immediately replaced by others. The bills and advances due and paid to-day, will be succeeded by fresh discounts and advances to-morrow ; so that, to find the true measure of banking risk, we must take the sum turned over in these trans-actions.

Taking your bills of exchange, for example, your in-vestment in them is turned over, on the average, four times in the year. Your banking risks on Bills of Ex-change alone, therefore, extend to £4,760,000 in the course of the twelve months. You discount fresh bills, and consequently incur fresh risks, to that amount, and thus invest and re-invest, in discounts alone, a sum equal to your entire capital and rest ten times a year.

The profits of an ably managed bank, holding deposits to five or six times the total of its capital and reserve, are no doubt large in aggregate : but they owe their largeness to their multitude, not to their scale. The £45,000 of net profit, which you annually disburse in dividends to your proprietors, if resolved into its ele-ments, would be found mainly to consist of millions of minute particles of interest and charges, which have accrued day by day on many thousands of accounts.

The ultimate atoms of banking profit are mainly to be found to the right of decimal point, even when that point has only a farthing for its integer.

The total in money, or monetarial value, received and paid by your thirty Branches, averages £4000 a day for each, and the average for your Head Office is £50,000, making in all a million a week, or a total annual movement of fifty millions. Where banking profits are reckoned by tens of thousands, therefore, they are extracted from tens of millions of pounds of transactions, the percentage of risk on which had needs be infinitesimal, and next door to nothing.

A prudent trader, taking annual stock of his affairs, would not consider 10 per cent. too much to write off his book-debts, in order to arrive at their probable value to realize: but if your book-debts—that is to say, your overdrawn accounts, advances, and discounts, had to be subjected to a like measure of abatement, you would have to write your paid-up capital off as lost and gone once a year.

PROVISION FOR LOSS. A Banker, in writing off his bad debts for the year, is apt to console himself with the reflection, in respect of some of them, that he can never make exactly such again, because he will know how to guard against them. That may be; but losses may already be in embryo which will come to him from directions as yet unsuspected. In making his annual provision for bad debts, therefore, he will rather be guided by the average of his past experiences, than by the figures for any current year. If these amounted, for example, to £5000, whereas his annual amount of bad debts over a period of years has averaged £7500, he will do well to set a sum aside which shall more nearly approach the latter than the former amount: because, if his losses are less than the average this year, they may be equally in excess of it next. He will thus give increased uniformity to his rate of dividend, and consequent stability to the price of the Bank's shares.

In dealing with accounts or bills individually, which have become more or less doubtful, a liberal treatment is always best. When you have to provide for loss on any given account or bill, do not minimize the risk; do not scale it at the least, but at the worst that may happen; and let your provision be in accordance with your principle. It is difficult to imagine a more depressing process than the perusal of a bad debts ledger, wherein the debts have been insufficiently written down. You open this mortuary of debt, with a faint hope, perhaps, that you may chance upon some account that has been over provided for, or some stray dividend which has been overlooked; but you will find this hope misplaced. These remains of departed accounts are more likely to require fresh grants from your profits to provide for their final interment. Looked upon as assets, they are as devoid of substance as the ghosts in Tartarus. Better, surely, at all times be in a position to inform your proprietors that your estimate of loss has been in excess, than that the reality has exceeded your worst anticipations, and that you have so many more thousands to write off? It will accord with their humour rather to write misfortune off at once, than by exasperating dribblets. If a tooth has to come out, it is better to have the operation perfected by one wrench than by a series.

There is a certain grimness of comfort experienced by the shareholders of a bank, when they know that their Directors uniformly take the worst view of things, and make such ample provision for bad debts, that there is never any residue of loss to provide for. In thus dealing with actual or anticipated disaster, your fund for losses, instead of being in a chronic state of exhaustion, will generally have a growing balance at its credit, to provide against exceptional mishap. Your holding of over-due bills, ill-starred advances, and moribund accounts, instead of being featured by a hopeless sterility, will rather suggest to the fancy a gathering of financial wreckage, from which, every now and then, there comes ashore the flotsam of an unexpected dividend, or the jetsam of some derelict security. A bad debt fund, thus nourished, will give you back of your abundance, and become to your Board an intermittent source of found money and pleasurable emotion.

DIVIDEND AND BONUS. It is the usage of some banks to distribute their annual profits to their proprietors entirely in the form of dividend. Others make the distribution partly in this form, and partly in the shape of bonus.

In favour of the latter course, it may be urged that you can with certainty fix upon some rate of dividend which you will be able to pay, under all circumstances. Your shareholders would thus know that, up to a certain figure, they might reckon upon a regular income from your shares, as surely as if it came to them from the Three per cents. The 'bonus' is thus supposed to be relegated to the uncertainties, and the edge of disappointment to be taken off, when this form of largess is not forthcoming.

I think this is a sanguine view to take of the feelings of shareholders, when the supposed default happens, and would suggest that your annual distribution of profits, whether it be partly by way of bonus, or wholly in the shape of dividend, should, as nearly as possible, be uniform, one year with another. The property of steadiness in your rate of dividend will be more esteemed by your proprietors, than if it varied from one half-year to another, and gave to the price of your shares a corresponding degree of change and uncertainty.

If you find, for example, that on the average of years your profits will sustain an annual distribution of 15 per cent., it would be well to adhere to that rate, even though you could in exceptional years divide considerably more;

because, in less fortunate times you may have considerably less to divide. Let your divisible profits for **two** consecutive years be, let us say :—

1st year £48,000, or 16 per cent. on capital.
2nd   "   £42,000, " 14   "   "

Average 15

Instead of dividing 16 per cent. the first year, and **14** the next, it would be a wiser policy to carry 1 per cent. forward from your fat year to supplement the profits of its less fertile successor, and thus pay 15 per cent. in both.

It has to be admitted that, theoretically, this course would be open to objection. The purist would say that you have no right to make an artificial and arbitrary division of annual profits. However much, or however little, you have to divide, it ought to be divided, without regard to what your next dividend may be.

If the majority of your shareholders were persons who thoroughly understood such matters, this contention would be more tenable: but your proprietors, as a body, are not versed in matters of banking finance. As a rule, they are conspicuously ignorant of this branch of knowledge. It is no disparagement to the average comprehension of country shareholders to affirm, that if you pay them 16 per cent. one year, and return to 14 the next, it will be difficult to persuade the bulk of them that the reduction has arisen from natural causes. They will witness with concern a corresponding fall in the price of the shares, and will be apt to fear that the Bank has met with serious disaster. Your high dividend of the one year will cause that of its successor to look doubly disappointing. It will seem to this section of your proprietors that you have put 2 per cent. into their pockets one year, only to take it out again the next. Moreover, for every pound of variation in dividend, you

18

may have caused many times the variation in the market price of their shares.

All this may be sound in theory, but the majority of your shareholders will have a disposition to look upon this way of managing their affairs as an upsetting and inconvenient thing in practice.

In common with other Banks you divide your net annual profits in the form of a percentage on your Capital alone.   But as your Rest is as much the property of your shareholders as the paid-up capital itself, your virtual rate of distribution to your proprietors on their own money, taking your annual distribution at £45,000, is 10 per cent., and not 15 ; as thus :—

> £300,000 Capital @ 10 per cent. = £30,000
> £150,000 Rest @ 10 per cent. = £15,000
> _____
> £45,000

A high rate of dividend has a certain influence, no doubt, on the minds of the outside public.   It is looked upon by many as evidence of a bank's stability and success.   On the other hand, there are those amongst your customers, who imagine that the terms on which you work their accounts must be usurious, to enable you to pay 15 per cent.   You and I, of course, know that this is a fallacy ; and that high dividends in banking do not arise from inordinate rates of profit, but from magnitude of operations.   A difference of an eighth per cent. in the interest on Goldworthy's deposit of £100, for example, would make a difference to him of an annual half-crown ; but the same fraction per cent. would make a difference to you, on the total amount of your deposits, of three thousand pounds a year.   A loss or a gain to Goldworthy has to be multiplied by twenty-four thousand, to find the resulting loss or gain to you.   Banking profit, as we have seen, is a noun of multitude—an aggregation of atoms; and banking transactions are conducted on terms which would be impossible, except for the prodigious multiplier provided by their volume.

A high rate of dividend, moreover, is apt to excite envy and lead to opposition. Fifteen per cent. per annum, in these days, is a high rate of interest for an ardent promoter to conjure with; and on the whole, it is at least an open question whether bank dividends had not better be based on Capital and Rest combined, than on Capital alone.

LETTER XXXVII.

THE REST.

He who, when he should not, spends too much, shall, when he would not, have too little to spend. FELTHAM.

YOUR Rest or Reserve Fund has been accumulated out of undivided profits, set aside from time to time to meet unforeseen losses, so that your usual rate of dividend may not be trenched upon should such losses arise.

This being the object of the fund, it ought to bear a certain proportion, not to the amount of your paid-up capital, but to the total of your assets; because that total is the true measure of your domain of loss.

Your resources represent three millions of money, invested in multifarious items of banking asset, and your Rest is put at 5 per cent. of this aggregate.

This percentage, like most of our other figures, is a suggestion merely. It is larger in some banks, and less in others; but for the sake of argument it may be taken as it stands. This at least is certain—the larger your rest, the higher your rate of dividend will be. The fund, whatever its amount, is practically a sum lent you in perpetuity without interest. As forming a portion of your working capital, you can safely invest it in the less available and more lucrative forms of advance. If invested to yield 5 per cent., it would bring you in £7500 a year, or an annual contribution of 2½ per cent. towards your dividend.

A large rest inspires belief in the continuity of your rate of dividend. In this way it gives support and steadiness to the market price of your shares. Your shareholders could not well have a safer, or, as we shall see, a more politic investment.

Nevertheless, there are those to be found in bank proprietaries, here and there, who are covetous of these rests or reserves of undivided profits, and would have an immediate division of at least a portion of them, if they had their way. Why, they urge, leave this large fund for the benefit of posterity? Why not leave future shareholders to provide their own reserve funds?

To test the soundness of these views, let us imagine that your shareholders suffer themselves to be persuaded that your bank can be worked equally well on a Rest of half its present amount; and that the other half, £75,000, ought to be divided amongst them rateably, and that it is divided accordingly. The distribution will yield a cash bonus of £2 10s. on every share held by your existing proprietors.

But in making them this presentation, you lose for ever the use of the £75,000 thus given away—a sum which, at 5 per cent., produced £3750, or 1¼ per cent. of your annual dividend; which would, therefore, have to be reduced from 15 to 13¾ per cent.

What effect this reduction will have on the market price of your shares, it is hard to say; but that it will at least be proportionate to the drop in the dividend, goes without saying. In all likelihood it will be considerably more; a drooping dividend has a more prejudicial and immediate effect on price than a rising one: but let us take the drop at its arithmetical equivalent—£2 10s. per share.

A man, then, holding a hundred of your shares will have received a bonus of £250. But if the market value of his shares has thereby become diminished to precisely the same amount, it is impossible to see what he has gained by the operation. His hundred shares, which were worth £3000, are worth only £2750 now, and the probability is that they will be worth a good deal less; but under no circumstances can he gain by the transaction. You cannot, even in banking, eat your cake and have it: you cannot enlarge your financial blanket by cutting a portion from one end to tack it on the other.

But if it is impossible to see how your shareholders could benefit by this self appropriation of fifty per cent. of the Rest, it is not difficult to see what they might lose by it.

In the first place: it will cause, as we have just said, a reduction in your usual rate of dividend. If this should be attributed on all hands to the actual cause, little harm might come of it; but it will not be so attributed. There is a widespread ignorance and open-mouthed credulity about banking affairs, which you have always to reckon with. It will suffice for the majority of people to know that the District Union Bank is paying a lower dividend than heretofore, to conclude that the Bank is not doing so well as formerly. Not content with this, they will proceed to hazard conjectures as to the cause. Some will assign it to bad debts, others to a falling off in its business, others to something else. But regarded in whatever light, a reduction in your ordinary rate of dividend will wear an unfavourable aspect to a large section of the community.

In the second place: you have to take into account what effect the reduction will have on the minds of those who can read a bank balance-sheet perfectly, and take the exact measure of its weakness or its strength. Such critics are limited in number, it is true; but they are on the increase, and their opinion has a weight which makes itself felt, and is apt to spread. To such observers, the abstraction of £75,000 from your Rest, to put into your own pockets, will present itself as neither more nor less than the voluntary extinction of one-sixth of your working capital, whereby the strength of your position will be impaired in a like degree. It will be impossible for them to regard the operation with favour, or to speak of it with approval. It will appear to them an impolitic weakening of your position, without even the poor excuse of an equivalent to justify it.

Once again : a large proportionate Rest is accepted by the public as evidence of prudence and ability in the management of a bank : and you will command a larger future for your business by maintaining your rest at £150,000, than by taking half of it back again to yourselves, and working on the other half. If you would have your business go forward and your custom increase, do not yourselves take a backward step. In banking, as in other things, nothing succeeds like success ; and the extinction of half your Rest will not have this appearance, put on it what complexion you may.

As an alternative course, you suggest that the £75,000, instead of being paid to your shareholders in cash, might be added to the amount of their shares, which would thus be raised from £10 to £12 10s. paid.

The alternative would have this advantage—it would leave the amount of your working capital unreduced and your financial position apparently untouched. But the operation, regarded in the light of a bonus, would, as in · the previous case, defeat itself Your revenue, it is true,. would be unaffected by it. Your divisible profits would still be £45,000 : but out of these you would have to pay dividend on the £75,000 added to your capital : so that your annual rate of distribution would sink from 15 per cent. to 12. The operation would, in fact, be as broad as long. A dividend of 12 per cent. on £12 10s. would be the exact equivalent of 15 per cent. on £10. To take from one pocket to put into another, is a futile way of enriching yourselves, and a mere fooling with figures.

You have yet another course to suggest, in the event of the attack on your Rest proving successful : you would create 7500 new shares, and distribute them gratis amongst your shareholders, first paying up £10 on each share out of that fund. This would enable you to give each of your shareholders one new for every four old shares held by him. He would thus receive a bonus equal to £7 10s. on each old share, taking the market price as before at £30. But the market price would not

continue at that figure. You would have created and
added £75,000 to your paid-up capital, without adding
a farthing a year to your revenue. Out of the same
balance of divisible profit, you will now have to pay
on a capital enlarged by one fourth. So that your rate
of dividend, as in the previous case, will drop from
15 per cent. to 12, and your apparent bonus will disappear in a corresponding shrinkage of price. One
hundred of your shares at the old price, made them
worth £3000 to the holder : and 125 of them at the new
price of £24, will make them worth no more to him.
His means, as far as they consist of your shares, will
not have been enlarged a single pound by the distribution, and the bonus of £7 10s. per old share will
prove itself a mere delusion and arithmetical Jack-o'-
lantern.

Nevertheless, of the three methods of partition, the
last would be the least objectionable. Like either of
the other processes, it would equally denude your Rest
of half its substance : but it would have this in its favour
—it would add three times its own amount to your
reserve liability, whereas the other methods of appropriation would add nothing to that reserve. They
would simply absorb the £75,000, and render back
nothing in return. They would pamper a present, at the
cost of a future appetite. They would not exactly kill
the goose that lays your golden eggs; but they would
do it grievous bodily harm.

A reduction of your Rest to one half its amount,
therefore, by whatever method the reduction is carried
out, involves matter for consideration which lies outside
the mere question of its practicability. An exercise in
the rule of subtraction will suffice for that purpose at
any time.

If you had determined from the outset that 2½ per
cent. on your assets would have provided a sufficiency
of Rest, and had stopped it accordingly at £75,000,
and divided all accumulations beyond that figure from
time to time as they arose; that would have been a

different matter. It is one thing to give a certain amount of security to depositors and stop there; but it has quite another effect upon the imagination to withdraw a security which you have once given.

At whatsoever percentage of your assets, therefore, you decide to put the limit of your Rest, that limit, once reached, had best be adhered to as a minimum, and the Fund thereby created held sacred from touch, except to provide for unforeseen disaster. To break into it in cold blood, for partition amongst yourselves, would be a delusive gain, and a short-sighted act of improvidence.

LETTER XXXVIII.

OPENING OF NEW BRANCHES.

The artist himself was at that time busy upon two great designs; the first to sow land with chaff, wherein he affirmed the true seminal virtue to be contained, as he demonstrated, by several experiments, which I was not skilful enough to comprehend.
A VOYAGE TO LAPUTA.

WHEN you receive a memorial 'numerously and influentially signed,' as the phrase is, inviting your Bank to open a Branch at some place, in opposition to an existing bank; it will be well, before you take any other step, to have the history of the document closely investigated. You will especially seek to know with whom the movement originated. There may be ground for such a memorial now and then, but such instances are rare. It will not seldom be found that the promoter of the memorial has an eye to the management of the new Branch for himself. He may be a school teacher, or a book-keeper out of place, or a trader on his last legs, or something else. He may be as unfit to be manager of a bank as to be Chancellor of the Exchequer; but that in no way abashes him. His concern is not with his fitness for the position, but with its fitness for him. It is such an easy berth: short business hours,—all the regular work done by clerks, except the 'sweating' of obnoxious customers,—a luxury which he will reserve to himself; a good salary; a house to live in; rent and taxes free, with fuel and light thrown in;—these are the delights which stir the covetous desires of your average memorial-monger, who would have you invade the territory of a neighbouring bank, in order to provide him with a situation. If questioned as to his qualifications for the position, he has no misgivings. He presumes that he will be instructed in everything, what to do, and he flatters himself that he will be found equal to the doing of it. In respect of his claims, he submits that the memorial itself settles that point. It is his parchment of title, whereby the position is conveyed to him for life by the memorialists.

There is unfortunately no difficulty in obtaining signatures to such things. People by scores will sign them, without a thought as to the consequences. It never occurs to them that their signatures may lead one bank to do grievous injury to another, not only without benefit, but with serious detriment to itself But this loose signing of documents, which may be fruitful of evil, is set down to careless good nature; as if calculated enmity could do more to set a couple of friendly institutions by the ears.

When the usual 'deputation,' therefore, come to present the memorial, and assure you that the other bank is most unpopular in the place, and that scores of its customers will come over to you as soon as you open there, you will receive their allegations with outward courtesy, but with inward distrust. You will promise to consider the matter. With this view, you will have the statements of the deputation carefully investigated in the locality itself. It may turn out by possibility that they are grounded on fact. The result of the enquiry may be that the resources of the existing bank are insufficient for the growing wants of the district, and that there is actual room and need for another bank.

But probability runs quite the other way. Your Inspector is more likely to find that the other bank has ample means and is fairly popular, except with the needy few, and that these are the only customers of theirs who are likely to come over to you in scores —an accession of custom which you will hardly look upon as a thing to be desired.

The influential signatories, it will be found, attached their names to the memorial without an idea of transferring their banking accounts to you. They signed it, they will tell you, because they were asked to do so, and thought it would be a good thing for the place; that was their sole motive.

No doubt circumstances will arise which will justify your opening a fresh Branch from time to time in places either destitute of banking accommodation, or whose monetary wants have outgrown the means of the existing banks. It may even be necessary sometimes to plant a new Branch at a given point, on purely strategic grounds. If on the line of towns A., B., and C. you have Branches at A. and C. only, you could not allow another bank to occupy B. You would have to do so yourselves, although you might have to work the Branch at a loss.

This is practically your position at Oxborough. Between it, on the main line to your next Branch, lies Midgely,—more than a village and less than a town—with its 500 people, resolved with one consent to have a bank in the place, if memorials and importunity can effect it.

You may assure them that the place is not large enough, as yet, to support the expenses of a bank, but that will not move them in the least. You may seek to prove that no bank would be foolish enough to neglect a chance of adding to its profits, but your reasoning will fall upon ears deaf to persuasion. Midgely has set its heart on having a bank, and a bank it will have; and if you persist in your refusal to open there, they must apply elsewhere.

Even if you accede to their desire so far as to give them a sub-branch, open one day a week, it will be a costlier step to you than you will ever be able to make them understand or believe.

Your Manager at Oxborough will have to give one-sixth of his time to that mite of an establishment. He will have to be absent one day out of six from the important business of Oxborough, in order to conduct the Lilliputian finance of Midgely,—a sacrifice of which you can estimate the true weight and value, but which you will fail to render obvious to the Midgelyites, who are not given to thinking lightly of their monetary affairs.

Your opening at Midgely, even one day a week, will go against the grain ; but if your choice comes to lie betwixt your going there, and allowing another bank to do so and appropriate your Midgely connexions bodily, the choice ceases to be optional. Better the Midgely business, minus fresh expense and trouble, than, so to speak, minus itself.

LETTER XXXIX.

THE DIRECTORATE.

Not unlike those which, at the instant and importunate sute of their acquaintance, refuse a cunning Pilot and chuse an unskilfull Mariner, which hazardeth the ship and themselves in the calmest sea. EUPHUES.

THE leading subject on which you will take counsel with your daily Board will be as to the safety and soundness of proposed discounts or advances as they arise from day to day. In matters of pure finance or administrative routine, the Directors will rather look to you for guidance, than seek to advise you; but as regards the safe employment of the funds of the Bank, their advice will be above price.

As men engaged in active business, they will be daily on 'Change, and will thus keep abreast of things. Whether money is being made or lost, in this direction or that, by this firm or another, they can hardly fail to hear of it, and either by direct knowledge, or through business friends, will be able to trace every rumour to its source and take its proper measure. You cannot yourself be a frequenter of 'Change. Even if that were desirable, you have other matters to supervise which will keep you a prisoner at the Bank during business hours. Your daily Board will transact your out-of-door work for you with greater efficiency than you could hope to do it yourself

The record of your daily proceedings is revised by your whole Board, which meets once a week for that and other purposes. Two of your six Directors retire annually by rotation, but are eligible for re-election,

286

and as a rule they are re-elected accordingly. Your form of government appears to be suitably adapted for the successful administration of a country bank.

In some banks, the retiring Directors cannot be re-elected for a time. They must retire from the service of the bank for at least twelve months. That term of retirement served, they are again eligible for election. The framers of this proviso no doubt believed that there was an element of safety in it. They conceived that a Board, the individual members of which were never changed, might avail themselves of their oneness, in the event of things going wrong, to withhold the fact from the knowledge of the shareholders ; whereas an annual change in the membership of the Board would render this form of reticence less feasible.

This was, to put the matter mildly, to take a disparaging view of directoral integrity. But letting that pass,—does the rule really afford the check for which it was designed ? In the case of a bank like your own, for example, if two of your Directors were obliged to go into honorary retirement every year, but could be re-elected the year following, the protection afforded by this arrangement against wrong-doing would obviously be slight. Your Board would virtually consist of eight members instead of six.

Unhappily, there have been instances in the course of the last half-century, in which Directors of banks have been guilty of conduct which it would be difficult to denounce in language of sufficient emphasis : but to infer from these few and exceptional cases that all banking Boards are tarred with the same brush, would surely be an unwarranted perversion of the law of evidence. But even if the inference were as just and reasonable, as it is untrue and ridiculous, the annual audit by public accountants of the books and balance-sheet of a bank has put an end for ever to successful collusion on the part of its Directors or Managers, to hoodwink its proprietary.

There is heard at your meetings of shareholders an occasional demand for 'fresh blood' on the direction. The cry, if traced to its source, will not seldom be found to have originated with someone who has a secret desire to join the Board himself. However this may be, the ground usually taken is, that a Board which never changes its members, unless by death or voluntary retirement, becomes virtually self-elective, with a tendency to intellectual stagnation and the impairment of business vigour.

If one of your Directors has become incompetent or ineligible, by reason of age or infirmity, or any other cause, it is not only the right but the duty of the shareholders to replace him ; but if the infusion of fresh blood is to be achieved by the discharge of able and experienced men, for the mere sake of change, or the gratification of furtive ambition, such a course on the part of shareholders may be as unwise as it would be ungenerous. It may involve the dismissal from their service, of gentlemen who are possessed of a knowledge of the accounts and business of the Bank, which it has taken them many years to acquire ; in order that their seats may be taken by other gentlemen, who for some years to come, can have no reliable knowledge of the accounts or business, or the general working and policy of the Bank.

No shareholder would adopt a policy of change like this in the conduct of his own business. He would not dismiss tried and experienced hands, in order to replace them with the unskilled and inexperienced, for the pure love of change.

Even where a Director has to retire for the year only, his retirement involves a certain waste of power. When he returns to office, his mind will have become a blank in respect of the operations of the Bank for a whole twelve months. Not a single bill will be in the bill-case which was in that repository at the date of his retirement, nor will the position of a single account in all probability be exactly what it was. The continuity of his knowledge of the daily transactions of the Bank in bills and advances will have been broken, and he will consequently return to the Board with his usefulness in council proportionately impaired.

There are those, it is true, who deem themselves qualified at a moment's notice, to undertake the management or chief direction of a bank, without any previous training in the conduct of a business which is liable beyond all others to swift destruction in inexperienced hands. And to this cause are mainly to be assigned the past calamities of banking on both sides the Tweed. Our bank failures, without exception, have been the result of either a deplorable ignorance, or a culpable disregard of the first principles of every-day banking. So far from the control or management of a bank being a thing which anyone can understand at sight, there is perhaps no business more difficult of ready grasp. I have given a long business life to the practice and study of it, but do not look upon my education as even yet complete. Every now and again I still come upon something new—some fresh ' wrinkle '—some side-light, which goes to enlarge or qualify, sometimes to upset, old and cherished impressions, and to divest experience of finality.

Your shareholders will do well, therefore, to have as few amateur financiers on the Board at any one time as may be. Vacancies in your direction will arise in the natural course of things, with sufficient frequency to prevent mental stagnation at the Board, and these must necessarily be filled up with ' fresh blood.' Such vacancies will be wide enough apart, to ensure at all times a majority of experienced men on your Direction ; so that the 'prentice hands upon it may have time to master some of their duties before they rise to command.

To force the hand of time, and anticipate natural change in this matter, is to venture upon a game of administrative hazard. You can inject fresh blood by force into the veins of your Board, no doubt, and thereby stimulate it to greater action ; but it does not follow that it will be a healthy action.　It is just as likely to result in friction and a war of opinion betwixt the old lights and the new.　Your Board might thus become divided against itself, and that uniformity of principle in the action of the Bank, which is of supreme importance to its highest interests, would be jeopardized.　The decision of to-day might be upset by the vote of to-morrow—the policy of one period by the opposite policy of another. The management of the Bank might thus become uncertain and capricious.　Your constituents would never rightly know how they stood with you, nor what to rely upon.　If this should happen, they will be apt in time to seek elsewhere for that steadfastness of purpose in the direction of a bank, which is essential to the smooth working of their own business arrangements.

There is, no doubt, as you observe, a feeling in some minds that the accounts of Directors had better be kept at any other bank than their own.　It is urged that they ought not to sit in judgment on their own accounts.

But the grounds for this objection are more fanciful than real.　It is not to be supposed that the Director of a bank would ever seek better terms for himself than would be granted to any other customer.　But, if he should, his colleagues would surely have the moral courage to refuse him ?　They would hardly expose themselves to the taunt that they favoured themselves more than they favoured other people.　For this reason alone, no Director is likely to seek exceptional terms for himself; and if he did, no Board, nowadays, with the inevitable yearly audit of the books and accounts before them, would dare to listen to him.　If a Director will comply with the rules of the Bank, as regards security and all other conditions, so that his account shall be as safe and profitable as any other account of its class, there can be no reason for his keeping it elsewhere. On the contrary, his own Bank has clearly the first claim to it.

Once in every year, accompanied by two of your Directors, who take the duty by rotation,'you make a round of visits to your Branches, in order to check the cash, and investigate the accounts, bills, and securities of each Branch on the spot.

The Board as well as yourself arrive in this way at a personal knowledge of your chief provincial customers, who must otherwise remain to you mere human abstrae-tions, with no more character or individuality about them than their names and avocations afford in the index to your ledgers. Instead of mere headings of ledger folios alphabetically arranged, they will thus become living entities, with whom you will have largely improved your chances of intelligent dealing and mutual business satis-faction in the future.

The majority of your customers will approve of being thus looked up, although some few may have substantial reasons for disliking it extremely. The major part will have a pride in feeling that their accounts will bear the closest scrutiny in the strongest light. They will deem it a compliment, moreover, that your Directors and your-self should come amongst them once a year, to see how things are getting on in ' the old place ;' and a compli-ment paid to their native town touches their municipal bosoms with a pleasing elation.

These visits, moreover, enable you to revise and rec-tify, from time to time, your record of the business capacities of the Managers and other members of your provincial staff. You will find some diligently forging ahead, in knowledge and ability ; others standing where they stood; and some few you may discover losing ground, it may be from age or from other causes.

With a customer's ledger account before you, and its daily working exposed to view, you have an unrivalled opportunity of putting a Branch Manager 'through his facings.' In many accounts, items will stand out from the rest, in regard to which you will look to him for en-lightenment. You will desire to know what such trans-actions mean. You will expect him to read them for you—to explain where the money they represent came from, or whither it went, and the why and the wherefore, as the case may be.

While you thus give an excellent fillip to his understanding and memory, the comparative readiness, fulness, and ability with which he shall answer your questioning, will assist you in assigning to him his just rank in your official scale of merit.

Moreover, these periodical visits will have a wholesome effect in keeping the rank and file of your country staff up to standard. It will be their natural desire to pass as efficients. If they find, therefore, that you are not above taking cognizance even of small things, and that you take especial note of careless handwriting, blotted books, frequent erasures, and waste and muddle wherever found, the Deputation will administer a tonic which will have a distinctly bracing effect. The delinquents will have an eye to next salary Board, and will not imperil their chances at that tribunal by persistence in habits, in respect of which you have left them in unequivocal possession of the sentiments of the Board and yourself

LETTER XL.

THE RIGHTS AND DUTIES OF SHAREHOLDERS.

There is no defence in walls, fortifications, and engines against the power of Fortune; we must provide ourselves within, and when we are safe there, we are invincible; we may be battered, but not taken.　　　　　　　　　　L'ESTRANGE'S SENECA.

WHEN a man becomes a shareholder in a bank he becomes to all intents and purposes a co-partner in the business transacted by it. He is as much concerned in its success, to the extent of his holding, as if the business were his own. The fact that he is only one partner amongst hundreds or thousands, as the case may be, neither releases him from responsibility, nor affects his rights as member of a co-partnership. He has joined a firm, no doubt a large one, in point of numbers; but he is just as much a member of it, as if his fellow-partners numbered only two or three.

It is necessary to press this point—obvious and commonplace as it may seem—because it has yet to be realized by many whom it largely concerns. There are shareholders to be found here and there, to whom their own Bank would appear to be a hostile institution, which it is their business to attack on the slightest pretext. The Naggleton of your annual meetings quarrels with the Rest as too large, or with the profits as too small. He quarrels with your Report. It is too concise; he wants to know a great deal more than what it tells him. He is disappointed with the dividend, and objects to the balance carried forward to next year as excessive. He cannot understand why the District Union Bank pays only 15 per cent., when it is well known that other banks pay 17½ or 20.

There must be bad management, or inexcusable losses, or an over-salaried staff, or something.

This line of hostile remark is lawful to every share-holder, but it is not always expedient. In easy times, this splenetic indulgence in adverse criticism, although it is impossible to see what good can come of it, may be unproductive of harm; but in times of monetary excite-ment, when the air is filled with rumour to the prejudice of banks, and whispers are heard of looming trouble and impending loss, such a line of questioning rebuke may be mischievous.

When such-like rumours, always dubious of birth, and sometimes malignant of purpose, reach the ears of a shareholder, it is at once his duty and his interest to communicate with the nearest Manager of the Bank, in the first instance, and ascertain the truth. For him to stand up, at one of your Bank meetings at such a time, without notice, to ask if it be true that you have lost a hundred thousand by Blank & Co., and another fifty thousand by Cypher Bros., both of which rumours are either sheer inventions or monstrous exaggerations; is only to play into the hands of the inventor of the calumny and give wings to his malevolence. The very putting of such a question carries imputation with it. The evil-minded will conclude that there must be something in it, with whatever emphasis of contradiction you may de-nounce it.

Even more mischievous may be the question put by some other reckless querist, who desires to know whether there is a run going on upon some of your Branches. The rumour may be as groundless as the other: but even if it were true, and it is thus proclaimed throughout your district that some of your Branches are being run upon, it would hardly be matter for surprise if they were all more or less run upon before a week was out. The force of example is in nothing more absolute than in a run—it spreads with the swiftness and virulence of contagion.

I repeat,—that whatever a shareholder may at any time

hear to the prejudice of his own Bank, it is not merely his interest, but his bounden duty, to convey the rumour in the first instance privately to the Manager, and not primarily to his fellow shareholders in public meeting assembled. 'It is an infatuated bird that fouls its own nest.'

Not that I would circumscribe by the breadth of a hair the privilege of shareholders to ask questions on points concerning their own interests: they have a right to know the truth, whatever it may be; and it will be the duty of the Board and yourself to reveal the truth to them at all times without circumlocution or evasion. I would merely have a shareholder to beware of asking questions in public to his own detriment, which he might with equal ease and with more than equal advantage ask in private. No doubt there are questions which it may be politic for a shareholder to put to you publicly, in order that you may publicly answer them; but he should be well assured of this before putting them; otherwise it may happen that in seeking to do the Bank service, he may do it grievous injury.

The shareholder afflicted with that form of eccentricity which incites him to intermittent attacks on his own property, has his counterpart in the man in Hogarth's picture, who is sawing through the perch on which he is himself astride.

Mr. Naggleton is at times moved with a desire to know the exact amount of bad debts which you have made during the twelve months covered by your statement of profits.

If your losses have been of abnormal amount, you will not wait for such a question to be put,—you will anticipate it: but with regard to your ordinary annual provision against loss, you cannot enter into particulars with him. You set aside, out of profits every year, a sum which will not only cover ascertained bad debts, but which shall provide for contingent losses as well— for losses which are not yet, but which may be. Looking, for example, at your holding of bills arising out of any particular trade or industry, in which it is known that heavy losses have been sustained, your Directors, without being able to single out any one bill, or series of bills, as likely to involve loss, might deem it prudent nevertheless to set aside a sum in blank, so to speak, to cover such eventualities. But this is a point upon which your Report would properly be silent: you could not refer to it, without saying either too little or too much. If too much, the credit of individuals might be compromised; if too little—if you merely hinted that such provision had been made—there would be no limit to conjecture on the subject. The amount you hold of such bills would first be guessed at, then steadily exaggerated, and finally enlarged to an alarming total.

For these reasons, and for others, your shareholders will do wisely to leave this particular point at all times in the hands of the Board. Let them rest content with the assurance of your balance-sheet, indorsed by the certificate of independent auditors, that before striking the balance of profits for the year, you have made ample provision for every bad and doubtful debt.

When a heavy local failure takes place, which affords irresponsible gossip a genial topic for reckless guess-work and mischievous suggestion, it will be wise to advise your Branches at once how you stand affected by the failure; otherwise your Managers will be unable to contradict any edition of the facts, however damaging, which may reach the too receptive ears of the more timid of your proprietary.

The shareholder in a Bank is a partner in a business which, to the extent of his holding, is carried on for his benefit. The greater the profits, the larger his dividend. It is a duty which he owes to himself, therefore, to seek to increase the business and thereby add to the profits of the institution.

There are still in most districts numbers of people who have never yet ‘kept a banker.’ These are they who

should move the special solicitude of the Bank shareholder; this is the quarry in which he should work. It
is his business to search out and bring the bankless in.
True, he is only one partner amongst a thousand others
in your Bank; but that does not release him from the
obligation of doing what he can for the common good.
Let him bring only one fresh customer to the Bank in
the course of every twelvemonths, and let us put the
addition thus made to your revenues at the modest
figure of twenty shillings a year; and let each of your
shareholders do the same; and the result, in the course of
five years, will be an increase of £5000 a year in your
profits; or an addition of 1½ per cent. to your annual
dividend.

This appears to you an over-estimate. You say that
in your proprietary hive at Oxborough the drones out-
numbered far the workers. But the extra activity of the
workers will sometimes out-balance the indolence of the
do-nothings, and the tale of expected work be thus
made up.

But to put the matter differently: let us suppose that
through the combined exertions and influence of your
customers and shareholders at Oxborough, a fresh
account or deposit came to your Branch there only once
in ten days? You will hardly regard this as an extravagant estimate: but the result would be thirty new
accounts or deposits in the course of the year for
Oxborough Branch, and consequently nine hundred for
your Branches as a whole.

As we have seen, the profits of banking are in a great
measure made up of inconsiderable particles. The
shareholders in Banks therefore are not to disregard the
worth of small things, and because they cannot do much,
conclude to do not'iing. Pence and farthings, as well
as pounds and shillings, go to swell the annual tale of
Bank profits.

In times of panic, it is the special duty of a shareholder **to** stand by his own Bank. If he saw his own

house on fire, he would at once seek to put out the flames. If he sees the Bank in which he is a proprietor attacked, with all the forces of panic fighting on the side of the assailants, it is surely his duty to lift a hand in defence of his own property.

If timid and foolish people are running for their deposits, a man of wealth and influence might be able to reassure many and disabuse them of their fears. He would not overstep the limits of discretion if, in cases when depositors have ceasèd for the moment to be accountable beings, he should even offer to guarantee their deposits; for which the assets of the Bank would be for him an ample cover and indemnity. And what the rich and powerful amongst shareholders might do, others less affluent or influential might do, each to the extent of his ability, even if that were limited to turning the alarms of the timid into ridicule, and laughing panic out of countenance.

Nevertheless, incredible as it may seem, it is at a critical time like this, that one of your shareholders loses his head and throws his fifty shares on the market for instant sale, thus causing a rapid fall in their market price. It would be in vain to represent to a person thus possessed, that the worst time to sell shares is when there are no buyers. His one object is to 'get out,' let the price go to what it will; and when he has driven it down some £5 a share, some one finds courage perhaps to relieve him of his holding.

Now no one would object to his parting with his shares at any sacrifice, provided he were the only sufferer. But in forcing a sale of his fifty shares, he has brought the price of all the shares held by his co-proprietors down to the level of his own. He has emancipated himself by inflicting six hundred times his own loss upon others. Against his loss of £250, you have to place a drop in the value of his neighbours' property to the extent of £150,000.

And the mischief may not end here; other nervous shareholders, seeing the rapid fall in the price of your shares, may likewise take fright, and your bell-wether be followed by a score of sheep like himself. Fresh batches of shares may thus be thrown upon the market and the price thrust further down.

The unexampled fall in the price of your stock will not escape the notice of the outside public; and if it leads them to the conclusion that its own shareholders have lost confidence in the Bank, who shall blame them? But such an impression, should it seize upon the minds of your depositors, at a time when banking credit is at a severe point of tension, might bring them upon you in numbers. True, you are always prepared and ready for the worst. With such a balance-sheet as yours, you may set any run at defiance. But a weaker bank, suddenly assailed, might be overwhelmed in this way— stricken down by the hand of one of its own co-partners. In his frantic haste to set himself free, he will have brought the fabric about his own ears. Should this be the result, there will be few to pity his dismay, when he finds that the sale of his shares has not released him from liability upon them for twelve months to come. It will then come home to him, when it is too late, that in his selfish haste to free himself from responsibility, at the expense of others, he has brought upon himself the very calamity, from which it was his effort and struggle to escape.

The shareholders in banks, if they would act wisely for themselves, will never attempt a sale of their shares in a time of panic.

If a fear has been put into their minds as to the soundness of the Bank, let them refer the matter to the nearest Manager and have it cleared up at once. They will thus at least give themselves the benefit of the doubt. By forcing a sale of their stock in the midst of a money crisis, they may render the catastrophe certain, which is as yet only in apprehension. They may get rid of their shares; but in doing so they may get rid of the Bank itself, and thus end their flight from responsibility at the bottom of a precipice.

And whilst you have thus sometimes to reckon with mutiny within the camp, you are exposed to other forms of attack from without.   You will not always escape calumny; and your assailant will bide his time to give it utterance at the right moment.   The Bank's difficulty will be his opportunity.

You hold that the man who would of malice aforethought seek to wreck a solvent Bank, has much the same claim to virtuous motive, as the ruffian has who would blow up a public building.   The difference between the two, you submit, is merely in degree.   The minor offence would not involve risk to human life: it would only render life not worth living, to hundreds of innocent people.

But calumny would be harmless if it were not spread about.   Do not give it circulation, and it will fall dead from the lips of the traducer.   It is therefore the special duty of all shareholders in banks, to abstain from the repetition of rumours to the prejudice of banking institutions, especially in times of monetary anxiety and alarm.

Your proprietors ought rather to act as the guardians and police of banking credit.   The people who glibly pass from mouth to mouth, slanders that might impair the standing of any credit institution, do so for the most part without evil intention ;   but whether a bank is brought down with intention or without, the result to its shareholders is equally cruel and disastrous.

The failure of a Bank, moreover, in the midst of a monetary crisis, adds fresh fuel of alarm to the prevailing excitement, and may cause runs upon other banks to their undoing ; and thus the banking system of a whole district might be brought to a standstill.   If this should come to pass, the predictions of evil so recklessly scattered by your gad-abouts, will have come home to roost. If any of these persons shall happen to be depositors in one . or other of the suspended banks, they will have locked their own as well as their neighbour's money up, more or less effectually, for an unknown period.   If borrowers from the Banks or discounters with them, they will have shut up the sources of such facilities and may have to come to a stand-still themselves—a result which most people will look upon as a righteous judgment. If they shall prove to be shareholders in any of the Banks, they will have ruinously depreciated the value of their own property. The stranglers of credit may thus find the noose tightening about their own necks. In any event, they will have helped to bring about a disaster, which will subject thousands of people in trade to serious inconvenience,—it may be to wearing anxieties and ruinous business loss ; whilst scores of hardworking clerks and officials, their wives and families, will be cast helpless upon the world.

Unfortunately you cannot limit the consequences of the stoppage of a bank, to those who bring the structure down about their own ears. A bank—especially a bank with numerous Branches—has wide ramifications :

> *It is a massy wheel*
> *To whose huge spokes ten thousand lesser things*
> *Are mortised and adjoined ; which, when it falls,*
> *Each small annexment, petty consequence,*
> *Attends the boisterous ruin.*

LETTER XLI.

THE FUTURE OUTLOOK.

The Golden Age, it is but too true, is not the lot of the generation in which we live ; but if it is to be found in any part of the track marked out for human existence, it will be found, I trust, not in any part which is past, but in some part which is to come. DEFENCE OF USURY.

IN dealing with possible fluctuations in the aggregate of your deposits, we assumed a maximum pressure of 10 per cent., or the withdrawal of £250,000 of the whole.

For nine years out of ten, looking at the past, this will probably exceed their utmost point of depletion ; but if the tenth year be visited with a commercial crisis, combined with a money panic, the average level of your deposits may suffer a more serious depression.

You ask, as regards this decennial year of affliction, what of the future ? Will things continue to move in the same grooves as heretofore, and each decade be rounded off by a paroxysm in the money market ?

It is hard to say : we can do little more than set before our minds the leading elements of the problem. We can inquire of the past in what it differs from the present, and of both what guidance they have for us in the future : but to give a categorical answer to your question would require the gift of prophecy.

As regards the present, then, we are still working our monetary system on practically the same basis, in respect of gold, as when the Act of 1844 was passed, although the deposits of the Banks have since then more than trebled in amount.

It is true that the reserves of the Banks, namely the

amount of Bank of England notes, and coin in hand, money at call and Consols, have largely increased, and that the average reserve now ranges, as we have seen, from 24 to 36 per cent. of the liabilities ; but only a small percentage of this average is held by the Banks in gold. A recent estimate by the Coinage Committee of the Institute of Bankers places the liabilities of the Banks at 575 millions, and the gold held by them at 25 millions, or 4½ per cent.* This is the golden pivot on which the vast wheel of our monetary system revolves.

It is beyond dispute, therefore, that if the Banks were called upon to discharge their indebtedness, exclusively in gold, on any one day, the transaction would be impossible ; but it is not less true that they could discharge the whole of their liabilities to the public in far less time than it has taken to build them up.

It is a property of money to create or cancel debt ; to convey capital or money's worth, from hand to hand, and from place to place, with ceaseless repetition, without undergoing diminution itself. It is the common carrier of capital. Its function is akin to that of the railway truck, which carries its customary load, performs its appointed run, and is ready for any additional number of loads and runs which may be required of it. The same hundred pounds with which a debt is cancelled, a payment made, or a purchase completed to-day, will suffice for similar uses to-morrow and for any series of to-morrows. If it changed ownership once a day, it would complete operations to three hundred times the sum of itself in the course of a year, and still be the same £100 in money, and ready to enter upon the same endless round of work.

And what is true in this respect of a hundred pounds, is equally true of five and twenty millions of pounds. They will suffice to cancel twenty-five millions of debt any day and be themselves undiminished by the process.

---

* Journal of the Institute, June, 1883.

Let the money owing to Bankers be repaid, in exact ratio and coincidence with their repayments to their depositors; and, as a mere matter of manipulation, our holding of gold would alone suffice to liquidate our 575 millions of banking indebtedness, in three-and-twenty days.

But this is mere playing with figures. The process is less suggestive of a sober act of business, than of Bobadil's method of destroying an army.

The realization and distribution of 575 millions of banking assets, in a given number of days, may be demonstrable, as an exercise in arithmetic; but looked at in a practical light, such an operation is a chimera, only surpassed in extravagance by the idea that the necessity for it should ever come to pass. The imagined process may nevertheless serve to shew how the constructive property of money enables us, as a community, to run into a mutuality of debt and aggregate of liability, so far beyond the amount which our reserve of gold would enable us to discharge at any one time.

But the financial skill which has enabled us, as a nation, thus to economize the use of gold well-nigh to vanishing point, has its disadvantages.

Whilst the public mind is at rest concerning monetary affairs, the immense operations of banking, trade and commerce go evenly and swiftly on; money passes readily from hand to hand, and the currency is equal to its work: and by currency or money I here mean only Bank of England Notes and specie. But when a time of discredit supervenes, the circulative power of the currency becomes impaired,—not necessarily from any reduction in its amount, but from a growing indisposition on the part of holders to part with it freely.

It follows that the same holding of currency or money, which would suffice for our national requirements at one time, might fall perceptibly short of these at another: because it is manifest that a currency which changed hands, let us say, once a week, would complete a larger tale of work than if it passed from hand to hand only once in ten days.

And this is virtually what happens when clouds appear on the monetary horizon and foreshadow a coming pressure. That visitation is usually heralded by a heavy fall in the exchanges,—the accredited barometer of the money-market,—and a rapid upward movement of the Bank rate. The enhancement of the rate has some such effect in retarding the movement of the currency, as the application of the brake has in lessening the speed of a railway train. It induces Bankers and other holders of money to slacken speed, and to part with their funds with increasing caution. The result is a 'tightness' in the money market, the initial twinge, it may be, of approaching panic.

The tightness has barely made itself generally felt, perhaps, before there is another rise in the rate : the feeling of uneasiness is enhanced : and the disinclination on all hands to part with money increases visibly.

And whilst the mobility of the currency is thus being impaired, a drain of gold may be diminishing its volume. For every million of bullion leaving the Issue Department, a million of Notes may be undergoing cancellation.

Meanwhile there is no abatement in the general demand for money. The business commitments of the community cannot be abridged in a day. The merchant requires his bills to be discounted, and his existing engagements to be met. Your manufacturers, farmers, and traders require and expect their customary facilities. The general pressure for money in fact rather increases, and the Bank rate goes steadily up.

The depreciation in the value of shares and other property—which is a feature and consequence of the crisis—now tempts the investing class of your customers to draw upon their credit balances. The more excitable of your depositors, startled perhaps by the failure of a bank somewhere,—it matters little where or which, when there is panic in the air—come for their money, to withdraw and hoard it.   The pressure becomes increasingly severe; and half a score of failures, more or less serious, in a few days, give intensity to the crisis.

One step further and we are on the edge of a precipice: another million of gold leaves the Issue Department, the rate is put up to 10 per cent., and the strain reaches that point of tension, when something must give way, or our monetary system go over the brink.

Fortunately, at the last moment, the Government of the day suspend the Act of 1844: and behold, before the day is out, the Panic has disappeared, like the baseless fabric of a vision.

And what has Government done? It has simply relieved the public mind of a dread which threatened our whole monetary system with paralysis.   It has made arrangements with the Bank of England, under which its notes may be had, on conditions—at a price; and that moment apprehension begins to subside, and the currency, freed from general arrest in bankers' safes, merchants' cash boxes, and the secret hiding places of the timid, begins to flow again through the arteries of our monetary system.

Briefly stated, these were some of the leading features of the panics of 1847, 1857 and 1866; and the lesson which they hold for us, would seem to lie mainly in the fact, that each panic was brought to a climax by a drain of gold.

Now a drain of gold is usually the result of overtrading or speculation.   That being the case, the question which we have next to ask is—Have we seen the last of overtrading and speculation?   We might almost as well ask,—Have we seen the last of human nature?   We have not seen the last of these things.   On the contrary, when they next take place they will probably be on a larger scale than heretofore,—a scale proportioned to the enormous increase in our commercial and monetary transactions since the time of our last panic. It is possible indeed to imagine such a conjunction of disturbing events and adverse influences, at some critical point in the future, as may result in more intense pressure upon our monetary system than it has ever suffered in the past; unless when the evil time comes, the Act of 1844 is promptly suspended, or judiciously amended meanwhile. •

As matters stand, the Ministry of the day must either look helplessly on during the march of a crisis, and see the country arrive at a condition of monetary dead-lock, or take the grave responsibility of suspending an Act of Parliament. Would it not be a more politic arrangement, by means of a short rider to the Act, to empower the Government, when things shall arrive, in their judgment, at panic point, to suspend the restrictive clauses of the Act,—the same high rate of discount, be it 8, or 10, or 12 per cent., being maintained, until any excess of issues thus occasioned shall have returned to the Issue Department and been cancelled? The probability is that no such excess would then ensue. What adds to the intensity and peril of a money crisis, is the well-founded dread that the time is at hand, when, owing to the operation of the Act, it will be impossible to obtain bank notes at any price or at any sacrifice: hence the forestalling and hoarding, in view of eventualities, which locks a large portion of the currency up, and practically withdraws it for the time being from circulation or use.

There is nothing revolutionary in the suggestion here made: on the contrary, it is precisely what has been done, and with the happiest results, on each of the three occasions on which the Act has been suspended. All that I would urge is that, in this respect, the measure shall be rendered self-acting, and not, as at present, self-destructive. Let its relaxation at the right moment be a fulfilment of the law and not a breach of it.

The Act makes no provision for an abnormal condition of things. Its working is faultless, so long as the times are easy, and there is smoothness in the money market; but when there comes a general breakdown of credit, the Act in its operation, so far from allaying public alarm, enhances it to a point bordering on frenzy, and then breaks down itself.

'Notwithstanding the beneficial operation of the Act of 1844,' says Mr. John Stuart Mill, 'in the first stages of one kind of commercial crisis, (that produced by over-speculation) it, on the whole, materially aggravates the severity of commercial convulsions: and not only are contractions of credit made more severe by the Act—they are also made greatly more frequent.'

The framers of the measure would appear to have taken for granted the perpetual sanity of all classes of the community in respect of monetary affairs, and made no provision for casual aberrations. The Act was not framed, so as to yield or bend for a moment to that final rush of unreason and alarm which culminates in panic, and like a tidal wave sweeps all before it, the Act itself included.

It may be said that it is for the public advantage that the strength or weakness of our banking system should now and then be put to the test. There is no objection to this. The objection is to the construction of the test, the peculiarity of which is, that its application is calculated to embarrass the soundest institutions equally with the weakest. In its operation it presses alike upon the prudent and the reckless. If there are any weak places in our banking system, a pressure of less than 10 per cent. will assuredly find them out. A five per cent. rate sufficed to sink the West of England Bank, and the City of Glasgow Bank went down in a monetary calm.

But banks and bankers are not alone concerned in the operation of the Act of 1844. They can, in most cases, protect themselves, by a peremptory recall of advances and curtailment of discounts; but this is only to pass the pressure on to merchants, manufacturers, traders, and others, so that it comes to rest in the end upon the shoulders of the business community.

The working of the Act in a time of excitement and

swiftly spreading apprehension, suggests to the imagination, a boiler with its safety-valve screwed down and a blazing furnace underneath : whereas the proposed power of relaxation would enable it, when the pressure became extreme, to blow off steam, instead of some day blowing our monetary system into space,—which it may conceivably do, the first time the suspension of the Act is too long deferred by an irresolute Government.

It may be urged that any relaxation in the stringency of the Act might lead to a suspension of specie payments. The reply is that we have put this hazard to the test on three memorable occasions, and that no such result has followed, or was ever within the range of probability. The danger to be feared did not lie in that direction. The danger was that if the Act had not been suspended when it was, the country was, on each occasion, within measurable range of the suspension of all payments whatsoever, in specie or anything else.

In pursuance of your inquiry then,—Have we seen the last of our money panics ?—it has to be confessed that we have not, thus far, found much encouragement for the future, in either the past or the present condition of things ; and we have yet to add to the adverse features of the situation, the humiliating fact that, even in this nineteenth century of civilization and culture, we are not yet exempt from the folly and mischief of runs.

In the scare which had its rise in the failure of the City of Glasgow Bank in Oct. 1878, only six years ago, and culminated in the stoppage of the West of England Bank in the following December, some of the most powerful banks in England were fiercely run upon, and notably those of unlimited liability. What had usually been deemed to afford the greatest security was, in 1878, suspected to afford the least. There was this peculiarity, moreover, in the direction taken by the movement: it did not assail the Banks that held deposits by tens or hundreds of thousands : it was the Banks that held deposits by threes and fives and tens of millions, which had to face the storm. We have to take into account therefore, that our next scare may take a lower and wider range. Having assailed the Titans of banking in vain, the next paroxysm of distrust may try conclusions with the smaller and more numerous class of banking institutions ; let us hope, with the like baffling result.

On the other hand, it is in our favour that there can never again be a failure like that of the City of Glasgow Bank, nor even a modified edition of Overend, Gurney & Co. The all but universal adoption of the Act of 1879, has rendered calamities like these beyond the reach of accomplishment by any stretch of human wickedness or imbecility. Bank failures we may have now and then, but not catastrophes like these. 'Our future failures, if any, will arise from imprudent bank- ing,—from the locking up of deposits in unavailable forms of security, to cover excessive rates of deposit interest ; but there is no reason to suppose that this description of banking prevails to any extent.

The existence of Leeman's Act is another point in favour of our future outlook. Under that Act, the broker who offers bank shares for sale must have the shares to sell. He must give the name of the seller, or the numbers of the shares to be sold. He cannot now execute unlimited 'bear' operations in the shares of any Bank which he may select for attack, and thus place its credit, and possibly its existence, at his mercy.

It was argued against the measure that only weak and badly managed banks had anything to fear from this process ; but that was not so. Moreover, badly managed banks may, with safety, be left to go to the wall, without this questionable form of propulsion. The Act was designed by the Legislature, to protect perfectly solvent Banks against a form of attack which, in critical times, might bring the strongest Bank into a position of embar- rassment and danger.

It is a fallacy to contend that the market has the same moral right to speculative dealings in the shares of

Banks as in those of Railway companies. However much you may depreciate the price of any Railway Stock by bearing operations, the undertaking itself remains intact : but it may be far otherwise with a Bank. It depends for its existence upon credit. Sap that, by fictitious sales of its shares in a time of monetary excitement, and bring its depositors upon it in a rush, and you smash up, it may be, a perfectly solvent institution.

It has been argued that the Act, by prohibiting 'operations for the fall' in Bank shares, leaves the shareholders in discredited or insolvent concerns in a fool's paradise, until it is too late to get rid of their responsibilities : but as they can only rid themselves of these by transferring them at the last moment to the shoulders of other people, a measure which puts this manner of escape from liability under modified restraint, will scarcely be looked upon by the community at large as a grievance to be removed.

Had the Act not been in operation in 1878, when some of the strongest banks in the country were assailed for weeks together with persistent virulence, it is at least conceivable that the scare of that time might have been so enlarged and intensified, as to lead to a crisis of destructive range and severity.

The panics of the future will be influenced to some extent in their direction and force by the action of the public press. Its universal eye will always be upon us. What any leading newspaper says to-day, as to the monetary outlook, will be repeated throughout the land in a million or so of broad sheets to-morrow morning. The press cannot, it is true, prevent the fabrication of malicious and mischievous rumour, but it can refuse to give it circulation. In the strained condition of things which precedes and heralds panic, what is to be said, for example, of some such paragraph as this—— 'Two Banks in ——shire are freely spoken about'? What advantage such a paragraph can yield to any one, passes comprehension ; but the evil it may do is not difficult of estimate. Before night of the day of publication, not two, but half-a-score of Banks will be freely spoken about, their depositors and shareholders needlessly alarmed, and fresh fuel added to the prevailing excitement.

The nearly universal adoption by Banks of ' reserved liability' is another element in the problem of the future. It will afford a solid ground of assurance to depositors in times of pressure and alarm. Capital in this form cannot, as they know, be called up and lost in the business of a bank. ˻It constitutes an inviolable reserve for their protection, and insures the safety of their deposits, whatever may happen to the Bank itself.

A further and abiding ground of confidence to depositors and the public, will be found in the compulsory audit, at least once a year, of the books, accounts and securities of every bank which has registered under the Act of 1879. It is beyond question that, if this safeguard had been in force since the institution of Joint Stock Banking, the most ruinous failures of the past would have been averted. It would have been impossible for any body of Directors to nurse enormous and ever growing accounts, year after year, long after they had become more than doubtful, without even a suspicion of the fact reaching the ears of shareholders; until the Banks themselves capsized and went down before their eyes. The ' fierce light' of the inevitable audit would have rendered impossible this cumulative form of banking ruin in the past, and will render it absolutely impossible in the future.

Nevertheless, we must not rely on either reserve liability or compulsory audit, as unfailing panaceas for panic in all time to come. There have been times, and there may be again, when sections of the community become deaf to reason. If there is panic about, no matter how baseless it may be, they are sure to catch it with greater or less severity. Be your reserve liability of what amount it may, or your financial position a very fortress and citadel of strength,—if they hear of people running for their money, no matter where, nor for what reason, they will run too.

My counsel to you, therefore, for what it may be worth, would be to maintain your finances at all times, and under all circumstances, in a position of impregnable strength; because panic, when it comes, will travel like other things now-a-days on electric wings. Be less anxious for your dividend than solicitous about your financial safety. Let that be assured, whatever the immediate effect on your profits may be. A dividend based on financial strength, may suffer occasional abatement; but one earned by a more adventurous policy, at the cost of financial weakness, is a precarious one at the best; at the worst, it may fail you altogether some day, and dividend, Bank, and Manager simultaneously disappear.

If the movement by depositors on the Banks in the December of 1878 had become general, and been coincident with a commercial crisis, a ten per cent. Bank rate, a rapid depletion of the reserve in the Banking Department, and a persistent drain of bullion, the ordeal for English banking might have been one of unexampled severity. In the struggle for existence which would have ensued, the question of the hour would have been, not the forthcoming dividends of the Banks, but the survival of the fittest.

Be especially on your guard in sluggish times of business and low rates of interest for money. The temptation to depart from the lines of prudent banking is then at its greatest. It is then, if ever, that a bank is drawn towards 'chancing it'—towards advances on securities of an outside character and uncertain negociability, in order to secure a larger return of interest.

We have seen what this may lead to, should pressure come upon a bank unawares. The stream of monetary events runs with smoothness to the very verge of the rapids, and you may adventure upon its current once too far. Your only safe rule is steadfastly to abide by the limits which you have assigned to your various forms of asset, so that you may always have your resources well in hand, come what may.

Let your device as a banker be that of the strong man armed, and your motto AYE READY. You will not otherwise be prepared, at all points and at all times, to encounter and overcome the difficulties which may be in store for English banking in the large uncertainties of the future. Above all things, in the regulation of your finances, place no reliance on the chapter of accidents for seeing you through. ' He digs in sand and lays his beams in water,' says Feltham, ' who builds upon events which no man can be master of.'

INDEX.

Land, Labor and Law.

A Search for the Missing Wealth of the Laboring Poor.

By W. A. PHILLIPS,

MEMBER OF CONGRESS FROM KANSAS, MEMBER OF THE COMMITTEES
ON PUBLIC LANDS AND CURRENCY AND BANKING.

---

1 volume, 12mo, cloth, - - - - $2.50.

In this book COLONEL WILLIAM A. PHILLIPS, one of the pioneer settlers of Kansas, a life-long friend of Horace Greeley, and in "Free-Soil" days the special correspondent of the New York *Tribune*, gives us a history of the various systems of land tenure in ancient and modern times, comparing them with the system of laws now regulating the holding and transfer of land in the United States. Colonel Phillips has enjoyed peculiar advantages for the study of the subject he has chosen, having served several terms in Congress, where he distinguished himself as a member of the Committee on Banking and Currency as well as of the Committee on Public Lands. This fact alone would warrant the calling of public attention to his book, but when it is remembered that the author is a writer of acknowledged ability, it will be within bounds to say that Colonel Phillips has made a most important contribution to the discussion of a subject that sooner or later is certain to become a "burning question" in American politics.

*** *For sale by all booksellers, or sent, post-paid, on receipt of price by*

CHARLES SCRIBNER'S SONS,

PUBLISHERS,

743 & 745 Broadway, New York.

TRIUMPHANT DEMOCRACY;

OR,

FIFTY YEARS' MARCH OF THE REPUBLIC.

BY ANDREW CARNEGIE.

1 volume, 8vo, - - - - - *$2.00.*

Mr. Carnegie, though born in Scotland, and a firm lover of the "old home," is a thorough republican in sympathy and in practice, and a radical of the radicals in his advocacy of a government of the people, by the people, and for the people. For royalty and its surroundings he has nothing but contempt, and his comparisons of monarchical forms and observances with republican simplicity and his scathing comments will be read with interest not only here but in England. Indeed, the work may be said to be intended primarily for British readers—to open the eyes of the masses in the United Kingdom to the wonderful advancement—physical, moral, political and intellectual—of the United States during the last half century, an advancement either little understood or wilfully misrepresented in Europe. Though various causes have contributed to this unexampled rate of progress, the principal one, in Mr. Carnegie's opinion, is the fundamental fact of the equality of the citizen in the Republic. To this grand principle all nations must eventually subscribe, he argues, and the sooner it is adopted by Great Britain the better for the country and the better for the people. Its author claims that it is pure missionary work on his part, and that his sole desire in its preparation has been to show his countrymen—and to prove by solid facts and figures—the superiority of republican over monarchical institutions. This is the true inwardness of his book and of its title—"Triumphant Democracy."

*** *For sale by all booksellers, or sent, post-paid, on receipt of price by*

CHARLES SCRIBNER'S SONS,

PUBLISHERS,

743 & 745 Broadway, New York.

THE COUNTRY BANKER,

HIS CLIENTS, CARES, AND WORK. FROM THE EXPERI-
ENCE OF FORTY YEARS.

BY GEORGE RAE,

Author of "Bullion's Letters to a Bank Manager."

WITH AN AMERICAN PREFACE BY BRAYTON IVES.

1 volume, 12mo, cloth, $1.50.

"Mr. Rae may be congratulated on having produced a book which can be recommended to the student who wishes to gain an insight into the subject."—*London Times.*

"We have seldom taken up a book on the business of banking which is at once so interesting and so full of shrewd common sense as this of Mr. Rae's."—*Economist.*

"The dry bones of banking theories and abstractions are here clothed with flesh and blood, and made to live and move full of life and animation."—*Liverpool Mercury.*

"One of the most valuable additions to banking literature of late years."—*Journal of the Institute of Bankers.*

"Mr. George Rae has, in the above book, contributed to banking literature probably the best work that has ever been written on the subject, not even excepting those of Mr. Gilbart."—*Bullionist.*

"It is entirely free from pedantry and abounds in definitions singularly terse and comprehensive."—*Glasgow News.*

"The subject may seem at the first glance to be a very dry one, but our author contrives to treat it in such a fashion as to make it exceedingly interesting."—*Scotsman.*

"A book of shrewdness, wit, and rare practical knowledge."—*New York Tribune.*

"Wherever we have dipped into the contents of the book we have felt the invigorating influence of a master mind in banking craft."—*The Banking World.*

".... It crystallizes into sparkling forms the experiences of a long banking life, and is equally interesting to bankers and to their customers, and has that first of literary virtues, sincerity."—*Liverpool Daily Post.*

** For sale by all booksellers, or sent, post-paid, on receipt of price by

CHARLES SCRIBNER'S SONS,

PUBLISHERS,

743 & 735 Broadway, New York.

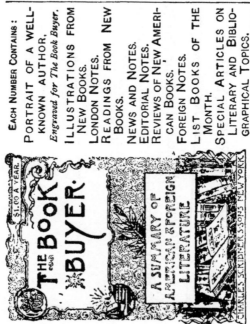

SUBSCRIPTION BLANK.

To CHARLES SCRIBNER'S SONS,

743 and 745 Broadway, New York.

Enclosed find One Dollar* for One Year's Subscription to THE
BOOK BUYER [ILLUSTRATED], to be mailed beginning

to the following address :

*The new postal notes, which may be obtained at your post-office for a fee of three cents, or
stamps in small denominations, offer convenient modes of remittance.

Lightning Source UK Ltd.
Milton Keynes UK
UKHW012044271218
334533UK00005B/435/P